Teach

Yourself

Visual Basic 6

Teach

Yourself

Visual Basic 6

Scott Warner

Osborne/**McGraw-Hill**

Berkeley New York St. Louis San Francisco Auckland Bogotá Hamburg London Madrid Mexico City
Milan Montreal New Delhi Panama City Paris São Paulo Singapore Sydney Tokyo Toronto

Publisher
Brandon A. Nordin

Editor-in-Chief
Scott Rogers

Acquisitions Editor
Wendy Rinaldi

Project Editor
Madhu Prasher

Editorial Assistant
Debbie Escobedo

Technical Editor
Brian Engler

Copy Editor
Nancy Warner

Proofreader
Joe Sadusky

Indexer
Jack Lewis

Computer Designer
Jani Beckwith

Illustrator
Lance Ravella

Series Design
Peter Hancik

Cover Design
Regan Honda

Osborne/**McGraw-Hill**

2600 Tenth Street

Berkeley, California 94710

U.S.A.

For information on translations or book distributors outside the U.S.A., or to arrange bulk purchase discounts for sales promotions, premiums, or fund-raisers, please contact Osborne/**McGraw-Hill** at the above address.

Teach Yourself Visual Basic 6

1234567890 DOC DOC 901987654321098

ISBN 0-07-882556-3

ABOUT THE AUTHOR

Scott Warner is a best-selling author or contributor to more than a dozen computer books. In addition, he writes applications in many different tools and languages, such as Visual Basic, Delphi, Powerbuilder, Oracle PL/SQL, HTML, and Java. Both he and his wife, Nancy, live in Phoenix, Arizona. They both have Computer Information Systems degrees from Purdue University. As a private consultant for the computer and publishing industries, Scott works with the latest technology on a daily basis, including the latest operating systems, programming tools, and consumer applications.

DEDICATION

I would like to dedicate this book to the Super Chief and Pudgy.
You know who you are.

Contents at a Glance

Contents

Acknowledgments

I would like to thank everyone at Osborne/McGraw-Hill for their hard work and dedication in making this book. I would especially like to thank the following individuals for guiding this book through the process of turning ideas into printed text:

▼ Madhu Prasher

▼ Wendy Rinaldi

▼ Debbie Escobedo

▼ Lysa Lewallen

In addition to those who helped publish this book, I would like to thank Brian Engler for reviewing this material for technical accuracy and James Ralston of The Oasis Group (www.oasisgroup.com) for providing input on technical issues.

Introduction

With the proliferation of computers into every part of our lives, the demand for software to accomplish everyday tasks grows at a rate that developers struggle to keep up with. In addition, many people have needs that are so unique it is impossible to buy software to meet them all. For those with programming experience, an easy solution is to write an application that meets all of their requirements. That way, they get exactly what they want and can change the program when their goals change. But what about those with little or no programming experience?

Visual Basic provides a set of tools that makes it easy to develop powerful Windows applications—fast. That's not to say that there is nothing to learn, but the learning curve is small—even for those with no programming experience. In fact, with this book and a free weekend, any one can be a Visual Basic programmer. With this knowledge, you can write applications to accomplish business tasks or just for fun.

HOW THIS BOOK IS ORGANIZED

This book teaches you how to master the Visual Basic skills necessary to use this powerful programming tool. Each skill is presented and explained. Then, a set of examples and exercises develops those skills through experience. Finally, the end of each chapter tests your overall knowledge of the skills covered in the chapter.

The material is presented sequentially, meaning that you should work through each chapter in order. At the beginning of each chapter is a review that makes sure you understand the important aspects of the previous chapter. Appendix A contains all of the answers and solutions to the exercises and skill checks in this book. Use it to check your work and gauge your progress. If you have trouble with a topic, read over it again and work through the examples and exercises a second time.

USING THIS BOOK AS A REFERENCE

This book teaches you the basic skills necessary for creating Visual Basic applications. While Visual Basic encompasses more than is discussed here, this book gives you the skills that are the building blocks of all that you can accomplish in Visual Basic. If you have trouble as you begin to write more complex applications, use this book as a reference to refresh your memory about how Visual Basic works. Because the book is arranged by task, you can easily find help on specific tasks that you have trouble completing.

Visual Basic **keywords** are highlighted throughout this book. Keep an eye on these keywords to understand how Visual Basic works. The highlighted keywords, combined with the glossary, make this book an excellent source for understanding terms used in Visual Basic.

1

Introducing Visual Basic

chapter objectives

I f you are reading this book, you are most likely new to Visual Basic. In addition, you may be new to the BASIC programming language. Microsoft's Visual Basic programming tool uses a language that is based upon the original BASIC programming language. However, it is in a visual environment that makes it easy for beginners—and old pros—to quickly create Windows applications.

Before you begin to create these applications, you will probably want an explanation of the way that Visual Basic works. This chapter introduces you to the basics of working in the Visual Basic environment. You will learn how to start and exit Visual Basic and use its various tools.

Visual Basic is one component of the Microsoft Visual Studio development platform. Each of the tools in Visual Studio uses basically the same type of environment. Learning one of the tools, such as Visual Basic, makes it easier to learn the other tools (Visual C++, Visual J++, Visual FoxPro, and Visual InterDev).

This chapter explains how applications are organized into projects and how to manage those projects. It also demonstrates how to print projects according to individual needs. Finally, you will learn how to build and run the applications that you create.

1.1 **S**TARTING AND EXITING VISUAL BASIC

Before you can use any of Visual Basic's tools or features, you must start Visual Basic. There are several different ways to start Visual Basic, including the following:

▼ Using the Start menu

▼ Using a program shortcut

▼ Opening a file that is a registered file type

Any of these methods starts Visual Basic. The first two methods are basically the same and cause the exact same results to occur. Using the third method has a slightly different result, which is discussed in the "Starting Visual Basic Using a Registered File Type" section.

STARTING VISUAL BASIC USING THE START MENU OR A PROGRAM SHORTCUT

The Start menu is a common method for starting applications. You may already use the Start menu to open applications such as Windows Explorer, Calculator, or WordPad. To start Visual Basic from the Start menu, follow these steps:

1. Click the Start button.
2. Click the Programs folder on the Start menu.
3. Click the Visual Basic folder on the Programs submenu.

Visual Basic is normally located in the Microsoft Visual Studio 6.0 folder in the Programs submenu, but its folder could be named something else if you did not accept the default during installation.

4. Click the Microsoft Visual Basic 6.0 icon in the submenu. Visual Basic starts and the New Project dialog box appears, as shown in Figure 1-1.
5. Select the Standard EXE icon from the New page of the New Project dialog box and click the Open button, or double-click on the Standard EXE icon.

To open Visual Basic using a program shortcut, replace steps 1 through 4 with the single action of double-clicking on a program shortcut that points to Visual Basic. The Visual Basic executable file is VB6.EXE. It should be located in one of the subfolders of the Microsoft Visual Studio folder, which is contained in the Program Files folder.

When Visual Basic is first started, the New Project dialog box appears with three pages: New, Existing, and Recent. You select a page to view by clicking on the appropriate tab. These pages allow you to choose which type of project you are going to work with, and possibly the exact project.

The Visual Basic programming environment should now be started with a new standard executable project. This project is named Project1 by default, and a single form (Form1) is created. Figure 1-2 shows what your screen should look like after starting Visual Basic and creating a new standard executable project.

FIGURE 1-1

The New Project dialog box allows you to choose the project that you will work on immediately after starting Visual Basic

▼

FIGURE 1-2

After starting Visual Basic, you are ready to begin designing your application

▼

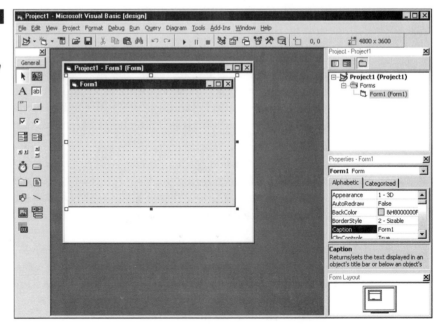

If you had chosen one of the other options for new projects, a form may not have been created by default. Other types of projects may not need a form. Forms are discussed in more detail in the "Working with Forms" section in this chapter.

In addition to creating new projects while starting Visual Basic, you can also work with files that you have already created. The following sections discuss opening files that already exist when starting Visual Basic. For information on opening files after you have started Visual Basic, see the "Working with Forms" and "Working with Projects" sections of this chapter.

If you don't want the New Project dialog box to appear when you start Visual Basic, click the Don't Show This Dialog In The Future checkbox. This causes Visual Basic to start a default project every time it starts. You can change this option back by choosing Options from the Tools menu and clicking the Environment tab of the Options dialog box. Then, click the Prompt For Project option button and click the OK button.

Using Existing Files

You don't have to create a new project every time that you start Visual Basic. The New Project dialog box also lets you choose from existing files. Click on the Existing tab in the New Project dialog box to open an existing file. The dialog box changes. It takes on the appearance of a Windows Open dialog box, as shown in Figure 1-3.

The Existing page of the New Project dialog box is the standard Open dialog box. To open a file, you select it and click the Open button—or just double-click it.

By default, only project files are shown on the Existing page of the New Project dialog box. If you want to open a file that is not a project file, select All Files in the Files Of Type dropdown list box.

Using the Most Recently Used Files

You may find that you typically work with only a few files or the file that you were working on the last time you used Visual Basic. To access the most recently used files, click the Recent tab in the New Project dialog box. Figure 1-4 shows that the Recent page lists the filename and the folder that it is saved in.

Projects created in an earlier session or by another programmer can be opened from the New Project dialog box when starting Visual Basic

▼

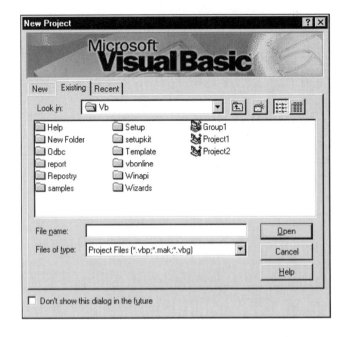

The files on the Recent page of the New Project dialog box are listed in the order that they were most recently used

▼

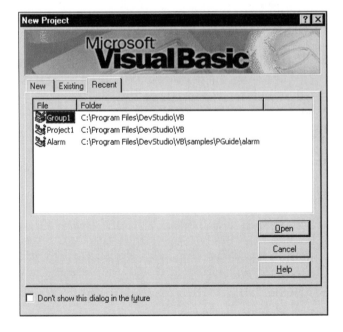

Select the file that you want to use and click the Open button or double-click the file. Unlike normal Windows list views, these files cannot be sorted by file name or folder. The files are only listed in the order that they were most recently used.

STARTING VISUAL BASIC USING A REGISTERED FILE TYPE

Windows allows file types to be registered. The registration is a definition that determines which icon is displayed with the filename and what program is used when opening the file. A file's type is determined by its extension—the three characters that appear after the period (or dot) in a filename. For example, Word documents end with .doc, such as Document1.doc. It is easy to identify and use registered files in Windows because of their identifying icon.

There are many advanced features of registered file types. You can define more than one action to be performed on file types. For example, a Visual Basic Project file has three different actions defined in its registration: Open, Make, and Run. This feature allows you to customize how Windows behaves when working with files. For more information on the Windows registry and registered file types, see Osborne's Windows 98: The Complete Reference.

Because projects and other Visual Basic files are registered file types, Windows knows to use Visual Basic to open these files. Double-click on any Visual Basic file to open it.

To open a file, you can right-click a file and choose Open from the shortcut menu. This method works on any Visual Basic file, whether it is a project file, form file, or any other type of Visual Basic file.

EXITING VISUAL BASIC

You should now be familiar with the ways you can start Visual Basic. The remainder of this chapter introduces you to the different parts of the Visual Basic environment. Before you continue, you might want to review the methods available to exit Visual Basic. Just like closing any other Windows application, the following actions close Visual Basic:

▼   Click the Close button

▼   Press ALT-F4

▼   Choose Exit from the File menu

▼   Choose Close from the Control menu

You can close Visual Basic by typing ALT-Q. This is not a Windows standard and may not work in other Windows applications.

If any changes have been made before you close Visual Basic, you are asked if you want to save those changes. Figure 1-5 shows the dialog box used to present this question. The list of changed items varies by the number of open files that have been changed.

Choose Yes to save these files or No to discard any changes. For more information about saving files see the "Working with Projects" section in this chapter.

FIGURE 1-5

Click the Cancel button if you don't want to save your changes or discard them
▼

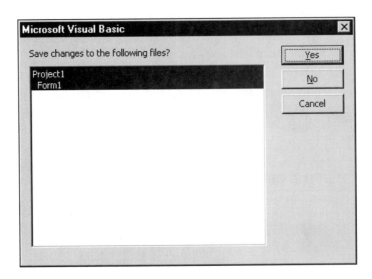

EXAMPLES

1. To start Visual Basic and open the Alarm sample project from the New Project dialog box, click the Existing tab of the New Project dialog box. Then, locate the project in the vb\samples\pguide\alarm directory where you installed Visual Basic. If the sample files were not installed, this file will not be there. Finally, select the project file and click the OK button.

2. To open the Alarm sample project using its registered file type, locate the project in the vb\samples\pguide\alarm directory where you installed Visual Basic. Then, double-click the project file. You could also right-click the project file and choose Open from the shortcut menu.

3. Exit Visual Basic by pressing ALT-Q or ALT-F4, clicking the close button, or choosing Close from the control menu or Exit from the File menu.

EXERCISES

1. Start Visual Basic and create an ActiveX Control project.

2. Use the Options dialog box to force Visual Basic to create a default project at startup.

3. Exit Visual Basic and don't save any changes if you are prompted to.

1.2 USING THE PROJECT EXPLORER

You use the Windows Explorer to view the contents of your computer. Explorer displays the contents of your computer in a hierarchical view. This view displays all of the devices and folders available to your computer and where they are contained. If you open an Explorer window, for example, you can easily locate your hard drive (C:) and the Windows folder. From this view, it is obvious that the Windows folder is contained on your hard drive.

The Project Explorer window lists the currently open Visual Basic projects and the files that they contain. More than one project can be open at a time, but each project's contents are listed directly below that project.

IDENTIFYING FILES CONTAINED IN A PROJECT

Figure 1-6 shows the Project Explorer window. It uses a tree view—like Windows Explorer—to list projects and their content. Projects are at the top of the hierarchy in the Project Explorer. After that, the contents of the project are listed.

The contents of a project can be categorized into types of objects and placed into object folders. Figure 1-6 shows a project that has forms and modules. Therefore, there is a forms object folder and a modules object folder. Clicking the plus sign to the left of the folder reveals the contents of that folder.

FIGURE 1-6

The Project Explorer window functions like Windows Explorer

▼

View object button

Toggle folders button

View code button

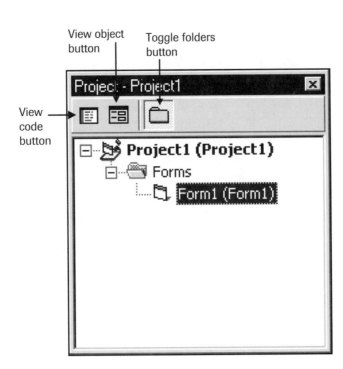

Tip

Click the Toggle Folders button to switch between viewing project files in object folders and not viewing them in object folders.

Table 1-1 describes the types of files that a project can contain. You will definitely use forms and modules when working with Visual Basic. Depending on how advanced your programs become, you may never use some of the other file types. However, it is a good idea to at least familiarize yourself with all of the types.

WORKING WITH THE PROJECT EXPLORER WINDOW

By default, the Project Explorer is docked on the top-right side of the Visual Basic window. The title bar of the Project Explorer window

Object	Description	File Extension
Forms	Forms are the windows and dialog boxes that make up an application.	.frm
Modules	Modules contain Visual Basic code that Visual Basic applications can use.	.bas
Class Modules	Class modules contain Visual Basic code that Visual Basic applications can use.	.cls
User Controls	User control files are used to create ActiveX controls.	.ctl
User Documents	User documents are used to create ActiveX documents.	.dob
Property Pages	These files are used to create property pages for complex control properties that cannot use a standard property page.	.pag
Related Documents	Documents that are related to a project. Only the path to the file is stored.	
Resources	Resource files store text and bitmaps for use by Visual Basic applications. This allows the same application to be used in different countries or regions.	.res

TABLE 1-1 *Items That a Project Might Contain* ▼

contains the word Project and the name of the active project. There are many options that can help make it easier to work with the Project Explorer window. The following sections describe those options.

Hiding, Moving, and Resizing the Project Explorer Window

There may be times when you don't need the Project Explorer and would rather have that space to view a form or some code that you are working on. To accommodate this, Visual Basic allows the Project Explorer to be hidden, moved, and resized. The following sections describe how to accomplish these tasks.

HIDING THE PROJECT EXPLORER WINDOW   Click the close button in the top-right corner of the Project Explorer window to hide it. You can also right-click anywhere on the Project Explorer and choose Hide from the shortcut menu. While the Project Explorer is no longer visible, it is not really closed. Visual Basic continues to keep track of all the objects in your project. Choose Project Explorer from the View menu to make it reappear—or press CTRL-R.

Click the Project Explorer button on the toolbar to make the Project Explorer window appear.

MOVING THE PROJECT EXPLORER WINDOW   Visual Basic allows the Project Explorer to be moved so that it can be placed where it works best for you. The following are the methods that can be used to move the Project Explorer window:

▼   Click the title bar and drag the window to a new location.

▼   Double-click the title bar to move the window to its last undocked location. The window can still be docked to any side of its parent window, which is the Visual Basic window.

▼   Right-click on the window and choose Dockable from the shortcut menu to move the window to its last undocked location. This makes the window no longer dockable.

Double-clicking the title bar a second time returns the Project Explorer to its previous docked location. This cannot be done after making the window undockable. Figure 1-7 shows a Project Explorer window that has been made undockable.

FIGURE 1-7

The Project Explorer window behaves differently depending upon whether or not it can be docked

▼

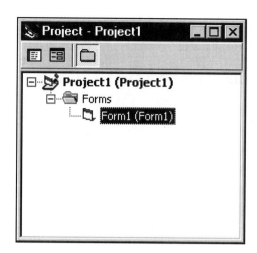

If the Project Explorer window cannot be docked, it is treated like every other child window. A child window can be minimized and maximized by using the minimize and maximize/restore buttons that appear in the title bar.

RESIZING THE PROJECT EXPLORER WINDOW   Complex projects might have many objects, which can make it difficult to view all of them in the Project Explorer. If this is the case, you can resize the window so that you can view more—if not all—of the objects. To resize the window, move the mouse pointer over one of the borders until it takes the shape of a double-headed arrow. Then click and drag the border to the size that you desire. Don't forget that an undockable Project Explorer window can be minimized and maximized. Maximizing the window allows you to quickly view the largest possible number of objects.

If the Project Explorer is docked and there are other windows docked around it, changing its size also changes the size of the other windows.

Opening Files in the Project Explorer Window

Now you know how to navigate the Project Explorer. You also know how to move it around, change its size, and even alter its behavior. Now, it's time to learn how to use it. The following sections explain how to use the Project Explorer to view the code and the objects that make up your project.

USING THE PROJECT EXPLORER TO VIEW OBJECTS   Visual Basic allows programmers to visually build applications by placing controls onto forms. To view these forms or any other visual object, select it in the Project Explorer and click the View Object button. This displays the Object window for the selected object. Chapter 3 discusses using forms and controls in Visual Basic.

Double-click an object in the Project Explorer to view it in its Object window.

USING THE PROJECT EXPLORER TO VIEW CODE   Visual Basic is a popular programming tool because it cuts down on the amount of code that must be written to make a Windows application. However, code is still a necessary part of making robust and useful Windows application. To view the code contained in a module or the code for any other object, select the object and click the View Code button. This displays the Code window, which allows you to edit the code associated with the selected item. Chapter 2 discusses the use of code in Visual Basic.

Double-clicking a module opens the Code window for that module. Double-clicking a visual object opens the Object window for the selected object.

EXAMPLES

1. To expand or contract the list of contents for a project, double-click on the project name or click the plus or minus sign next to the project name.
2. To view a form, select the form and click the View Object button or double-click the form.
3. To view the code for a form, select the form and click the View Code button.

EXERCISES

1. Hide the Project Explorer.

2. Make the Project Explorer reappear.

3. Make the Project Explorer undockable.

4. Maximize the Project Explorer.

5. Restore (unmaximize) the Project Explorer.

6. Make the Project Explorer dockable and return it to its original location.

1.3 *WORKING WITH FORMS*

Forms are the basis for almost all Visual Basic applications. They are used to design the windows and dialog boxes that users interact with when using an application. The following windows interact with each other to let you customize the appearance of your forms:

▼ Form window

▼ Form Layout window

▼ Properties window

The Form window—generically referred to as the Object window—and the Form Layout window are discussed in this section. The Properties window is discussed in the "Using the Properties Window" section of this chapter.

USING THE FORM WINDOW

You work with forms in the Form window, which looks like a window within a window. The inner window, which is labeled Form1 in Figure 1-8, is the actual form.

In this window, you can change the size of the form. To do so, move the mouse pointer over one of the sizing handles. The sizing handles are the eight small squares around the outside of the form. When the mouse pointer changes to a double-headed arrow, click and drag the side of the form to the size that you want.

FIGURE 1-8

Forms can be modified to meet your needs in the Form window

▼

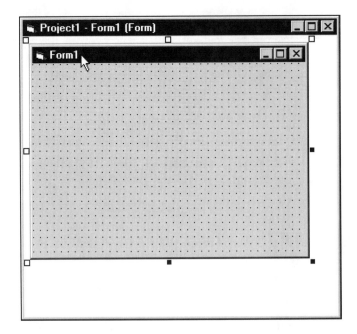

A form's minimize and close buttons are disabled in the Form window, but the maximize button still works. This allows you to have the window maximized when the form first appears.

Visual Basic provides you a tool to help you determine the size of your forms. The object size box appears at the far right of the Standard toolbar. It indicates the width and height of the selected form in *twips*. **Twips** are Visual Basic's unit of measurement—1440 **twips** is one inch, and 567 **twips** is a centimeter.

Width   Height

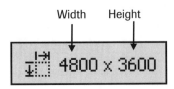

USING THE FORM LAYOUT WINDOW

If a form is maximized when it first appears, it is not necessary to specify a location for the window to appear. It simply takes up the whole screen. However, many times a form is not maximized when it first appears. Visual Basic allows you to specify the location that the window first appears by using the Form Layout window, which is shown in Figure 1-9. Be sure to read the "Determining the Startup Position of a Form" section for more information on specifying the location of a window. The Form Layout window can be hidden, moved, and resized like the Project Explorer.

The Form Layout window displays the location of all open forms. You can identify the different forms, because the name of the represented form is displayed. If there are multiple forms open, the selected form appears to be on top of the other forms in the Form Layout window. To change the location of a form on the desktop, click the form and drag it to a new location. This only changes the location of the window at runtime. The form will not move to a different location in the Form window.

FIGURE 1-9

The Form Layout window graphically represents the location of a form on the user's desktop
▼

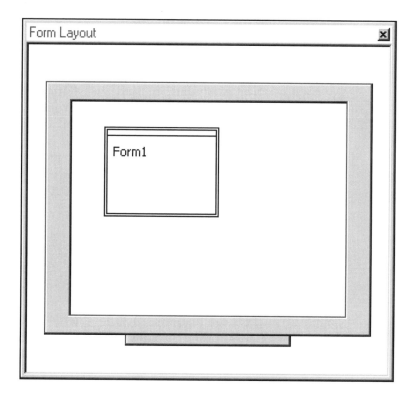

Form Layout

Form1

Even if a form's Form window is not selected, you can click it in the Form Layout window and drag it to a new location. This does not change which Form window is selected.

Visual Basic provides you with a tool to help you determine the location of the form relative to the upper-left corner of the desktop. The *object coordinates* box is located just to the left of the object size box. It indicates the distance that the form is from the left side and top of the desktop. This measurement is also displayed in **twips**.

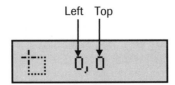

Determining the Startup Position of a Form

There is one important feature that you must use to be able to manually determine where a form appears on the desktop. By default, forms appear in the Windows default location. This location is determined by the Windows operating system and is out of your control. To force the form to appear where you have specified in the Form Layout window, right-click on the form and choose Manual from the Startup Position submenu of the shortcut menu. Now the form will appear in the location you have specified when it is run.

From the Startup Position submenu, choose Center Screen to force the form to appear centered in the desktop or Center Owner to force the form to appear centered in its parent window.

Using Resolution Guides

Applications are often designed on a computer with a monitor that is set at a higher resolution than the computers that will be using the application. This can lead to forms that are too large to be completely viewed without scrolling through a window or moving it around. The Form Layout window has a feature called *Resolution Guides* to help prevent this.

Resolution Guides outline the size of resolutions that are smaller than the size of your current monitor resolution. If your monitor is set to a resolution of 800x600, for example, the Resolution Guides show the borders of a 640x480 resolution. The borders of your current resolution or any higher resolutions are not shown. Right-click on the Form Layout window and choose Resolution Guides from the shortcut menu to activate this feature. Figure 1-10 shows the results.

EXAMPLES

1. To change the size of a form, click on a sizing handle and drag the side of a form to the desired size.

2. To change the location of a form, click on the form in the Form Layout window and drag it to the desired location.

FIGURE 1-10

Resolution Guides make it easier to design for smaller resolutions

▼

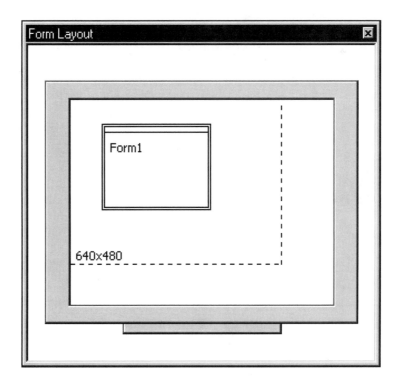

EXERCISES

1. Change the size of a form to four inches wide by two inches high.

2. Maximize and restore a form.

3. Change the location of a form to 1000 **twips** from the left side of the desktop and 1000 **twips** from the top of the desktop.

4. Change the location of a form to the center of the desktop.

5. Hide the Form Layout window and then make it reappear.

1.4 USING THE PROPERTIES WINDOW

The Object window and the Form Layout window allow you to make changes to the size and location of forms. You can even use the object size box and object coordinates box to help you be more precise in your changes. But while these two features make it easy to quickly identify the size and location of a form, they don't make it any easier to make the form the exact size that you want or place the form in the exact location that you want. It can be tedious to drag the form around until you get the exact measurements that you want.

There is a way to specifically set the size and location of a form. Width and height are properties of size, and left and top are properties of location. Therefore, Width, Height, Left, and Top are properties of a form. In addition to these four properties, forms have many other properties that affect their appearance and behavior.

WORKING WITH THE PROPERTIES WINDOW

The Properties window behaves like the Project Explorer and Form Layout windows. It can be hidden, moved, resized, docked, and undocked. Figure 1-11 shows the Properties window for a blank form.

Tip

The Description Pane shows a brief description of the selected property. This will probably be helpful while learning Visual Basic, but later you may think of this as wasted screen space. To remove the Description Pane, right-click on the Properties window and choose Description from the shortcut menu.

FIGURE 1-11

The Properties window lists the properties of the currently selected object

▼

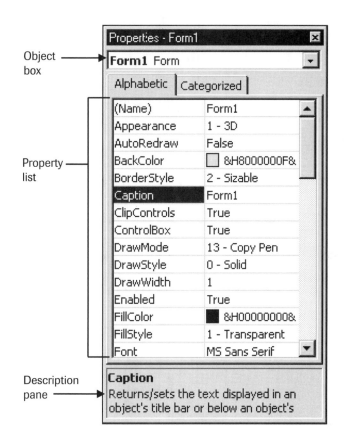

Properties are listed alphabetically. Use the scrollbar to move through the list of properties if they are longer than the window. You can also sort the list by category by clicking the Categories tab. This separates the properties into categories like Appearance, Behavior, Font, and so on. Each category has a plus or minus sign beside it that you can click to expand or contract that category. Figure 1-12 shows the Properties window with the Appearance category contracted and the Behavior category expanded.

The Object Box lists the selected object. That object can be a form or a control that has been placed on a form. You can use the Object Box to select other controls on a form, but not to select other forms.

FIGURE 1-12

*Categories classify
properties
according to how
they affect
the form*
▼

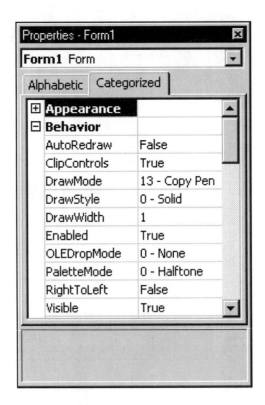

SETTING PROPERTIES

You can scroll through the Properties windows and view all of the properties for a form, but the real purpose of this window is to let you change these properties to suit your needs. There are different types of properties, and each is set in its own way. The following sections discuss how to set the different types of properties.

Setting Free Text Properties

The simplest type of property is *free text*. In other words, you just type in the value that you want. Some examples of this are a Name, Caption, Width, and Height. To set this type of property, follow these steps:

1. Select the property.

2. Type the new value.

3. Press the ENTER key or select a different property.

While you can type anything that you want for the value of a free text property, it may not be valid. For example, you can't type letters into the value for the width of a form. Figure 1-13 shows the dialog box that Visual Basic uses to inform you of an invalid entry. The property returns to its original value after you click the OK button.

Setting Enumerated Properties

Some properties have a finite number of values that they can have. For example, the **Enabled** property is either **True** or **False**. To Visual Basic, this means that it is set to either -1 or 0. Properties of this type use numbers to identify their possible values. That might seem simple enough to remember for **True** or **False**, but what about properties that have more than two possible values? It could be very confusing to remember what ten different numbers stand for.

To make them easier to work with, these types of properties use *enumerated data*, which means that a text value is assigned to each of the possible values. The following shows the possible values for the startup position of a form:

Value	Enumerated Constant	Description
0	VbStartUpManual	Manual
1	VbStartUpOwner	Center Owner
2	VbStartUpScreen	Center Screen
3	VbStartUpWindowsDefault	Windows Default

The possible values for this property don't give much indication of what they mean. That is the reason for the constant, which can be used to set these properties in code (see Chapter 2). Figure 1-14 shows that when you set a property of this type the possible values and a description are listed in a dropdown list box. Select a value from the list to set the property.

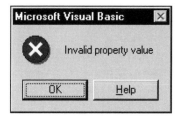

FIGURE 1-14

A downward facing arrow on to the right of a property indicates that you choose from a list of values

▼

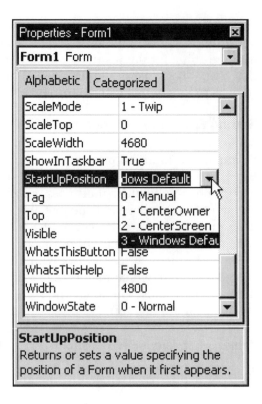

Double-click enumerated property values to toggle through all of the possible choices.

Setting Properties with Property Pages

Some properties are more complex than others are. More complex properties may require the use of property pages to select a value for them. An ellipsis appears to the right of the property if it has a property page. Click the ellipsis to open the property page. Figure 1-15 shows the property page for the **Font** property.

After you make your changes, you click the OK button to set the property to the new value or the Cancel button to leave the property

FIGURE 1-15

The Font property page allows you to make multiple changes for a single property

▼

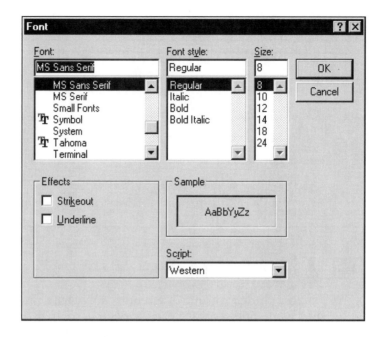

unchanged. The value in the property list will only indicate a small part of the value for that property.

Note

A property page can have tabs that separate it into multiple pages.

EXAMPLES

1. To change the name of a form, select the form and click the **Name** property in the Properties window. Then, type **frmMyForm** and press the ENTER key.

2. To set the **Moveable** property of a form to **False**, select the form and double-click the **Moveable** property in the Properties window. If it is already set to **False**, don't do anything.

EXERCISES

1. Change the **Caption** of a form to My Form.

2. Use the Properties window to change the startup position of a form to the center of the screen.

3. Change the **Font** of a form to size 10, bold Courier.

4. Set the **BackColor** property to the color of an active title bar.

5. Set the **BackColor** property to white.

6. Hide the Description pane and make it reappear.

7. Hide the Properties window and make it reappear.

1.5 *U*SING THE TOOLBOX

To this point, you've worked only with forms; but forms alone don't make an application. The controls that are placed on a form give the form the ability to interact with users and therefore become useful. The Toolbox, which is shown in Figure 1-16, allows you to place controls onto forms.

Note   *The size and location of the Toolbox can be customized just like the Project Explorer, Properties, and Form Layout windows.*

PLACING CONTROLS ON FORMS

The controls in the Toolbox are placed on forms. Then you use the Properties window and the Code window to customize the behavior of the controls. Chapter 2 and Chapter 3 discuss these topics in further detail. To place a control on a form, follow these steps:

1. Open a form in the Object window.

2. Select a control by clicking it once.

3. Click on the form where you want the top-left corner of the control to be.

4. Holding the mouse button down, drag the mouse to where you want the lower-right corner of the control to be.

5. Release the mouse button.

FIGURE 1-16

*The Toolbox
contains Visual
Basic controls*

▼

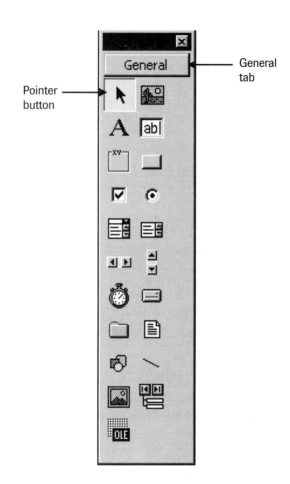

General
tab

Pointer
button

When you release the mouse button, the control appears on the form in the area that you just selected. If, after selecting a control, you decide that you want to use the mouse on the form without placing a control, click the Pointer button. Then no controls are selected.

Tip

Double-click a control to immediately place it on the active form. This method places the control in the center of the form and uses the default size for the control.

To identify a control, place the mouse pointer directly over it. This causes a ToolTip to appear. ToolTips describe the control or button that they are associated with. You can turn ToolTips on and off using the General page of the Options dialog box.

CUSTOMIZING THE TOOLBOX

By default, each project starts with the twenty most commonly used controls in the Toolbox. Depending on how you use Visual Basic, these may be the only controls you need to use; but you will most likely need to use additional controls. Thus, the Toolbox can be customized for each project by adding controls.

Each project has its own custom Toolbox. Changes that you make in one project's Toolbox do not affect other projects' Toolboxes.

Adding Controls to the Toolbox

Visual Basic comes with many controls that are not automatically included in the Toolbox. Follow these steps to add controls to the toolbox:

1. Choose Components from the Project menu.
2. Select the controls that you want to add from the Components dialog box shown in Figure 1-17.
3. Click the OK button to add the selected controls and close the Components dialog box.

You can create your own controls or buy controls from other developers. To add these controls, click the Browse button and select the control file.

Click the Selected Items Only checkbox to show only the controls that are selected for the current project.

Adding Tabs to the Toolbox

There is a raised area at the top of the Toolbox with the word General on it. This is a tab, and all of the default controls appear on the General tab. If it helps you keep track of the controls that you are using for a project, you can create new tabs and add new controls to those tabs. To add a new tab, follow these steps:

1. Right-click on the Toolbox.
2. Choose Add Tab from the shortcut menu.
3. Enter a name for the tab in the dialog box shown in Figure 1-18.
4. Click the OK button.

FIGURE 1-17

The Components dialog box allows you to add controls to the Toolbox
▼

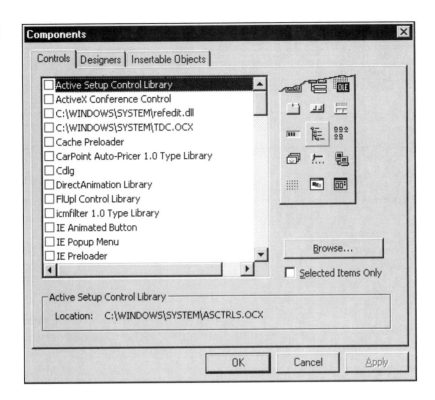

Select the new tab by clicking on it at the bottom of the Toolbox. A Pointer button is automatically added to every new tab. To add controls to the new tab, select the tab and follow the steps outlined in the "Adding Controls to the Toolbox" section.

To remove a tab, right-click on the tab and choose Delete Tab from the shortcut menu. Deleted tools on the tab are moved to the General tab.

FIGURE 1-18

Visual Basic prompts you for a name for the new tab
▼

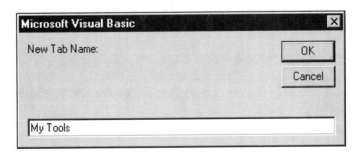

EXAMPLES

1. To select a control, click on the control in the Toolbox.

2. To deselect a control, click the Pointer button.

3. To add a Label control to the middle of a form, open a form and double-click the Label control in the Toolbox.

EXERCISES

1. Place a TextBox control on a form.

2. Place an Image control on a form.

3. Add the Microsoft Common Dialog control to the General tab of the Toolbox.

4. Add a tab called Internet to the Toolbox.

5. Add the Microsoft Internet controls to the Internet tab of the Toolbox that you added in the previous step.

6. Delete the Internet tab.

1.6 *WORKING WITH PROJECTS*

All Visual Basic applications are based upon projects. A project file (VBP) doesn't contain any forms, controls, or code. It contains a list of all the objects and files that are used in the project. These objects include all of the items listed in the Project Explorer plus all of the controls that are being used. Saving a project updates this information. This structure allows you to use forms and other objects you create in more than one project. For example, you could create one logon form and use it for all of your projects.

Caution

If you use objects, such as forms, in multiple projects, you must be careful about what type of changes you make. A change that makes the form work well in one project might make another project stop working.

Before you begin working on projects, you should make some basic decisions about how you are going to manage your files. Making these decisions early can save you a lot of time.

ORGANIZING PROJECTS

Many times, due to time constraints, people jump right into developing an application without planning the management of their development. This error can cause a lot of headaches. Careful planning can benefit even the smallest project. It will help protect your code and the time you have invested.

While planning is very beneficial to your personal projects, it is absolutely essential to *group* projects. There must be a mechanism in place to manage who develops which files when. Communication between team members is crucial to avoid repeating work or, even worse, losing work.

Using Directories to Organize Files

The simplest thing that you can do to plan your projects is to decide upon a directory structure for your projects. This structure can be developed to only address projects, or it can also include separate planning for forms and controls. Figure 1-19 shows a directory structure that stores all files for a project in a single directory.

In this structure, a project folder is created for each project. The folder is named after the project and all files concerning the project are stored in that folder. You can also add folders inside of the project folder.

Use separate folders for different versions of a project. It will take up a lot more space on your hard drive, but it will be very helpful if you ever need to go back to a previous version.

If you create forms or controls that you reuse in other projects, this method could become confusing quickly. Create special folders to keep reusable objects separate. Figure 1-20 shows one way you could manage projects, forms, and controls.

This method allows you to manage reusable objects without associating them with a specific project. These examples in no way

FIGURE 1-19

Files can be organized by project only

▼

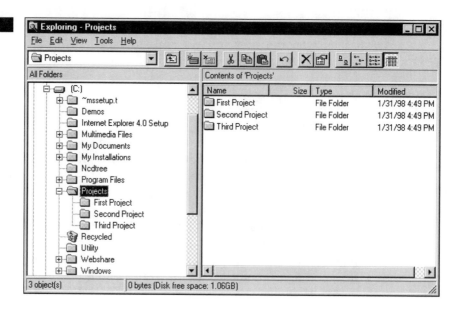

FIGURE 1-20

Keep track of your reusable objects by giving them their own folder

▼

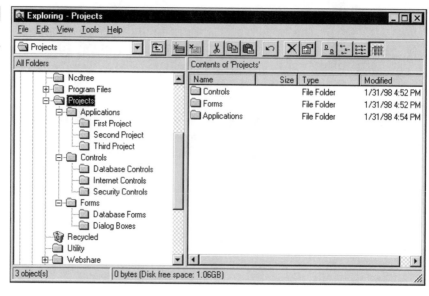

exhaust the possibilities for managing your projects. You don't have to use either of them, but you should use some type of organized system.

Collaborating with Others

Keeping track of your own projects can be quite a task. Introducing other developers makes it even more difficult. Many problems can arise from having multiple developers. Most are a result of two or more people working on the same file.

Communication is the key to avoiding problems when working in a team environment. The best way to protect project files in a team environment is to use version control software, such as Microsoft Visual Source Safe.

Version control software allows developers to lock files while they are working on them. This prevents others from modifying files that you are working on. Such software can also keep previous versions of files for your reference.

CREATING PROJECTS

New projects can be created when you first start Visual Basic. You can also create projects after starting Visual Basic. To create a new project, follow these steps:

1. Choose New Project from the File menu.
2. If you already had a project open, you may be asked if you want to save any changes. Click the Yes or No button to continue.
3. Select the type of project that you want to create in the New Project dialog box shown in Figure 1-21.
4. Click the OK button or double-click your selection.

Now that you have created your project, you should save it. When saving a project, you are saving the project file and the files of the objects used in the projects. Follow these steps to save a project:

1. Choose Save Project from the File menu.
2. Select a name and location for the files in the project, such as form files. See Chapter 2 for more information on naming objects and files.
3. Repeat step 2 as many times as necessary.
4. Select a name and location for the project file.

FIGURE 1-21

*The New Project
dialog box is
different after you
have started
Visual Basic*
▼

The next time you save the project you will not be prompted to select a name and location for all of the files, unless you have added a new file to the project. Adding and removing objects is discussed in the following section.

Adding and Removing Objects in Projects

The default project is created with a single form. Most projects require the use of more than one form and sometimes the use of other types of objects. To add an object to a project, choose the type of object you want from the Project menu. The choices are as follows:

▼ Form

▼ MDI Form

▼ Module

▼ Class Module

▼ User Control

▼ Property Page

▼ User Document

▼ ActiveX Designer

▼ File

If you choose to add a file, you can select the Add As Related Document checkbox in the Add File dialog box. This adds the file to the project as an outside document that is related to the project. You might do this with a Word document or an Excel spreadsheet. When you view this file from the Project Explorer it is opened with the application that created it.

Use the second button on the standard toolbar to add a new object to a project.

There may be times when you want to remove an object from a project. To do so, select the object in the Project Explorer and choose Remove from the Project menu. The Remove command is followed by the name of the selected object. Removing a file from a project does not delete the file.

Files can be added, saved, and removed by right-clicking on them in the Project Explorer.

Using Project Groups

In some cases, you may have several related projects that you want to work on simultaneously. This is done using *project groups*. A project group can be made up of many different projects, but one of them must be designated the *startup project*. The startup project is the project that Visual Basic uses when you choose the run command while working with a project group.

To create a project group, you must add one or more projects to your Visual Basic session while you are working with a project. Follow these steps to add a project and create a project group:

1. Choose Add Project from the File menu.

2. Select a New, Existing, or Recent project to add from the Add Project dialog box shown in Figure 1-22. This dialog box is very similar to the one used when starting Visual Basic.

3. Repeat step 2 as many times as necessary.

4. Choose Save Project Group from the File menu.

5. If you added any new files while creating your project group, you are prompted to save them. Choose a name and location for the project group file.

Right-click on a project in the Project Explorer and choose Set As Start Up from the shortcut menu to make it the startup project. From that same menu, choose Remove Project to remove a project from the group.

Tip

Add new projects by using the first button on the standard toolbar. This button has a dropdown menu that lets you choose to create a Standard EXE, ActiveX EXE, ActiveX DLL, or ActiveX Control project.

EXAMPLE

An example of a directory structure that separates a project into three development stages is shown in Figure 1-23.

Initially, the project files are stored in the Development directory. As development continues and the project is ready for testing, the files

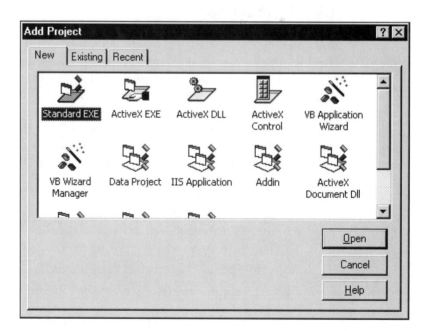

FIGURE 1-23

Directory structure for the development of projects

▼

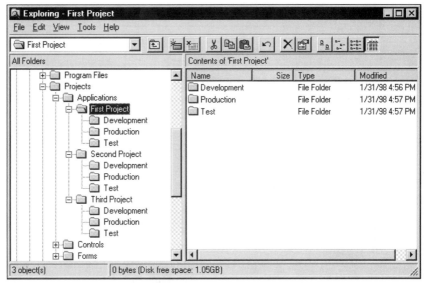

are moved into the Test directory. Testing is performed on the files in the Test directory. Changes suggested by testers are made to the Development files. When developers are comfortable with the changes, the modified files in the Development directory are moved to the Test directory—replacing the files that testers used to come up with their suggestions. Eventually, the files in the Test directory are ready to be distributed to users. At that time, they are moved to the Production directory. Now, the process can begin again, using any new requirements presented by users.

EXERCISES

1. Create a new project and save it as FirstProject in a folder that you have created for your projects.

2. Add a new form to FirstProject.

3. Add a new user control to FirstProject.

4. Create a project group using FirstProject and a new project called SecondProject.

5. Remove the user control from FirstProject.

1.7 PRINTING PROJECTS

Projects can be printed to help you review them or distribute hard copies to others. This printed material can also be used for documentation purposes. Printing Visual Basic projects involves more than simply issuing a print command. You must specifically tell Visual Basic what to print. As with other Windows applications, you can also specify which printer to use.

SELECTING WHAT TO PRINT

Visual Basic can print an entire project or a single line of code. It is up to you to determine what you need. To begin the process of printing, choose Print from the File menu. Figure 1-24 shows the Print dialog box.

In the Range section of the Print dialog box, choose to print selected code, the current object, or the entire project. Then, choose what you want printed and the print quality to be used. Click the OK button to print the project according to your selections.

Select the Print To File checkbox to send the contents of the print job to a file. If you choose this option, you will be prompted to supply a name and location for the file.

FIGURE 1-24

The Print dialog box deals with one project at a time ▼

Print - Project1.vbp ☒

Printer: HP LaserJet

Range
- ○ Se̲lection
- ● C̲urrent Module
- ○ Current P̲roject

Print What
- ☐ F̲orm Image
- ☑ C̲ode
- ☐ Form As T̲ext

Print Quality: High ▼   ☐ Print to Fi̲le

OK

Cancel

Setup...

Help

SETTING PRINTER PROPERTIES

Most Windows applications that allow you to print also allow you to specify which printer you would like to use and make changes to the settings for that printer. Visual Basic gives you this ability. There are two ways to access the printer setup:

▼ Click the Setup button in the Print dialog box.

▼ Choose Print Setup from the File menu.

Either method opens the Print Setup dialog box shown in Figure 1-25.

This dialog box is not specific to any one printer. Regardless of the type of printer used, it has the same appearance and the same choices. The most important selection in this dialog box is the Name of the printer. You choose this from a dropdown list box that lists all of the printers installed on your computer. Then, you choose the paper size, paper source, and orientation for your print jobs.

Note *Click the Properties button of the Print Setup dialog box to set properties that are specific to the printer you choose.*

FIGURE 1-25

The Print Setup dialog box works for all printers

▼

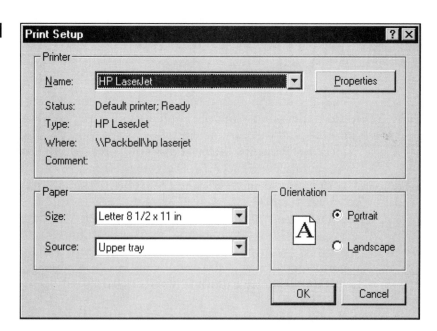

EXAMPLES

1. To select a different printer, open the Print Setup dialog box and click the arrow at the right side of the Name dropdown list box. Then, select the name of a different printer.

2. To change the orientation of your print jobs from Portrait to Landscape, click the Landscape option button on the Print Setup dialog box.

3. To change the resolution of the material sent to your printer, select a different value in the Print Quality dropdown list box on the Print Setup dialog box.

EXERCISES

1. Print only the image of a form.

2. Print the code of an entire project.

3. Print the image and code of a form.

4. Open the Properties dialog box of your printer.

1.8 *B*UILDING AND RUNNING *APPLICATIONS*

Building an application *compiles* the code into a format that Windows can understand. Compiled applications are then distributed to users—who can run the compiled applications. *Syntax* errors, which are incorrect words in the code or in the wrong order, are identified when you compile a project. *Logic* errors refer to your application not performing as planned. They must be identified through testing and debugging procedures. See Chapter 12 for more information.

Projects can be run from within a Visual Basic session, which means that the code is compiled and the application is started. This lets you preview and test your application. It is also how debugging is performed. Some of the options for building applications affect the way that applications are run in Visual Basic.

BUILDING APPLICATIONS

To prepare an application to be distributed to users, it must be *built* or compiled. Building an application generates an executable file that is used to start the application. To compile a project, follow these steps:

1. Open the project that you want to compile.
2. Choose Make *Project Name* from the File menu, where Project Name is the name of the project that you are compiling.
3. In the Make Project dialog box shown in Figure 1-26, choose a name for the compiled application and where to save it.
4. Click the OK button.

Note

To compile all of the projects in a project group, choose Make Project Group from the File menu.

FIGURE 1-26

The Make Project dialog box determines the name and location of the compiled project
▼

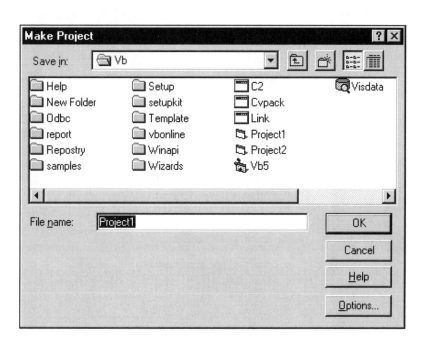

This compiles the project using the default settings. To change the compiler settings, click the Options button on the Make Project dialog box. This opens the Project Properties dialog box shown in Figure 1-27.

The Make tab of the Project Properties dialog box allows you to include version information with your compiled projects. For example, you can provide a version number and specific comments, such as Company Name, Legal Trademarks, and Product Name. The version number consists of a Major, Minor, and Revision number. Click the Auto Increment checkbox to have the revision number increased by one every time that you make the project. A project's title and the icon used to represent it can also be changed on this tab. Icons are chosen from the icons that are used in the project.

Click the Compiler tab to change the way that your project is compiled. The most important decision to make here is whether to compile to native code or pseudo-code (p-code). All Visual Basic applications require the file MSVBVMx0.DLL to operate, where x refers to the Visual Basic version that the application was created in. Projects compiled to native code don't require any additional supporting files to operate, but projects compiled to p-code require additional support files

FIGURE 1-27

When opened from the Make Project dialog box, the Project Properties dialog box displays the Make and Compile tabs

▼

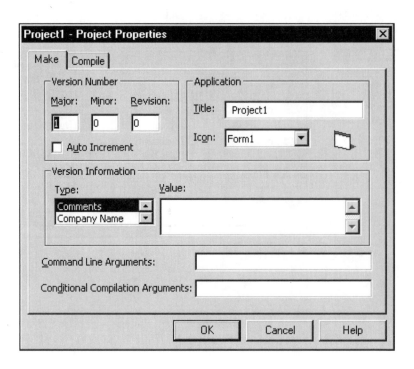

to be functional. If you choose to compile to native code, you must make some choices about how the project is optimized, as shown in Figure 1-28.

When compiling to native code, you can choose to have the compiler build the project to be fast, small, or not do anything special. You can even have it favor a particular processor (Pentium Pro).

> **Note** *The Make and Compile properties of a project can be accessed any time by choosing Project Properties from the Project menu. This opens the full Project Properties dialog box, which includes the General, Make, Compile, and Component tabs.*

RUNNING APPLICATIONS

Making a project allows it to be run outside of a Visual Basic session. However, this is inconvenient when developing and testing an application. It is easier to make changes to your project and

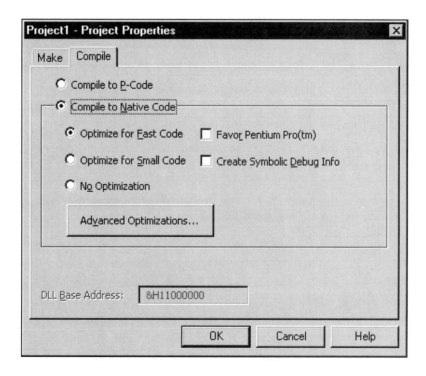

immediately run them to see the effect of the changes. Then, you can make more changes and continue this process until you are happy with the results.

Before running your project, there are a couple of options that you should be aware of. Figure 1-29 shows the General tab of the Options dialog box. The Compile section has two options that are used when running your projects: Compile On Demand and Background Compile.

Select the Compile On Demand checkbox to have Visual Basic compile only the code that it needs to run the application. For example, if an application has four forms and you only use two of them while running it from Visual Basic, only the two used forms are compiled. The Background Compile option uses idle time to compile an entire project, whether or not the parts are used.

Note

The Background Compile option can only be selected if the Compile On Demand option is selected.

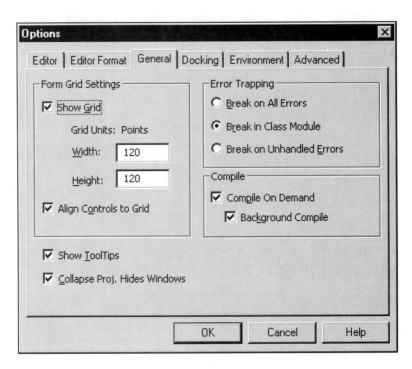

FIGURE 1-29

Compile options on the General tab of the Options dialog box

▼

These options are selected by default. This gives you the best performance when running your applications. You can run your application using any of the following methods:

▼ Press F5

▼ Click the Run button on the toolbar

▼ Choose Start from the Run menu

To have your entire project compiled before it is run—regardless of the setting in the Options dialog box—choose Start With Full Compile from the Run menu or press CTRL-F5.

EXAMPLES

1. To auto increment the revision number of a project every time that it is compiled, select the Auto Increment checkbox on the Make tab of the Project Properties dialog box.

2. To compile a project so that it favors the Pentium Pro processor, select the Favor Pentium Pro checkbox on the Compile tab of the Project Properties dialog box.

EXERCISES

1. Generate an executable that uses native code on the root of your hard drive called Native.

2. Generate an executable that uses p-code on the root of your hard drive called Pseudo.

3. Run a project compiling only the necessary code.

4. Run a project compiling all of the code before it starts.

Mastery
Skills Check

1. Which tab on the New Project dialog box gives you the quickest access to the last project that you worked on?

2. How do you view the code for a form?

3. How do you develop forms for a user that has a lower resolution than you do?

4. Name all of the properties that control the appearance of a form.

5. How many controls are in the Toolbox?

6. Can you create a new project while you have a project open?

7. How do you print the images for all of the forms in a project?

8. How do you run a project after compiling all of the code for that project?

2

Adding Code and Using Events

chapter objectives

Visual Basic is a powerful development environment because it allows applications to be developed visually. You drag and drop controls onto forms. Then, you arrange and size controls on a form to create the interface for your Windows applications. However, the forms and controls by themselves do not create very useful applications. Code must be added to forms and controls to give them more complex functionality. Programming code is a set of instructions that tells the computer what to do.

When developing Windows applications, *events* are used as triggers to perform the actions of a program. Pressing a button, changing the size of a form, or just moving the mouse causes an event. This is where the real power of Visual Basic development comes from: combining events with code to produce powerful applications. These applications are called *event-driven* applications because the events that users perform make the application work.

Review
Skills Check

You should be able to correctly answer the following questions before beginning this chapter:

1. What are the three ways to start Visual Basic?

2. How do you view a form in the Object window?

3. Can you specify the position at which a form appears?

4. What is used to set complex properties?

5. How many ways are there to add a control to a form?

6. Do Project files contain code?

7. How many projects can Visual Basic print at once?

8. Are all projects compiled the same?

2.1 USING THE CODE WINDOW

Forms and other visual objects are designed in the Object window. The Object window acts like a canvas that forms can be painted on.

However, no code can be added in the Object window. In order to add code, the Code window must be used. Figure 2-1 shows the Code window.

VIEWING CODE

A project is made of objects such as forms, user controls, and modules. A standard module is a file with nothing in it but code. In addition, forms, user controls, and other project objects have code modules. To view these objects' code modules, select the object and click the View Code button in the Project Explorer. A Code window can only display the code for a single object. If you want to view the code for two different forms, they must each be opened in their own Code window.

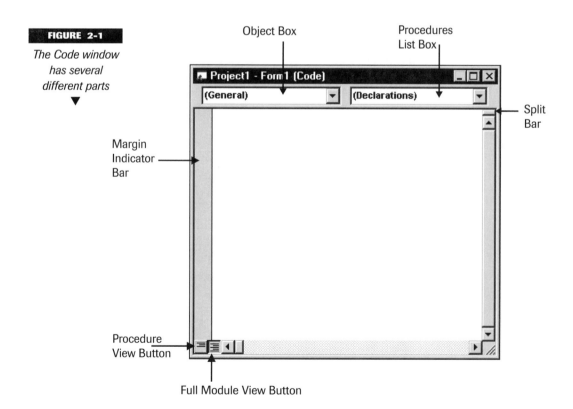

FIGURE 2-1

The Code window has several different parts
▼

Using the Object Box

The Object Box indicates which section of the code module is displayed. Form modules contain the following:

- ▼ general section
- ▼ section for the form
- ▼ section for each control on the form

Select a section to view the code for that section. To view the code for a command button named cmdClickMe, for example, you would select it from the Object Box. The Code window would then display the code for that command button.

Standard modules and Class modules both have a general section; Class modules also have a class section.

The Code window lists all of the code for a module. The Object Box and the Procedure/Events Box only change the area of the module that is displayed in the Code window. To view a single procedure at a time, you must click the Procedure View button. This forces the Code window to only display the procedure that is selected in the Procedure/Events Box. Click the Full Module View button to display all of the code again.

Using the Procedure/Events Box

Sections of code group different procedures that are part of the same object. A command button might have three procedures, for example. Selecting the command button in the Object Box moves the cursor of the Code window to the first procedure that was defined for the command button. When this happens, that procedure becomes selected in the Procedure/Events Box. If the selected object has no procedures defined for it, a definition for the object's default procedure is created—although it contains no code.

Procedure names are bolded in the Procedure/Events Box for procedures that contain code.

Procedures often correspond to events that occur for a control. When a control is selected in the Object Box, all of its events are listed in the Procedure/Events Box. These are called *event procedures,* and each control has a default event. The default event procedure for a command button is the **Click** event. This event is triggered when a user clicks the command button, which causes the code in this procedure to execute. Depending on the *scope* of a procedure, other procedures/events may be able to force it to execute. The scope of a variable or procedure refers to *when* it exists and *what* parts of an application has access to it while it exists. Scope is discussed in further detail in the "Using Scope" section of this chapter.

By default, Standard Modules don't list any event procedures in the Procedure/Events Box because they don't have events. These code modules only have user-created procedures, which are listed after they are created.

ENTERING AND EDITING CODE

Code is entered in the Code window just as you do in any other text editor or word processor. You place the cursor where you want to place the code and begin typing. Just like word processors that help with spelling and grammar, Visual Basic's Code Editor helps with syntax and word usage.

Press CTRL-SPACEBAR to have Visual Basic finish the word that you are typing in the Code Editor.

Setting Editor Options

Many Editor options help you automatically complete your code or warn you of possible problems. Other Editor options control the way code is listed in the Code window. These features can be very helpful, but you may not like all of them. To turn an option On or Off, choose Options from the Tools menu and click that option's checkbox. Figure 2-2 shows the Editor tab of the Options dialog box. The following sections explain each option.

Many of the Editor options can be accessed from the Edit menu and the Code window's shortcut menu if they are turned Off.

AUTO SYNTAX CHECK This option checks each line of code as it is entered. If a problem is found, you are immediately notified and the

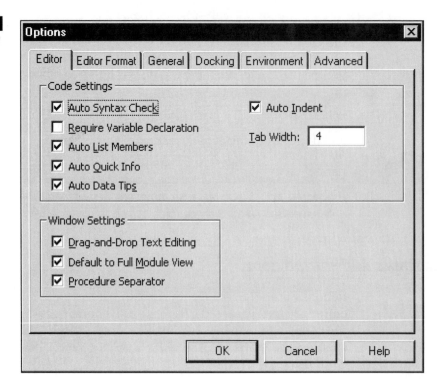

FIGURE 2-2

Code settings and window settings are controlled on the Editor tab of the Options dialog box

▼

format of the code in question changes. For more information on formatting in the Code Editor, see the "Setting Editor Format Options" section later in this chapter.

REQUIRE VARIABLE DECLARATION   This option requires explicit variable declarations in modules. The **Option Explicit** statement is placed at the beginning of all modules when it is selected. This means that all variables must be declared. The"Using Variables" section of this chapter discusses declaring variables and data types.

AUTO LIST MEMBERS   This option lists possible endings to a statement that you are typing. If this feature is active, for example, and you type the name of a command button followed by a period, then the properties and methods of the command button are listed. A period after an object allows you to access that object's properties and procedures (methods), which can be collectively referred to as an object's members. You can then choose which member to address from the list or press the ESC key to type it yourself.

Tip

If you press the ENTER key to select a member from the auto list, the selected member is added and a new line of code is started. To select a member and stay on the current line, press the SPACEBAR.

AUTO QUICK INFO   Procedures and functions can have many parameters. Remembering all of them can be a daunting task, especially for those that are rarely used. This option displays a ToolTip after you enter a function name. The ToolTip lists the parameters it requires.

AUTO DATA TIPS   This option displays the value of a variable in a ToolTip if you place the cursor over it, but it only works when debugging an application. Chapter 12, "Debugging Visual Basic Applications", discusses debugging in greater detail. The "Watching Variables" section of that chapter shows how to view the values of variables while your application is running.

AUTO INDENT   This option forces subsequent lines of code to be indented to the point of the previous line of code. If your first line of code is indented two spaces, for example, each time you enter a line of code and press the ENTER key the next line is automatically indented two spaces.

TAB WIDTH   This option controls how many spaces are added to code when you press the TAB key. The default is 4 spaces and can vary from 1 to 32.

DRAG-AND-DROP TEXT EDITING   This option allows selected text to be dragged to a new location in the current Code window or another Code window.

DEFAULT TO FULL MODULE VIEW   This option causes all of a module's code to be displayed when the module is opened in the Code Editor. If not selected, only one procedure at a time is displayed. Changing this option does not affect Code windows that are currently opened.

PROCEDURE SEPARATOR   This option causes lines to be drawn between all of the procedures in a module, making it easier to identify where a procedure ends and a new one begins.

Setting Editor Format Options

The way that text is formatted in the Code Editor can make it easy to identify the different elements that exist in Visual Basic code. Different fonts and colors give a visual cue as to what the purpose of the text is. For example, text that contains a syntax error defaults to red, while comments default to green. Figure 2-3 shows the Editor Format tab of the Options dialog box. This is where the Code Editor formatting options are set.

In addition to formatting options, the Editor Format tab of the Options dialog box controls the display of the Margin Indicator Bar.

FIGURE 2-3

The Editor Format tab shows a sample of how code elements appear in the Code window
▼

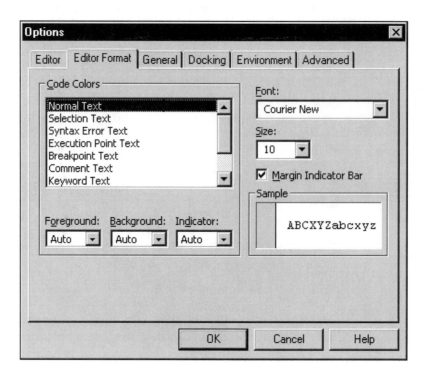

To make a change to the appearance of a code element, select the element in the Text List and choose the formatting options that you desire. Use the Sample display to preview your changes.

EXAMPLES

1. To view the Click procedure for a command button, double-click a command button that is on a form and select Click from the Procedure/Events Box.

2. To prevent Visual Basic from making suggestions for finishing statements, deselect the Auto List Members checkbox on the Editor tab of the Options dialog box.

3. To have normal text appear white on a blue background, open the Editor Format tab of the Options dialog box. Then, select Normal Text in the Text List and choose White as the Foreground color and Blue as the Background color.

EXERCISES

1. Change the Tab Width of the Code window to two spaces.

2. Disable the ability to drag and drop text in the Code Editor.

3. Switch between Procedure view and Full Module view.

4. Make the size of syntax error text equal 12.

2.2 *USING NAMING CONVENTIONS*

You should utilize a method of naming conventions when assigning names to objects and variables in a project. This makes reading and understanding your code easier for you and others, because control types and data types are discernible from the names they identify. While naming conventions should provide a *guideline* for naming objects and variables, they should not restrict the ability to appropriately name items.

Naming conventions do not have to be specific to a development tool. Variable data types are generally consistent across different programming languages. This allows the same naming convention to be used in different development tools.

Keep in mind that there are many different methods that can be used to create a naming convention. This chapter focuses on adding a prefix to names that indicate what type of object or variable they are. This method is flexible enough to handle new types as they occur and allows for quick identification. The following sections discuss and suggest a method for naming objects and variables.

NAMING OBJECTS

Controls are given a name using the Name property in the Properties window. A naming convention makes it easy to identify the type of object you are referring to in your code. This makes code easier to read and can help find problems in your code faster. Table 2-1 lists commonly used prefixes for many different controls.

While these prefixes are not official standards, they are the most commonly used. If you encounter any controls that are not listed, you can always come up with your own two- or three-letter prefix. For custom controls that you purchase, you can add the company's initials to the prefix.

There may be times that you are referencing a control when you won't know the control type in advance. In this case, you could use a ctr prefix. This prefix suggests that a control is being referenced without being too specific.

NAMING VARIABLES

Variables should be named using a prefix. The prefix can be determined by the following options:

▼ the data type of the variable, which is discussed in the "Understanding Data Types" section of this chapter

▼ the scope of the variable, which is discussed in the "Using Scope" section of this chapter

Control	Prefix	Example
3D Panel	pnl	pnlGroup
Animated button	ani	aniMailBox
Checkbox	chk	chkReadOnly
Combobox, dropdown list box	cbo	cboEnglish
Command button	cmd	cmdExit
Common dialog	dlg	dlgFileOpen
Communications	com	comFax
Data control	dat	datBiblio
Data-bound combo box	dbcbo	dbcboLanguage
Data-bound grid	dbgrd	dbgrdQueryResult
Data-bound list box	dblst	dblstJobType
Directory list box	dir	dirSource
Drive list box	drv	drvTarget
File list box	fil	filSource
Form	frm	frmEntry
Frame	fra	fraLanguage
Gauge	gau	gauStatus
Graph	gra	graRevenue
Grid	grd	grdPrices
Horizontal scroll bar	hsb	hsbVolume
Image	img	imgIcon
Key status	key	keyCaps
Label	lbl	lblHelpMessage
Line	lin	linVertical
List box	lst	lstPolicyCodes
MAPI message	mpm	mpmSentMessage
MAPI session	mps	mpsSession
MCI	mci	mciVideo
MDI child form	mdi	mdiNote
Menu	mnu	mnuFileOpen

TABLE 2-1 *Suggested Object Naming Conventions* ▼

Control	Prefix	Example
MS Flex grid	msg	msgClients
MS Tab	mst	mstFirst
OLE	ole	oleWorksheet
Outline	out	outOrgChart
Pen BEdit	bed	bedFirstName
Pen Hedit	hed	hedSignature
Pen ink	ink	inkMap
Picture	pic	picVGA
Picture clip	clp	clpToolbar
Report	rpt	rptQtr1Earnings
Shape	shp	shpCircle
Spin	spn	spnPages
Text box	txt	txtLastName
Timer	tmr	tmrAlarm
UpDown	upd	updDirection
Vertical scroll bar	vsb	vsbRate
Slider	sld	sldScale
ImageList	ils	ilsAllIcons
TreeView	tre	treOrganization
Toolbar	tlb	tlbActions
TabStrip	tab	tabOptions
StatusBar	sta	staDateTime
ListView	lvw	lvwHeadings
ProgressBar	prg	prgLoadFile
RichTextBox	rtf	rtfReport

TABLE 2-1 *Suggested Object Naming Conventions* (continued) ▼

Table 2-2 lists the prefixes typically used for variables. In addition to the prefix, variable names should be as descriptive as possible. Use more than one word if necessary. For example, if you have a string variable for the manufacturer of a car, use the variable name strCarManufacturer. When using more than one word in a variable, capitalize the beginning of each word. If you use abbreviations for very long variable names, be sure to develop a standard for such abbreviations.

Data Type	Prefix	Example
Boolean	bln	blnFound
Byte	byt	bytRasterData
Collection Object	col	colWidgets
Currency	cur	curRevenue
Date/Time	dtm	dtmStart
Double	dbl	dblTolerance
Error	err	errOrderNum
Integer	int	intQuantity
Long	lng	lngDistance
Object	obj	objCurrent
Single	sng	sngAverage
String	str	strFirstName
User-defined Type	udt	udtEmployee
Variant	vnt	vntCheckSum

TABLE 2-2   *Suggested Variable Naming Conventions* ▼

Tip

Include a u *at the beginning of a user-defined type variable when you still want the underlying data type to be clear.*

EXAMPLES

1. To create an OK and CANCEL button on a form, place two command buttons on a form. Select each button and change its Name and Caption properties. Name one button "cmdOK" with a caption of "OK" and name the other "cmdCancel" with a caption of "Cancel".

2. Identify a custom command button that you purchased from the ACME Software Company by using the prefix "cmdAS".

3. Name a variable that holds a **True** or **False** value as to whether or not something exists "blnExists".

4. Name a variable that holds a **True** or **False** value as to whether or not an exception to something exists "blnExceptionExists".

EXERCISES

1. Why are naming conventions used?

2. What is the commonly used prefix for the name of a form?

3. What is the commonly used prefix for the name of a Label control?

4. What is the prefix for a variable that holds a currency value?

5. What is the prefix for a variable that holds a user-defined string value?

2.3 USING VARIABLES

Variables are used to store values in an application. Many different types of values can be stored in variables. Types of values are called *data types*. While it is not absolutely required, it is good practice to declare all of your variables and assign them a data type. Declaring a variable is the process of specifically telling Visual Basic the name of a variable that you are going to use. This declaration can also assign a data type to the variable. There is a much lower chance for errors when you declare variables.

Values stored in variables can be manipulated to change their value or derive new values. The types of operations that can be performed on variables depend upon their data type.

The location and structure of a variable declaration determines *when* variables are accessible and *what* parts of an application can access them. This is called the *scope* of a variable. Scope is discussed in greater detail in the "Using Scope" section of this chapter.

UNDERSTANDING DATA TYPES

A variable's data type determines what kind of values it can hold. Each data type has its limitations and advantages. Some can only hold very small values—requiring minimal amounts of memory—making them faster to use. Others can hold very large values—requiring more memory—making them slower than the smaller types.

Finding the right data type is important to your application. You must be sure that a variable can hold any value it might encounter, which will create the fastest application possible. Table 2-3 summarizes the available data types. Smaller storage approximately translates into better performance.

You should now have a feel for Visual Basic data types. The following sections discuss declaring and using variables, as well as assigning data types. Use Table 2-3 as a reference when deciding upon a data type for a variable.

If you are unsure of the maximum value for a variable, use the data type that handles the largest value possible. Placing a value into a variable with a data type incapable of handling the value will cause an error.

DECLARING AND USING VARIABLES

A variable declaration is a statement to the program that a variable exists and is going to be used in the program. This declaration usually indicates the *type* of variable that is being declared, although it is not

Data Type	Storage	Range
Byte	1 byte	0 to 255
Boolean	2 bytes	True or False
Integer	2 bytes	−32,768 to 32,767
Long (long integer)	4 bytes	−2,147,483,648 to 2,147,483,647
Single (single-precision floating-point)	4 bytes	−3.402823E38 to −1.401298E-45 for negative values; 1.401298E-45 to 3.402823E38 for positive values
Double (double-precision floating-point)	8 bytes	−1.79769313486232E308 to −4.94065645841247E-324 for negative values; 4.94065645841247E-324 to 1.79769313486232E308 for positive values
Currency (scaled integer)	8 bytes	−922,337,203,685,477.5808 to 922,337,203,685,477.5807
Decimal	14 bytes	+/−79,228,162,514,264,337,593,543,950,335 with no decimal point; +/−7.9228162514264337593543950335 with 28 places to the right of the decimal; smallest non-zero number is +/−0.0000000000000000000000000001
Date	8 bytes	January 1, 100 to December 31, 9999
Object	4 bytes	Any Object reference
String (variable-length)	10 bytes + string length	0 to approximately 2 billion characters
String (fixed-length)	Length of string	1 to approximately 65,400 characters
Variant (with numbers)	16 bytes	Any numeric value up to the range of a Double
Variant (with characters)	22 bytes + string length	Same range as for variable-length String
User-defined (using Type)	Number required by elements	The range of each element is the same as the range of its data type.

TABLE 2-3   *Visual Basic Data Types* ▼

required to. The following sections discuss declaring variables and using the different data types.

Using Implicit Declaration

Variables do not have to be declared, although it is good programming practice to do so. If you use a variable in code with no declaration, it takes on the data type of the value that is assigned to it. This is called *implicit declaration* because the declaration of the variable is implied. Declaring variables this way can be useful, but it can also lead to unwanted errors. For example, one of the benefits of declaring variables is that Visual Basic checks the spelling of variables in code against the variables that you have declared. Visual Basic doesn't actually think the variable is spelled wrong, it only knows that the variable name that you tried to use isn't declared.

If you want to use implicit declaration, your program cannot use the Option Explicit statement, which requires variables to be declared.

This method of variable declaration should be avoided. A better way to assign values of an unknown data type is to declare the variable using the **Variant** data type (see Tables 2-2 and 2-3). That way, you can assign any type of value to the variable and Visual Basic still helps you avoid errors in your code.

Using Explicit Declaration

The Require Variable Declaration option on the Editor tab of the Options dialog box forces variables to be specifically declared before they can be used. This is called *explicit declaration*. Placing an **Option Explicit** statement at the beginning of a module also forces all variables to be declared within that module.

Enforcing explicit declaration is performed separately on each module, which means that every module must contain the **Option Explicit** statement to use this option. Any modules that do not contain this statement will allow implicit declaration.

Because implicit declaration is allowed, this does not mean that explicit declaration is not allowed. However, Visual Basic does not flag misspelled variables as nonexistent without the explicit option. It uses the misspelling as an implicit declaration.

Declaring Variables

Declare variables using the **Dim** statement:

```
Dim yourVariableName [As Type]
```

The Dim statement should only be used when declaring local variables. Module-level variables and global variables should use the Public or Private statement.

Replace yourVariableName with the name that you are using to identify the variable. The As Type section in the **Dim** statement is optional. Without it, the variable is declared using the **Variant** data type. Variable names must comply with the following guidelines:

- ▼ begin with a letter
- ▼ cannot exceed 255 characters
- ▼ cannot contain periods

In addition to the guidelines above, variable names must also be unique within their scope. For example, a form or a procedure can't have two variables declared with the same name.

Variables exist as long as the procedure or object in which they exist. So, if a variable is created when a procedure is called (executed), it ceases to exist when the procedure stops.

Variables declared using the Static keyword continue to exist after the procedure ends. This is useful if a variable should only be available within a particular procedure, but must hold its value even after the procedure ends. That way, the next time that the procedure runs, the static variable still contains the previous value.

Using Different Data Types

Each data type has its own unique features. Choosing the appropriate data type allows values to be stored efficiently and prevents data from becoming corrupted. The following sections summarize the major data types.

USING THE BOOLEAN DATA TYPE   A Boolean variable has two possible values: **True** or **False**. This makes the Boolean data type ideal for any values that are True/False, Yes/No, or On/Off. When converting numeric values to a Boolean data type, 0 becomes **False** and all other

values become **True**. The following are example Boolean
variable declarations:

```
Dim blnStatement As Boolean
Dim blnTestedForDefects As Boolean
Dim blnLightStatus As Boolean
```

Caution

*Make sure that there are only two possibilities for values stored in Boolean
variables, because a Boolean only has two possible values.*

USING NUMERIC DATA TYPES   Numeric data types store numbers. There
are several different types of numeric data types depending on the size
and format of the values being stored. For information on how to
manipulate numeric values stored in variables, see Chapter 5. The
following are example declarations of numeric data types:

```
Dim bytCurrentSelection As Byte
Dim intCounter As Integer
Dim lngBigCounter As Integer
Dim sngStatePopulation As Single
Dim dblCountryPopulation As Double
Dim curMutualFunds As Currency
```

USING THE STRING DATA TYPE   String variables hold non-numeric values.
This data type can hold numeric values, but mathematical operators
can't be used to manipulate the values. The declaration for string
variables can also specify a definite size for the string variable by
adding an asterisk and the size to the end of the **Dim** statement. These
are called fixed-length strings. The following are examples of string
variable declarations:

```
Dim strFirstName As String
Dim strMiddleInitial As String * 1
Dim strLastName As String
```

There are also operators and functions that can manipulate string
variables. For more information, see Chapter 4.

A numeric variable can be assigned a value from a string variable if the value of the string variable is a valid numeric value.

USING THE DATE DATA TYPE   Dates are stored using the **Date** data type. Values can be assigned to date variables using date literals, which is any valid date format surrounded by pound signs. For example, #10/31/98# or #October 31, 1998# could both be assigned to a date variable. The following are examples of date variable declarations:

```
Dim dtmStartDate As Date
Dim dtmEndDate As Date
```

USING THE OBJECT DATA TYPE   The **Object** data type allows Visual Basic objects—and objects from other applications—to be created in code and/or assigned to a variable. This is a versatile data type for working with objects, but whenever possible you should use the object's data type.

USING THE VARIANT DATA TYPE   The **Variant** data type can store values of any data type. It adjusts according to the value that is assigned to it. When declaring a variant variable, the As Type section is not necessary. The following are examples of variables declared as variant:

```
Dim vntTemporary As Variant
Dim vntNewValue
```

Values stored in a variant variable can be manipulated, but any operators used must be able to be used on the stored value.

Converting Data Types

Values can be converted to specific data types using conversion functions. These functions can only convert values that are appropriate for the data type that a value is being converted to. Table 2-4 summarizes the conversion functions.

The following are examples of the syntax for conversion functions:

```
strFirstAnswer = CStr(vntInput)
curWeeklyPay = CCur(intHoursWorked * sngPayRate)
```

Conversion Function	Converts Value To
Cbool	Boolean
Cbyte	Byte
Ccur	Currency
Cdate	Date
CDbl	Double
Cint	Integer
CLng	Long
CSng	Single
CStr	String
Cvar	Variant
CVErr	Error

TABLE 2-4 *Conversion Functions* ▼

USING ARRAY VARIABLES

Arrays allow multiple values to be stored in a single variable. An array variable uses an index to keep track of its values. Each value can be set or retrieved using the array variable name and the index number. The following is the declaration for a variable that can contain an array of string variables:

```
Dim strExampleArray(9) As String
```

This example can hold 10 different values, because the array index starts at zero and goes up to the upper limit that you specify in the declaration. If you want the array index to start and stop at specific numbers, you can define the variable to do so, such as the following:

```
Dim intNumberArray(1 To 10)
Dim dtmDateArray(54 To 87)
```

To set or retrieve any values from an array, you use the array variable name with an index number. The following shows an array that is created and populated with names:

```
Dim strNameList(1 To 4)
strNameList(1) = Scott
```

```
strNameList(2) = Nancy
strNameList(3) = John
strNameList(4) = Josie
```

Arrays can be multidimensional. To create a two-dimensional array, you would declare it using two numbers in the index separated by a comma.

EXAMPLES

1. The **Byte** data type can hold values from 0 to 255.

2. To force all variables in a module to be declared, add the **Option Explicit** statement to the general section of the module.

3. The variable name strMy.Name is not valid because it contains a period.

4. The following function statement returns a Boolean value of **False**:

   ```
   CBool(0)
   ```

5. The following function statements return a Boolean value of **True**:

   ```
   CBool(1)
   CBool(-12)
   CBool(843)
   ```

6. The following is the declaration for a two-dimensional array that can hold the days of each month:

   ```
   Dim strDaysOfMonth(1 To 12, 1 To 31) As String
   ```

EXERCISES

1. What is the maximum value of a variable with an **Integer** data type?

2. Is 55intSpeedLimit a valid variable name?

3. Declare a numeric variable that holds a two-digit number.

4. Declare two variables; one that holds the name of a city and one that holds a two-letter abbreviation for a state.

5. Which function converts variables to a **Date** data type?

6. Assuming the following, how would you retrieve the value FRI?

```
Dim strDaysOfWeek(1 To 7) As String * 3
strDaysOfWeek(1) = "MON"
strDaysOfWeek(2) = "TUE"
strDaysOfWeek(3) = "WED"
strDaysOfWeek(4) = "THU"
strDaysOfWeek(5) = "FRI"
strDaysOfWeek(6) = "SAT"
strDaysOfWeek(7) = "SUN"
```

2.4 *U SING SCOPE*

The *scope* of a variable or procedure refers to when it exists and what parts of an application has access to it while it exists. Scope is defined in the declaration of a variable or procedure. Procedures require that scope is included in their declaration, but the scope of variables can be implied by the absence of a defined scope.

USING SCOPE WITH PROCEDURES AND FUNCTIONS

Procedures and functions are code that is called upon to perform certain tasks. Code might be called upon to open a window when a button is pressed or rearrange the controls on a window when it is resized, for example. An important aspect to procedures is their scope, which determines their availability in an application. Limiting the scope of a procedure can protect sensitive data or prevent unwanted errors.

Using Private Procedures and Functions

A **Private** procedure or function can only be called from within the same module. In other words, the code module for Form A could not call a **Private** procedure in the code module for Form B. The following are declarations for a **Private** procedure and a **Private** function:

```
Private Sub MyPrivateProcedure()


End Sub
```

```
Private Function MyPrivateFunction() As Variant

End Function
```

Any attempt to call a **Private** procedure or function from an outside module results in an error.

Using Public Procedures and Functions

Public procedures and functions can be called from any module. This is what makes it possible to build a code module that can be used across multiple applications. For example, you could create a code module that contained financial functions that you often use in your applications. By declaring the functions as **Public**, they can be called by any other code module. You simply include the module in all projects that use the functions. The following are procedures and functions declared as **Public**:

```
Public Sub GetInitializationData()

End Sub


Sub MyPublicProcedure()

End Sub

Public Function GetHeadCount() As Integer

End Function

Function MyPublicFunction() As Variant

End Function
```

*Leaving the **Private** or **Public** keyword out of the declaration makes the procedure or function **Public** by default.*

USING SCOPE WITH VARIABLES

Variables also have a scope. While procedures and functions might contain variables, the scope of the procedure or functions does not affect the scope of the variable. The introduction of scope to variables creates the potential for an addition to any naming convention that you might be using for your variables. You may want to indicate the scope of all variables, or only certain types of variables.

Using Procedure-level Variables

Variables that are declared within a procedure are referred to as *procedure-level* variables. They are created when the procedure—or function—is called, and they are destroyed after the procedure runs. The following is an example of procedure-level variables:

```
Private Sub DemoProcLevelVariables()
  Dim intCounter As Integer
  Dim strGrade As String * 1

End Sub
```

The variables declared within the procedure above can only be accessed from within that procedure. They are not available to any other procedures or functions, not even within the same module. No change to any naming convention is necessary, because the variable is local to a single procedure. Therefore, there are no other variables of the same scope to confuse the variables with.

Using Module-level Variables

Variables declared as **Private** in the declarations section of a module are available to any procedure within that module, but not to any other modules. That means any procedure within a module can access and manipulate these variables. The following is an example of module-level variable declarations:

```
Private mvntScratchPad As Variant
Private mcurCost As Currency
```

The above is placed in the declarations section of a module. An *m* has been added to the beginning of each variable to indicate its scope. That way, it is obvious when you are working with module-level variables.

Using Global Variables

Global variables are declared in the declarations section of a module. Their declaration includes the **Public** keyword to indicate that they are available to all modules within an application. The following is a declaration for global variables:

```
Public gdtmLastActivity As Date
Public gintChancesLeft As Integer
```

These variables can be accessed and manipulated by all modules in an application. The *g* is added to the beginning of the variable to show that it is a global variable. This makes it easier to identify the scope of variables in code.

Limit the number of global variables that you use. Good programming practice dictates that they be used only sparingly because they have great potential to cause problems in code.

EXAMPLES

1. The following is the declaration for a **Private** procedure:

   ```
   Private Sub DoSomething()

   End Sub
   ```

2. The following is the declaration for a **Public** function that returns a string value:

   ```
   Public Function ParseString() As String

   End Function
   ```

3. The following is the declaration for a **Public** procedure that contains procedure-level variables:

   ```
   Private Sub CountMoney()
     Dim curDenomination As Currency
     Dim intNumberOfBills As Integer

   End Sub
   ```

EXERCISES

1. Write a declaration for a **Public** procedure named MyFirstProcedure.

2. Write a declaration for a **Private** function named MyFirstFunction that returns a **Variant** data type.

3. Declare a module-level variable named dblCalculatedValue.

4. Declare a global variable that stores the results of a question during a lie-detector test.

2.5 *U*SING SUBROUTINES AND FUNCTIONS

Subroutines and functions are the heart of coding in Visual Basic. Procedures perform tasks and possibly manipulate values stored in variables or in a database. Functions are similar to procedures, but they return a value—which means that functions can be used to place values into variables. Both subroutines and functions can accept values as part of their procedure call. These values are called *parameters* or *arguments* and can be used to change the behavior of a procedure according to the values that are passed to it.

Note

It is good practice to comment your code. An ' added at the beginning of a line of code causes the line to be treated as a comment. Comments are used for documentation only and do not affect the execution of the program.

USING SUBROUTINES

Subroutines execute the code that they contain when they are called. A subroutine is called by placing its name into a line of code. For example, the following line of code executes a subroutine called DoNothing that accepts no parameters:

```
DoNothing
```

The following line of code calls a subroutine called DoSomething that takes an integer value as a parameter:

```
DoSomething(7)
```

Calls to subroutines are often located in *event* procedures, which are subroutines that are triggered by an event. Events are caused by Windows users. Events are discussed further in the "Using Events" section of this chapter.

USING FUNCTIONS

Functions are subroutines that return a value when called. They can be used to process parameters and return a value. That value can then be stored in a variable. The return value of a function is returned by setting the function name equal to the value that the function should return. The following example is a function that takes a first and last name to return a full name:

```
Function GetFullName(strFirstName As String, strLastName As String)
   GetFullName = strFirstName + " " + strLastName
End Function
```

This is a very simple example. The function would be more useful if it accepted another parameter that determined if the function returned the name as the first name and then the last name or the last name, a comma, and then the first name. That would require the use of conditional operators, which are discussed in Chapter 6.

USING EVENTS

Events are the basis of most Windows applications. Windows made event-driven applications a reality, because Windows itself is driven by the occurrence of events: moving the mouse or clicking the mouse button. This puts the user in control of the application. The actions of the user cause events to occur. These events then cause procedures to be performed, which is how the work of the application is performed.

An easy way to see what the events of an object are is to select the object in the Object Box of the Code window. Then, you can view all of the event procedures in the Procedure/Events Box. Selecting an event from this list box creates the declaration for that event in the Code Editor, allowing you to add the code you would like to execute when that event occurs. The following is the event procedure for when a command button is clicked:

```
Private Sub cmdExitButton_Click()

End Sub
```

The code that is added to this procedure is executed when the cmdExitButton command button is clicked.

Tip

To add code to the default event of an object, double-click the object in the Object window. This causes the event procedure to be declared in the Code window so that you can add code for the event.

EXAMPLES

1. To call a subroutine named SaveSettings that takes no parameters, use the following:

   ```
   SaveSettings
   ```

2. The following is the declaration for a **Private** subroutine that accepts an integer parameter:

   ```
   Private Sub UseIntegerValue(intValue As Integer)

   End Sub
   ```

3. The following is a function that increments a counter by the number that is passed to it using a variable that it keeps track of:

   ```
   Function IncrementCounter(intIncrement As Integer)
      Static intCounter As Integer

      intCounter = intCounter + intIncrement
      IncrementCounter = intCounter
   End Function
   ```

4. Double-click on a command button to declare a procedure for its **Click** event.

EXERCISES

1. Does a subroutine return a value?

2. How do you return a value from a function?

3. Write a function call to a function named GetAccountBalance that accepts an integer account number and places the return value in a currency variable.

4. Does an event cause code to be executed?

Mastery Skills Check

1. What window is used to view and edit Visual Basic code?

2. How can code be written so that variable types are obvious without seeing the variable declaration?

3. Do all variables have to be declared?

4. Can variables declared in one module be used anywhere in an application?

5. What causes an event?

3

Using Intrinsic
Visual Basic Controls

chapter objectives

3.1 Using the Label and TextBox Controls

3.2 Using the Command Button Control

3.3 Using the Frame, Checkbox, and Option
Button Controls

3.4 Using the ListBox and ComboBox Controls

3.5 Using the Drive List Box, Directory List Box, and
File List Box Controls

3.6 Using Formatting Controls

3.7 Using Control Arrays

3.8 Using Tab Order

ntrinsic Visual Basic controls are the controls that come *built in* to Visual Basic. Microsoft created these commonly used controls for developers to utilize without having to spend time writing complex ActiveX controls of their own. *Controls* are placed on forms to allow users to interact with an application. Common controls include labels, text boxes, command buttons, checkboxes, option buttons, and list boxes. These controls are used in almost every Windows application. Visual Basic provides these controls in its toolbox so that they can be placed on forms and customized.

In addition to the unique features of each individual control, all controls have common properties and abilities that allow them to be manipulated in a similar fashion. This makes it possible to use the same method (using the Properties window or reusing code) to format different controls and work with them in code. The similarities can be just as important as the unique features that make controls so useful.

Review
Skills Check

You should be able to correctly answer the following questions before beginning this chapter:

1. How do you require that all variables in a module be explicitly declared?

2. Are naming conventions used for objects or variables?

3. What types of data can a variable hold?

4. Does scope affect where a variable can be used?

5. Do all subroutines correspond to a Windows event?

3.1 $\quad$ **USING THE LABEL AND TEXTBOX CONTROLS**

Labels are normally used to identify controls that don't have captions, such as text boxes. Text boxes allow users to enter information. Programs can then use this inputted information in various ways. Label and text box controls are normally used together to clarify the type of information that should be entered into a text box, but they can be used separately.

Let's start by creating a simple application that we can build on throughout the chapter. Follow these steps to create this application:

1. Start a new Standard EXE application.

2. Save the new project—the form as About and the project as Controls Tutor.

3. Create another new form and save it as Main.

4. Change the Name property of the project to ControlsTutor.

5. Change the Name property of the About form to frmAbout.

6. Change the Name property of the Main form to frmMain.

ADDING LABELS TO FORMS

Adding labels to a form is just like adding any other control to a form. Chapter 1 showed you how to add controls to a form. Place three Label controls on frmAbout, so that it looks like Figure 3-1.

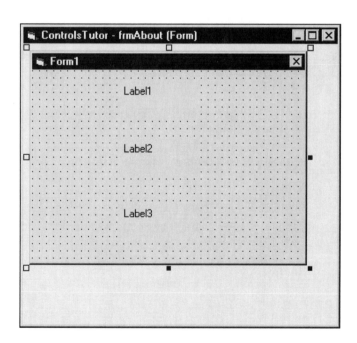

This form contains information about the application. It is used to tell the user who wrote the application, when it was written, or any other information that you feel might be useful. The following sections show how to customize the Label controls.

Setting Properties for Labels

At this point, the About box has three labels. Let's start with the one at the top of the window. Select it and change the properties to match the following:

Property	Value
Name	lblTitle
Caption	Controls Tutor

Next, you should open the Font property page and make the font as large as possible, with bold styling. After doing this, you may have to resize the label so that all of the text is visible. There are two ways to resize a control:

▼ Select the control and drag one of its sides with a sizing handle.

▼ Change the Width or Height property of the control.

The AutoSize property causes controls to automatically increase their size so that anything being displayed within them is fully visible.

Select the label in the middle of the form and change the following properties:

Property	Value
Name	lblAbout
AutoSize	True
Caption	Written by Scott L Warner for Teach Yourself Visual Basic

Change the following properties for the label at the bottom of the form:

Property	Value
Alignment	2 – Center
Appearance	0 – Flat
BackColor	Button Face
Name	lblClose
Caption	OK

In addition to changing the preceding properties, increase the font size to 14. Now, all of the properties are set for the labels of the About box, which should look similar to Figure 3-2.

Adding Code for Labels

Generally, labels do not have any code associated with them. They are mainly used to describe other controls, but it is possible to add code to labels. Our project is going to have code for lblClose that closes the About box and opens the Main form. To add the code, complete the following steps:

1. Select frmAbout in the Project Explorer.

FIGURE 3-2

Changing properties can affect the appearance of a control
▼

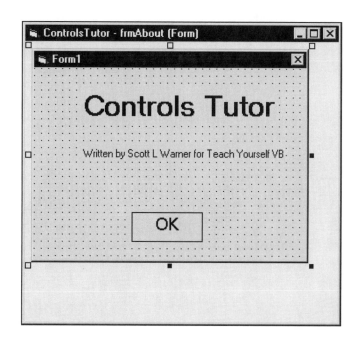

2. Click the View Code button.

3. Enter the following code:

```
Private Sub lblClose_Click()
    frmMain.Show
    Unload Me
End Sub
```

The declaration makes this subroutine an event procedure, with lblClose identifying the object and **Click** specifying the event. When you enter this procedure, the Object Box is changed to the lblClose object and the Procedure/Events Box is changed to the **Click** event.

The first line of code opens the Main form. **Show** is a form method that loads the form into memory and displays it. A *method* is just another name for a procedure that is used when the procedure is part of a specific object. More than one control can have the same method. For example, most controls have a **SetFocus** method, which moves the focus to that control when called.

You can find all of the methods for an object by selecting the object and pressing CTRL-J. A dropdown list box opens with all of the properties and methods for the object. The methods are each listed next to a green icon.

The second line of code closes frmAbout. **Unload** is a procedure that unloads a form from memory, which also makes it disappear from the screen. To use this procedure, put it in on a line in your code and place a form name after it. The keyword **Me** refers to frmAbout, because this procedure is part of that form. The actual form name could have been used, but by using **Me**, no changes to the code are necessary if the form name changes.

Double-clicking on the label opens the Code window and automatically declares the default Click event procedure.

Finally, change the **BorderStyle** of frmAbout to 0 – Fixed Dialog and the **Caption** to About. Run the application. The first thing that you see is the About box. Click the OK label to close the About box and open the Main form. It's not very exciting yet, but you just wrote a simple Windows application—and it only took two lines of code.

ADDING TEXT BOXES TO FORMS

Instead of displaying information about your application when it starts, you might want to force the user to supply a name and a password in order to continue. This adds a level of security to your application, and the information can be kept in variables for use in other parts of the application—for example, you might want to utilize the user name in a personalized message box. To create a login dialog box, complete the following steps:

1. Add a regular form to the Controls Tutor project.

2. Save the form as Login.

3. Change the following properties of the form:

Property	Value
Name	frmLogin
BorderStyle	3 – Fixed Dialog
Caption	Login
Height	1850
Width	3840

Place two Label controls and two TextBox controls on the form. Make the following changes to the properties for one of the labels:

Property	Value
Name	lblUserName
AutoSize	True
Caption	User Name:
Left	120
Top	135

Then, make the following changes to the properties of the other label:

Property	Value
Name	lblPassword
AutoSize	True
Caption	Password:
Left	120
Top	525

The next section covers the changes that need to be made to the TextBox controls.

Setting Properties for Text Boxes

Set the following properties for a text box to make it the text box for the User Name:

Property	Value
Name	txtUserName
Height	345
Left	1300
Text	
Top	120
Width	2300

Make the following changes to the properties for the control that holds the password:

Property	Value
Name	txtPassword
Height	345
Left	1300
Text	
Top	510
Width	2300

Your form should now look like Figure 3-3. This form is not complete; we'll finish it in the "Using the Command Button Control" section of this chapter.

It's usually not a problem if others know what someone's user name is, but passwords always need to be kept private. To prevent the password from displaying as it is typed in, the **PasswordChar** property of txtPassword is set to asterisk (*). That way, any character entered in the txtPassword text box is displayed as an asterisk.

Although an asterisk is the most commonly used value for the PasswordChar property of a text box, any character can be used.

If you don't feel that a label is enough for all users to understand what should be entered in a textbox, you can add a ToolTip to the text box. To do so, enter some descriptive text for the **ToolTipText** property of any TextBox control. When a user places the mouse pointer over the text box, the ToolTip text is displayed.

FIGURE 3-3

Text boxes make it possible for users to supply input

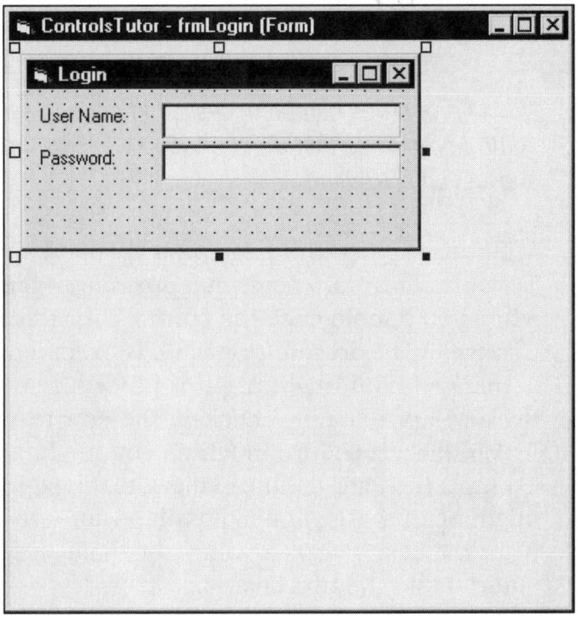

▼

ControlsTutor - frmLogin (Form)

Login

User Name:

Password:

Adding Code for Text Boxes

The value that is contained in a text box is held in the **Text** property. This is how you access the text in this type of control. The following code snippet places the values in txtUserName and txtPassword into **Public** variables:

```
Public strUserName As String
Public strPassword As String

strUserName = txtUserName.Text
strPassword = txtPassword.Text
```

The period (.) between the control name and the property is used to associate property names with specific controls. It is called *dot notation*. Most control properties can be accessed in code this way. This allows properties to be changed because of an action by the user. For example, dialog boxes with a More button appear to grow larger and add more controls when the button is clicked (like the Find and Replace dialog box in Microsoft Word). Actually, the other controls were always there. A piece of code similar to the following just made the form large enough to see the other controls when you clicked the button:

```
frmFormName.Height = 5000
```

Note

Not all properties can be accessed in code at run time. In addition, some control properties that don't existing while designing a form do exist when the application is running.

In this project, there is no need to add any code to either of the TextBox controls. The *default procedure*—the procedure that is declared when you double-click the control—for the TextBox control is the Change event procedure, which is executed after the text in the control is changed. You might use this procedure to write code that validates the new text—that is, checks if the new text is acceptable.

Another procedure in which you might add code is the DoubleClick event. If the user double-clicks a text box, for example, a dialog box might open that contains possible values to enter into the text box. After the user selects a value, the dialog box closes and the value is entered into the text box.

EXAMPLES

1. To change the properties of a label on a form, click on the Label control and change the properties in the Properties window.

2. To remove the default text from a TextBox control, select the control and delete whatever is in the **Text** property.

3. To add code to a control, select the control in the ObjectProcedure/Events Box and then select an event procedure from the Procedures box.

EXERCISES

1. How do you make a Label control automatically adjust its size to display all of its text?

2. What happens if you double-click a Label control?

3. How do you place the value from a text box into a variable?

4. What happens if you double-click a Text Box control?

3.2 *USING THE COMMAND BUTTON CONTROL*

Command buttons are usually referred to as buttons. Buttons are a result of the visual, event-driven nature of Windows. Where users once had to type a command, they now press a button. This makes learning and working with applications easier because users don't have to memorize commands.

In many cases, there are two standard buttons: an OK button and a Cancel button. After entering information or making choices on a form, the user clicks the OK button to accept the information on the form or the Cancel button to reject the information. An example of this is when Visual Basic prompts you for the name of a new tab for the Toolbox. You enter a name and click the OK button to create the tab using that name. If you click the Cancel button, the tab is not created and nothing happens—even if you entered a name.

ADDING COMMAND BUTTONS TO FORMS

Command buttons are added to forms just like any other control. When using command buttons it's a good idea to come up with a few standards. Decide on a size, font, and standard location to use for your command buttons, and maintain this consistently throughout your application. This gives your applications a professional appearance and makes it easier for users to find common buttons, such as OK or Cancel.

Captions for command buttons should be as descriptive as possible. This can cause command buttons to be larger than the standard size you have decided upon. Don't worry about it; it's more important that the user know what the button is for than it is to make it a particular size.

To demonstrate the use of command buttons, let's do some more work on the Login form that we built in the "Using the Label and TextBox Controls" section. The following section will place an OK and Cancel button at the bottom of the Login form and set their properties.

Setting Properties for Command Buttons

Choose a button to be the OK button, and make the following changes to its properties:

Property	Value
Name	cmdOK
Caption	OK
Default	True
Height	400
Left	360
Top	960

Any time the user presses the ENTER key, the OK button's **Click** event is triggered. This happens because the **Default** property is set to **True**. However, if the user moves the focus to another command button—selects a different command button—before pressing the ENTER key, the **Click** event of the selected command button is triggered. Focus always refers to the currently selected control. Users change focus by clicking on a control or pressing the TAB key.

Only one command button on a form can have its Default property set to True. If the Default property is set to True for one command button, the Default property is automatically set to False for all other command buttons on the same form.

Next, select the other button as the Cancel button and make the following changes to its properties:

Property	Value
Name	cmdCancel
Cancel	True
Caption	Cancel
Height	400
Left	2040
Top	960

Command buttons have a property that allows a button to be specifically designated as the Cancel button. This property is appropriately called the **Cancel** property. The **Cancel** property—when set to **True**—triggers the button's **Click** event any time the user presses the ESC key. Like the **Default** property, only one button on a form can have this property set to **True**. Of course, you can still click the button with the **Cancel** property assigned to **True** with the mouse pointer to get the same result.

There are other button properties that can be used to customize their appearance. For example, you can add pictures and even change the picture according to the state or condition that the button is in. After you become an experienced user, you may want to explore these properties.

Adding Code for Command Buttons

The Login form is almost complete. Figure 3-4 shows that it can now accept a user name and password. It can also let the user accept their entry or reject it—almost. Code must be added to the command buttons for them to function properly.

Before adding code to the command buttons of the Login form, open the Project Properties dialog box and make this form the Startup

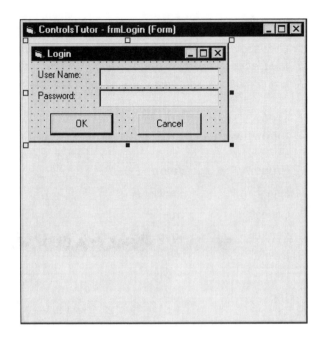

Object. When the project runs, the Login form will open. Also add the
following variables to the declarations section of the Login form:

```
Public mtxtUserName As String
Public mtxtPassword As String
```

These variables are available only while the Login form exists,
but they are accessible from anywhere within the project. Double-
click the OK button to open the Code window. The **Click** event
procedure is automatically declared for you. Add the following code
to this procedure:

```
Private Sub cmdOK_Click()
    mtxtUserName = txtUserName.Text
    mtxtPassword = txtPassword.Text
    frmMain.Show
    Unload Me
End Sub
```

If the user clicks the OK button, the user name and password are
placed into module-level variables and the Main form is displayed.
Finally, the Login form is closed.

The following code should be placed in the **Click** event procedure for the Cancel button:

```
Private Sub cmdCancel_Click()
    Unload Me
End Sub
```

This causes the Login form to be unloaded, which also closes the application because it was the only form. You still could have loaded the Main form without placing any values in the module-level variables, but if the user cancels the login process, they probably don't want to use the application. Run the project a couple of times and try both of the buttons.

EXAMPLES

1. Create a new form and add two buttons to it. Select one of the buttons and change its **Default** property to **True**. Then, select the other button and change its **Default** property to **True**. Finally, re-select the first button and notice that its **Default** property was changed to **False** because only one command button can be the default.

2. Double-click a command button to declare its default event procedure—the **Click** event procedure.

EXERCISES

1. What does setting the **Cancel** property to **True** do for a command button?

2. Can the **Default** and **Cancel** properties both be set to **True** for a command button?

3. Declare the **Click** event procedure for a button named cmdClickMe.

4. Add a call to the procedure DoSomething to the **Click** event of cmdClickMe. DoSomething does not take any parameters.

3.3   *USING THE FRAME, CHECKBOX, AND OPTION BUTTON CONTROLS*

Checkboxes and option buttons are both used to give users predefined choices. Users can only choose from the available options. These options are placed within a frame, which includes a *caption*. The caption indicates to the user what choice they are making. For example, a frame with a caption of Age might contain several option buttons that indicate age ranges. Figure 3-5 shows this example.

Option buttons are *mutually exclusive*, which means that choosing one automatically excludes the others as possibilities. Checkboxes are not mutually exclusive, but can still be grouped with a frame. Users can choose as many checkboxes as they want.

ADDING OPTION BUTTONS TO A FORM

Let's expand on the Login form by adding some option buttons that allow the user to specify what type of user they are. First, we need to enlarge the form and move the command buttons. Change the Height property of the form to 4500. Then move the command buttons by making the Top property 3600 for both of them.

Tip

To set a property value for several controls at the same time, select all of the controls that you want to change by holding down the SHIFT key while clicking each control. Then, set the property in the Properties window.

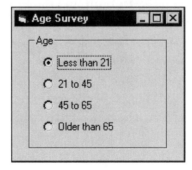

Draw a Frame control on the form and set the properties for it as follows:

Property	Value
Name	fraUserType
Caption	User Type
Height	1550
Left	100
Top	1000
Width	3500

The Login form should now look like Figure 3-6.

Next, add three option buttons to the form, placing them within the Frame control. Setting the properties for the option buttons is discussed in the following section.

Setting Properties for Option Buttons

Let's define three types of users for our application: Regular User without Admin Rights, Regular User with Admin Rights, and Super

FIGURE 3-6

Frames group option buttons and provide a description for the user

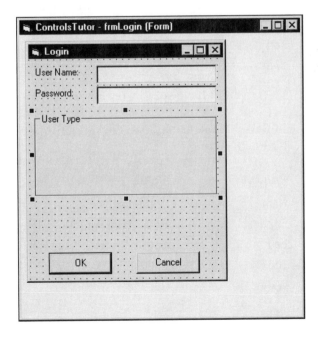

User with All Rights. These types don't have any actual meaning; they're just for this demonstration. Make the following changes to the first option button:

Property	Value
Name	optRegWithoutAdmin
Caption	Regular User without Admin Rights
Left	400
Top	1200
Value	True
Width	3000

The **Value** property of an option button indicates whether or not it is selected. This property is set to **True** when the option button is selected and **False** when it is not selected. Make the following changes to the properties of the next option button:

Property	Value
Name	optRegWithAdmin
Caption	Regular User with Admin Rights
Left	400
Top	1600
Width	3000

You could have set this option button's **Value** property to **True**, but that would have changed the first option button's **Value** property to **False**. Make the following changes to the properties of the last option button:

Property	Value
Name	optSuperUser
Caption	Super User with All Rights
Left	400
Top	2000
Width	3000

Your Login form should now look like Figure 3-7. This group of option buttons is fully functional; there is no code needed to make these controls operate.

Adding Code for Option Buttons

There may be certain situations when you want to add code to option buttons, but it shouldn't happen often. Option buttons automatically display the type of behavior you would want to program into them; the **Value** property is set to **True** when an option button is clicked, and the **Value** property for all other option buttons on the form is set to **False**.

Option buttons are used in code, but it's usually code for other controls, such as command buttons. This type of code requires the use of control statements, which are covered in Chapter 6. To get the value of an option button in code, use dot notation, like the following:

```
blnVariable = optRegWithoutAdmin.Value
```

FIGURE 3-7

*Option buttons
work without
extensive coding*

▼

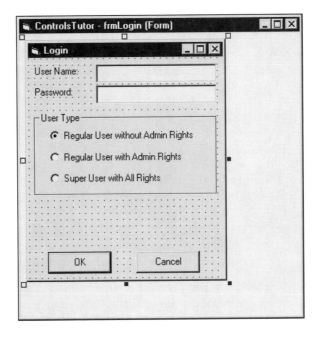

ADDING CHECKBOXES TO FORMS

Checkboxes are very similar to option buttons, but checkboxes have three possible values: **Unchecked**, **Checked**, and **Grayed**. An **Unchecked** value for a checkbox is the equivalent of a **False** value for an option button, and **Checked** is the same as **True**. Grayed is an intermediate state where the checkbox is neither **Checked** nor **Unchecked**.

Unlike option buttons, checkboxes are not mutually exclusive; more than one checkbox on a form can be **Checked** at once. Checkboxes are also often used when there is only a single option. The Checkbox control allows a single option to be **Checked** and **Unchecked**; once an option button is **Checked**, the only way to **Uncheck** it is to check a different option button.

Setting Properties for Checkboxes

Add two checkboxes to the Login form and make the following changes to the properties of the first checkbox:

Property	Value
Name	chkCheckMessages
Caption	Check for New Messages
Left	400
Top	2600
Width	3000

Then, change the properties of the other checkbox to match the following values:

Property	Value
Name	chkSendData
Caption	Send Diagnostic Data to Support
Left	400
Top	3000
Width	3000

These are the properties that are changed the most when working with checkboxes. As with the option buttons, these choices are made up for this project to demonstrate the use of checkboxes. Figure 3-8 shows what the Login form should look like now. The next section briefly discusses using checkboxes and their values in code.

Adding Code for Checkboxes

The **Click** event procedure of a checkbox can be used to activate or deactivate options associated with that checkbox. In other code, the **Value** property of checkboxes is used to control processing. Control statements are not essential when processing the data from checkboxes. For our example, let's add a couple of **Integer** variables to the Login form and place the values from the checkboxes into them during the **Click** event procedure of the OK button. The Click procedure would now look like the following:

```
Private Sub cmdOK_Click()
    mtxtUserName = txtUserName.Text
    mtxtPassword = txtPassword.Text
    mintCheckMessages = chkCheckMessages.Value
    mintSendData = chkSendData.Value
    frmMain.Show
    Unload Me
End Sub
```

FIGURE 3-8

Checkboxes allow multiple options to be selected simultaneously
▼

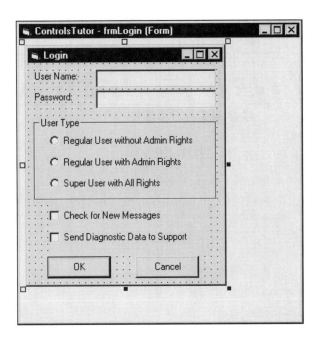

EXAMPLES

1. To select an option button named optFirstOption in code, use the following statement:

```
optFirstOption.Value = True
```

2. To cause only one option button to be selected at any one time, place the option buttons on a form. That's it; the mutually exclusive behavior of option buttons is automatic.

3. To cause a checkbox named chkFirstOption to be in a Grayed state, use the following code:

```
chkFirstOption.Value = 2
```

EXERCISES

1. Place four option buttons on a blank form.

2. Do option buttons have a double-click event?

3. Do checkboxes have a double-click event?

4. How do you reference the value of an option button or checkbox?

3.4 *USING THE LISTBOX AND COMBOBOX CONTROLS*

List boxes and combo boxes are used to give users choices. These function in a fashion similar to checkboxes and option buttons, but they present the choices in a different manner. The main difference between the list box and combo box controls is the amount of space that they consume on a form. This may be a factor in determining which one you use.

ADDING LIST BOXES TO FORMS

List boxes display items on a form. They have the appearance of a multiline text box, but they cannot be edited. Users select an item or items from the list and these selections are used in the application. The biggest limitation of a list box is size; it takes up a lot of room on a form.

Save the Controls Tutor project; we'll get back to it shortly. Create a new Standard EXE project. Save the form as frmListbox and save the project as List Controls. Then, add two ListBox controls to the form and follow the instructions in the next section.

Setting Properties for List Boxes

List boxes have the same size and location properties of all the other controls, though size and location aren't the properties that make this control useful. Use the mouse to arrange the list boxes on the form until it looks similar to Figure 3-9. Also, change the name of the list box on the left to lstOptions and the one on the right to lstSelectedOptions.

FIGURE 3-9

Items can be displayed in list boxes

▼

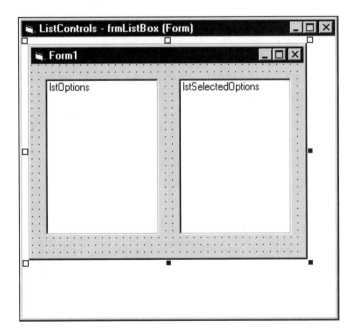

In this example, we're going to add items to lstOptions. To do so, complete the following steps:

1. Open the dropdown list box for the List property of lstOptions.

2. Select the first item in the list, as shown in Figure 3-10.

3. Type the following items into the list, pressing CTRL-ENTER after each item to go to the next line:

   ▼ Option A

   ▼ Option B

   ▼ Option C

   ▼ Option D

   ▼ Option E

4. Press the ENTER key to close the list box.

The list box now displays the items that you entered. While this looks nice, it probably won't do you much good when you go to write code for these items. List boxes also have an **ItemData** property that stores numeric values for each listed item. You could use the combination of the **List** and **ItemData** property, for example, to list employee names in the **List** property and place their employee IDs in the **ItemData** property. That way, users could select a name from the list and your program would know the ID for that employee.

Complete the following steps to add values to the **ItemData** property:

1. Open the dropdown list box for the **ItemData** property of lstOptions.

2. Select all of the items in the list—they should be all 0's.

3. Type the numbers **1** through **5** into the list, pressing CTRL-ENTER after each item to go to the next line.

4. Press the ENTER key to close the list box.

Now, Option A has an **ItemData** value of 1, B has a value of 2, and so on. Those are the essentials of setting the properties for a list box, but there are several other interesting properties that can be used, as described in the following sections.

FIGURE 3-10

The first item in the
list defaults to the
control name
▼

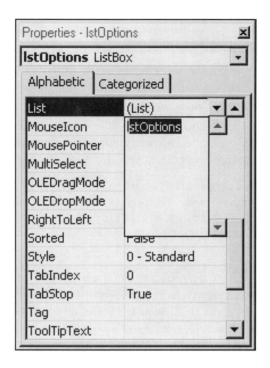

USING THE MULTISELECT PROPERTY   By default, only one item at a time can be selected in a list box. This is the case when the **MultiSelect** property is set to **None**. When it is set to **Simple**, more than one item can be selected at a time, but they must be individually selected using either a mouse click or pressing the SPACEBAR. The **Extended** setting for the **MultiSelect** property allows multiple items to be selected.

USING THE SORTED PROPERTY   Setting the **Sorted** property to **True** causes Visual Basic to handle all of the processing necessary to keep the list of items sorted in alphabetical order. This includes changing the index numbers that are used to access list items in code, which is covered in the "Adding Code for List Boxes" section.

USING THE STYLE PROPERTY   The **Style** property allows items in a list box to be displayed with a checkbox next to them, for example, when a user selects options in an installation application. Selected items have a check in their checkbox and unselected items do not.

When the Style property is set to Checkbox, the MultiSelect property must be set to None. However, more than one item can still be selected.

Adding Code for List Boxes

In this section, we're going to write code that adds items from lstOptions to lstSelectedOptions when double-clicked. Open the Code window for frmListBox and add the following procedure:

```
Private Sub lstOptions_DblClick()
  lstSelectedOptions.AddItem (lstOptions.List(lstOptions.ListIndex))
  lstSelectedOptions.ItemData(lstSelectedOptions.NewIndex) = _
    lstOptions.ItemData(lstOptions.ListIndex)
End Sub
```

These two lines of code transfer the **List** and **ItemData** values from lstOptions to lstSelectedOptions. The line continuation character (_) is used here to show one line of code on two lines. While there are only a few lines of code, a lot is happening here. First, the **AddItem** method of the lstSelectedOptions is being called. That method accepts two parameters: a string value and an integer value. The string value must be included and is added to the **List** property of the list box. The **List** property is an array of values; the first value in the list has an index of 0, the second 1, the third 2, and so on. When the string is added to the **List**, it is assigned the next available *index* in the **List** array. The index refers to the item's location in the list of values. If an integer value is included as a parameter, it is used as the index where the new value is inserted into the **List** array.

If you specify an index number when adding an item to a sorted list box, the sorting feature may not work properly from that point on.

In this example only the string value is included. The string value is added using the dot notation to access the **List** property array (lstOptions.List()) of the lstOptions list box. Also using dot notation, the index of the currently selected item (lstOptions.ListIndex) is used to specify which value from the **List** array is added to the second list box. To get the current index, the **ListIndex** property is used. This property is only available at run time.

After the code adds the item currently selected in the lstOptions list box to the lstSelectedOptions list box, the second line places the **ItemData** value for that item into the corresponding **ItemData** value. Like the **List** property, the **ItemData** property is also an array. The values in these arrays correspond to each other. This means that the **ItemData** for the value in **List**(3) is **ItemData**(3). Using the **NewIndex** property, which is a run-time property that specifies the last index number added to a list box, the **ItemData** property of lstSelectedOptions is updated with the **ItemData** value for the **List** value that was just added.

This code does nothing to prevent values from being duplicated in the lstSelectedOptions list box. To prevent that from happening, control statements (discussed in Chapter 6) have to be used.

To remove an item from a **List**, use the **RemoveItem** method. This method takes an index number as a parameter and removes the item at that location in the **List** array. Add the following procedure to have the ability to remove items from the lstSelectedOptions list box:

```
Private Sub lstSelectedOptions_DblClick()
    lstSelectedOptions.RemoveItem (lstSelectedOptions.ListIndex)
End Sub
```

This code could also be used with command buttons placed in between the two list boxes, as shown in Figure 3-11.

USING COMBO BOXES

Combo boxes are very similar to list boxes. They have many of the same properties and methods, but they display their list to users in a different manner than list boxes. Users can also make their own entries into combo boxes. The name *combo box* comes from the fact that the control is a combination between a dropdown list box and a list box. This control can actually take one of three different forms, which is controlled by its **Style** property:

▼ Dropdown Combo

▼ Simple Combo

▼ Dropdown Listbox

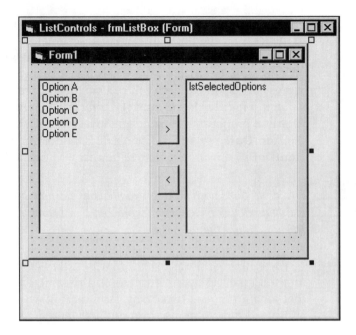

Figure 3-12 shows a form with each type of combo box. Combo1 is a dropdown combo; Combo2 is a simple combo; Combo3 is a dropdown list box.

A dropdown combo allows users to select from a list or to enter their own text. This is a good choice if you want to present the user with many choices and only have a small area to use. Users can also enter their own text in this control if none of the choices in the dropdown list is what they are looking for.

Simple combo boxes take up the same amount of space as a regular list box. Actually, simple combo boxes take even more space because they have a text box at the top that user can enter their own value in. This type of combo box behaves exactly like the dropdown combo.

By default, simple combo boxes do not display their list box. You must increase the height of the control for the list box portion to display.

Dropdown list boxes behave just like regular list boxes. Users can only choose from the items that are listed and cannot make their own entries. This control is simply a space-saving version of a list box.

FIGURE 3-12

The style of a combo box affects its appearance and behavior

▼

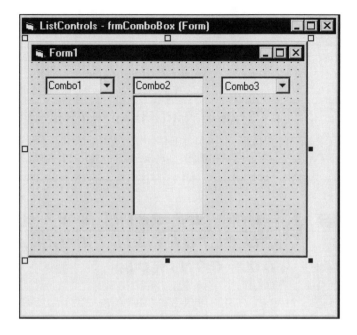

All three styles of combo boxes are used in code in basically the same way that a list box is used. However, dropdown and simple combo boxes allow users to enter their own text. If users enter text, the **ListIndex** property is -1 and the text can be retrieved using the **Text** property of the control.

EXAMPLES

1. The following procedure would cause an item to be copied from one list box to another when a button is clicked:

```
Private Sub cmdCopyItem_Click()
lstSelectedOptions.AddItem
(lstOptions.List(lstOptions.ListIndex))
lstSelectedOptions.ItemData(lstSelectedOptions.NewIndex)
= lstOptions.ItemData(lstOptions.ListIndex)
End Sub
```

2. To add an item to a list box in a procedure, use the **AddItem** method.

3. If a user types a value into a combo box instead of choosing from the combo box list, the **ListIndex** property is -1.

1. What parameters does the **AddItem** method accept?

2. How do you remove an item from a list box in a procedure?

3. What does the **List** property hold?

4. What does the **ItemData** property hold?

5. If a user enters a value into a combo box, how do you know it is a user-entered value? How do you use that value?

3.5 # USING THE DRIVE LIST BOX, DIRECTORY LIST BOX, AND FILE LIST BOX CONTROLS

Three of Visual Basic's standard controls interact with the file system to display hard drives, directories, and files. These controls have a variety of uses and are often used together. The following sections discuss each of these controls and illustrate how to use these controls.

USING THE DRIVE LIST BOX

The DriveListBox control displays the disk drives that are attached to a computer in a dropdown list box. All devices that have a drive letter are displayed, including hard drives, floppy drives, CD-ROM drives, and network drives. An icon is displayed next to the drive letter that indicates what type of device the drive is, as shown in Figure 3-13.

The **Drive** property is the important property for the drive list box. It is only available at run time. You can use the **Drive** property to set the drive letter in code. This property is normally used to set the **Path** property of the directory list box, which is discussed in the next section. The following code sets the **Drive** property of a drive list box to the D: drive:

```
drvDriveListBox.Drive = "D:"
```

When setting the Drive property of a drive list box, the colon that appears after a drive letter is optional.

Note

FIGURE 3-13

Drive list boxes show all resources that have been assigned a drive letter

▼

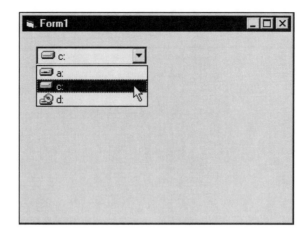

USING THE DIRECTORY LIST BOX

The directory list box is a special list box that displays the directory structure of a disk drive using a specialized list box. Directories are displayed as folders in a hierarchical structure. Subdirectories appear as closed folders beneath their parent directory, which appears as an open folder. Figure 3-14 shows a drive list box set to the C: drive and a directory list box with a path of C:\Windows\System.

The path of a directory list box can be determined using the **Path** property, which is a run-time-only property. This property can also be set in code. A common method for doing this is to place a drive list box and a directory list box on a form and use the following code to change the path of the directory list box any time a new drive is selected in the drive list box:

```
Private Sub drvDriveListBox_Change()
   dirDirectoryListBox.Path = drvDriveListBox.Drive
End Sub
```

Note   *The Path property of a directory list box can be set to a qualified network name. A qualified network name doesn't use a drive letter; it uses two backslahes and the name of a resource, such as \\servername. Specific directories for a resource can also be specified, such as \\servername\files\accounting.*

FIGURE 3-14

Directory list boxes show directories as folders

▼

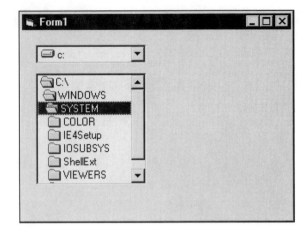

After adding this code to the **Change** event procedure for a drive list box, the **Path** property of the directory list box referenced in the code is changed to the drive selected in the drive list box. Coding the **Change** event procedure of a drive list box to update the **Path** property of a directory list box does not affect the default path of a directory list box. The path that the application is in determines this. If the application is in the C:\Program Files directory, the **Path** property of a directory list box is initially set to C:\Program Files.

If you want to specify the initial drive of a drive list box or path of a directory list box, use the Load event procedure of the form that the controls are on to set these properties when the form is loaded.

USING THE FILE LIST BOX

A file list box displays the files of a particular directory. This control has several properties that can limit the types of files that are displayed. The **Archive**, **Hidden**, **Normal**, and **System** properties determine if the file list box displays those types of files. They are **Boolean** properties, meaning that they are **True** (display that file type) or **False** (don't display that file type).

Like the ListBox control, the FileListBox control has a MultiSelect property that determines if more than one file can be selected.

Files can also be limited using a pattern in their file name. This is accomplished with the **Pattern** property. The default for this property is *.*, which displays all files. The asterisk is a *wildcard* character, which represents any character. Change the **Pattern** property to limit files by the beginning of their file name (for example, test*.*) or their file extension (for example, *.bat).

Like the directory list box, the file list box has a **Path** property, which is available only at run time. The **Change** event procedure can be used to synchronize the **Path** property of the directory and file list boxes, such as in the following code:

```
Private Sub dirDiectoryListBox_Change()
    filFileListBox.Path = dirDirectoryListBox.Path
End Sub
```

The DriveListBox, DirectoryListBox, and FileListBox controls can be placed on a form to create a dialog box that lets you select files. Figure 3-15 shows a form with DriveListBox, DirectoryListBox, and FileListBox controls. The code shown in this section could be added to keep these controls synchronized, so that the directory list box displays the folders of the drive selected in the drive list box and the file list box displays the files contained in the folder selected in the directory list box.

Tip

Use the drive list box, directory list box, and file list box to build a customized dialog box for opening files.

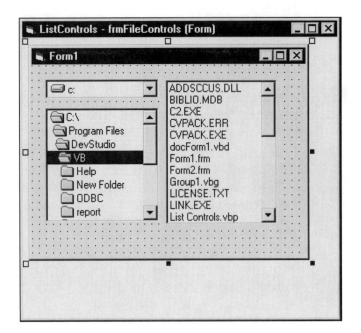

FIGURE 3-15

*View files using the
FileListBox control*

▼

EXAMPLES

1. To use a DriveListBox control, place it on a form and set the properties for appearance and position. The drive list box automatically lists all of the drive letters.

2. Use the **Change** event procedure of a drive list box to set the **Path** property of a directory list box to a newly selected drive.

3. Use the **MultiSelect** property to control how many files can be simultaneously selected in a file list box.

4. Set the **System** property of the FileListBox control to **False** to prevent system files from being displayed in a file list box.

5. To get the name of the currently selected file in a file list box, use the **List** and **ListIndex** properties—just like a regular list box.

EXERCISES

---

1. Can the **Drive** property of a drive list box be set while designing a form?

2. What property of the directory list box determines which directory is displayed?

3. What event procedure is triggered when the current directory is changed in the directory list box?

4. How would you display only the files with a TXT extension in a file list box?

5. Is the **Path** property of the directory list box and the file list box available at design time or run time?

3.6 *USING FORMATTING CONTROLS*

To this point, you have been given exact measurements to use when placing controls on forms. When building your own applications, you'll have to come up with these measurements yourself. The easiest way to do this is to just move the controls around on the form until it looks good. Visual Basic provides some tools that you can use to position your controls when building an application. These tools are discussed in the following sections.

Formatting tools base their changes on the control that most recently had focus.

ALIGNING CONTROLS

Many times, a form has several controls that need alignment, which is difficult to do by hand. To have Visual Basic align controls for you, complete the following steps:

1. Select multiple controls by either holding the SHIFT key down while clicking on each control or clicking on a form and dragging the mouse over all of the controls.

2. Choose Align from the Format menu.

3. Select the type of alignment you want to apply (to the selected controls) from the submenu.

To prevent yourself from accidentally moving controls around on a form, choose Lock Controls from the Format menu. Choose Lock Controls again to unlock the controls.

SIZING CONTROLS

When using the same type of control many times on a form, it can be tedious to make them all the same size. To quickly make several controls the same size, complete the following steps:

1. Select multiple controls by either holding the SHIFT key down while clicking on each control or clicking on a form and dragging the mouse over all of the controls.

2. Choose Make Same Size from the Format menu.

3. Select the type of sizing you want to apply (to the selected controls) from the submenu.

SPACING CONTROLS

Placing several controls on a form in a row is a common practice. To evenly space these controls, you could take the **Top** property of the first control and add a certain number to it. Then, you could do the same thing to the next control and so on until all of the controls were evenly spaced. But if you didn't like the way it looked, you would have to do it again. Complete the following steps to let Visual Basic do the work of spacing the controls for you:

1. Select multiple controls by either holding the SHIFT key down while clicking on each control or clicking on a form and dragging the mouse over all of the controls.

2. Choose Horizontal Spacing or Vertical Spacing from the Format menu.

3. Select the type of spacing you want to apply (to the selected controls) from the submenu.

You can also choose Center In Form from the Format menu to center selected controls either horizontally or vertically on a form.

ORDERING CONTROLS

There may be situations when you place controls on top of each other. For example, two controls might be displayed at the same location on a form, but at different times. Depending upon the order in which the controls were added to the form, you may have to move one control in front of another or vice versa. To change the order of selected controls, complete the following steps:

1. Select a control or controls.

2. Choose Order from the Format menu.

3. Choose to either Bring To Front or Send To Back the selected controls.

EXAMPLES

1. Place several command buttons of different sizes at various locations on a form. Then, select all of the buttons and choose Left from the Align submenu of the Format menu. The command buttons align their left sides with the command button that was selected last.

2. Place command buttons of various sizes on a form. Then, select all of the buttons and choose Both from the Make Same Size submenu of the Format menu. The command buttons all become the same height and width as the last button that was selected.

3. Place command buttons on a form. The buttons should be unevenly spaced. Then, select all of the buttons and choose Make Equal from the Vertical Spacing submenu of the Format menu. The command buttons are then evenly spaced vertically on the form.

EXERCISES

1. Place several controls on a form and use the Align submenu of the Format menu to align the controls in different ways.

2. Place several controls on a form and use the Make Same Size submenu of the Format menu to make the controls the same size.

3. Place several controls on a form and center them horizontally on the form.

4. Lock the controls on a form so that they cannot be moved or resized.

3.7 *U*SING CONTROL ARRAYS

Array variables hold many values in a single variable. Each value is assigned an *index number,* and that is how individual values are retrieved. Controls can also be stored in an array. To create a control array, more than one control of the same type must be given the same name. When a control is first given the same name as another control, the dialog box shown in Figure 3-16 appears to verify that you meant to create a control array.

Press the Yes button to create an array or the No button to not create an array. After creating a control array, this dialog box is not shown for any other controls that you add to the array.

Tip

To quickly create a control array with many controls, create one control and copy it by pressing CTRL-C. Then, add new controls to the form by pressing CTRL-V until you have the desired number of controls

SETTING PROPERTIES FOR CONTROL ARRAYS

Controls that are in an array have the same properties as controls that are not in an array. The difference is that controls in an array use the **Index** property, which is normally not used. The first control in an array has an index of 0; the next has an index of 1; and so on.

When setting properties at design time, select a control and use the Properties window. The names of control arrays in the object box of

FIGURE 3-16

Visual Basic makes you aware that two controls will have the same name

▼

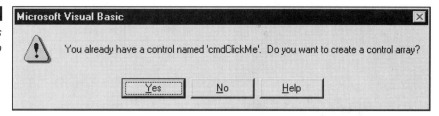

the Properties window are followed by parentheses enclosing a number. That number is the index for the control.

Note

The index for a control array can be retrieved from the Index property. This property is available at both design time and run time.

Address control arrays in code the same way that you use array variables—by using their index within parentheses. To change the **Caption** of an option button that is the first control in a control array, you would use the following code:

```
optOptionButton(0).Caption = "New Caption"
```

This is the same way that you would use any other properties or methods of any control in the same array, changing the index accordingly. See Chapter 6 for ways to quickly process array variables and control arrays.

HANDLING EVENTS FOR CONTROL ARRAYS

Control arrays don't have any additional events, but their events do accept an additional parameter. With many controls having the same name and triggering the same events, you must have some way of knowing exactly which control triggered an event. This information is supplied by the **Index** parameter. The following shows the declaration of the **Click** event for an option button that is part of a control array:

```
Private Sub optOptionButton_Click(Index As Integer)

End Sub
```

You can use the **Index** to perform the processing according to which control triggered the event. This keeps all of your code for multiple controls in a single procedure, which makes the code easier to maintain.

EXAMPLES

1. Use the **Index** property to work with controls that are part of a control array.

2. To change the **Caption** of the first and last command buttons in a control array with four controls, use the following code:

```
cmdCommandButton(0).Caption = "First"
cmdCommandButton(3).Caption = "Last"
```

3. To change the **Caption** of a command button in a control array when it is clicked, use the following code:

```
Private Sub cmdCommandButton_Click(Index As Integer)
    cmdCommandButton(Index).Caption = "Clicked"
End Sub
```

EXERCISES

1. Can a control array contain more than one type of control?

2. How can you tell if a control is part of an array?

3. What is the parameter that is passed to the events of control arrays?

4. How would you change the **Width** and **Height** of a command button when it is clicked if it is part of a control array?

3.8   *USING TAB ORDER*

When using Windows applications, you can use the TAB key to move the focus from one control to another. This is a feature that many users have come to depend upon. Well-planned forms can be worked with using only the keyboard, by using the TAB key to move from one control to the next. For example, when filling out a form that asks for a name and birthday, such as Figure 3-17, you can use the TAB key to move the focus from one control to another. The focus should originally be on the text box for the first name, then middle initial, last name, and birthday.

By arranging the controls of a form in a logical manner and designing the form so that the controls are used in a particular order, the need for using the mouse is eliminated. Eliminating the use of the mouse makes users more efficient when working with forms.

Planning forms to take advantage of tab order does not eliminate the ability to use the mouse to complete tasks. It adds another way of completing a task, which gives users another option for doing their work.

SETTING TAB ORDER

The tab order of controls on a form is determined using the **TabIndex** property.. Visual Basic sets the **TabIndex** property of each control that you place on a form, starting with 0 for the first control and adding 1 for

FIGURE 3-17

Controls on a form should have a logical order

▼

ListControls - frmTabOrder (Form)

Form1

First Name

Middle Initial

Last Name

Birthday

the control after that. The Menu, Timer, Data, Image, Line, and Shape controls are not included in the tab order and do not have a **TabIndex** property.

Invisible and disabled controls cannot receive focus. They remain in the tab order, but they are skipped when it is time for them to receive the focus. Frame and Label controls are also skipped in the tab order, but they do serve a special purpose, which is discussed in the following section.

Note   *Visual Basic automatically renumbers the TabIndex property of controls to reflect controls being inserted or deleted. The TabIndex property is also renumbered if you change its value for one of the controls on a form.*

USING ACCESS KEYS

Access keys are a quick way to move the focus to a particular control. The access key for a control is the letter that is underlined in the control's caption. To designate a letter as the access key, place an ampersand (*&*) in front of it. For example, the **Caption** *&*Click Me on a command button appears as Click Me. You could press ALT-C to move the focus to that command button.

When a label or frame has an access key, that access key is used to move the focus to the next control in the tab order. So if a label had a **TabIndex** of 3 and a text box had a **TabIndex** of 4, pressing ALT and the label's access key moves the focus to the text box.

Note   *Labels have a UseMnemonic property. When set to True, labels can use the ampersand to set access keys, but when set to False, the ampersand is displayed as text and does not set an access key.*

EXAMPLES

1. Place four controls on a form and change the **TabIndex** of the second control that you placed on the form to 3. Notice that the **TabIndex** for the other controls was automatically renumbered.

2. Run the form from the previous example and TAB through the controls. It should go from the first control you placed on the form to the third, to the fourth, and then to the second before it starts all over again.

EXERCISES

1. Which property determines where a control is in the tab order?

2. Are all controls included in the tab order?

3. Is an invisible control still in the tab order?

4. How do you set access keys for controls?

5. How do you display an ampersand in a label?

Mastery
Skills Check

1. How can users be allowed to enter data on a form?

2. What is the event most commonly used for command buttons?

3. What is the difference between a checkbox and an option button?

4. What is the difference between a list box and a combo box?

5. What does a directory list box display?

6. What is the quickest way to make a group of controls the same size?

7. Can more than one control have the same name?

8. What determines which control gets the focus when the TAB key is pressed?

4

Working with Strings

Strings are synonymous with text. Values stored in *string variables* can be placed into the Text property of any control that displays text, or any other property or variable that holds textual values. Variables declared as strings come in two varieties: fixed-length and variable-length.

After declaring string variables, values can be assigned to them in a variety of ways. Values can be supplied using a quoted string, variables, or properties. Several different values can be combined to create a single string or only a section of a string can be used. Strings can be compared to other strings to match them exactly or identify patterns.

Review

Skills Check

You should be able to correctly answer the following questions before beginning this chapter:

1. What data type is the Text property of text boxes?

2. Can command buttons have access keys?

3. What is the difference between an option button and a checkbox?

4. How do you access the values contained in list boxes and combo boxes?

5. What is displayed in a directory list box?

6. What is the quickest way to make a group of controls the same size?

7. Do controls in a control array have to be the same type of control?

8. If the **tab order** for one control is changed, does the **tab order** for the rest of the controls need to be changed also?

4.1 *U*SING STRINGS

Strings or **string** variables are capable of storing any character. It could be letters, numbers, or symbols. Most of the time strings are used to store textual data, such as a name or description. This is the type of data that they were designed to handle and they do it better than any other variable.

*Numbers can be stored in **string** variables but no mathematical functions can be performed on them.*

DECLARING STRINGS

Variable-length and fixed-length **string** variables differ in the size of string that they can hold. Variable-length strings can hold about two billion characters; fixed-length strings can hold around sixty-four thousand characters.

The *declaration* determines which type a **string** variable is. Strings are variable-length by default. Their size varies with the amount of data that is stored in them. The following are examples of variable-length string declarations:

```
Dim strFirstName As String
Private mstrQuery As String
Public gstrMessage As String
```

Declarations for fixed-length variables must include the size of the variable. The size is included at the end of the declaration following an asterisk:

```
Dim strState As String * 2
Private mstrSocialSecurityNumber As String * 9
Public gstrInventoryCode As String * 15
```

These declarations are for **string** variables of length 2, 9, and 15 characters, respectively. If fewer characters than the declared size are placed into these variables, spaces are added to the end of the variable to fill all of the available space. So, assigning a single letter to strState (declared in the preceding code) stores that letter and a single space.

*Store numbers that should never have math operations performed on them—social security number, phone number, zip code—in **string** variables. This eliminates the possibility of a number being altered by a mathematical function.*

ASSIGNING VALUES TO STRING VARIABLES

Values are assigned to **string** variables by setting them equal to a string of characters enclosed within quotations. The following sets the variable strState equal to the state abbreviation for Arizona:

```
strState = "AZ"
```

After this statement is executed, strState holds the value AZ. The quotation marks are required for this statement to work properly.

Without the quotation marks, this statement wouldn't necessarily cause an error, but it wouldn't work. Remember that if the Option Explicit statement doesn't appear in the declaration section of a module, that variable doesn't have to be declared. That means that Visual Basic would interpret AZ (without the quotations) as a variable and would not cause an error. The value of strState would be assigned the value of the variable AZ, which has no value—**NULL**.

There may be times when you assign the value of one **string** variable to another, and the quotations aren't necessary. For example, assigning a local variable to a global variable might look like the following:

```
Public gstrCurrentAnswer

Private Sub cmdAnswerQuestion_Click()
    Dim strAnswer
    strAnswer = txtAnswer.Text
    gstrCurrentAnswer = strAnswer
End Sub
```

Because strAnswer is a variable, it requires no quotations. The value that is held in strAnswer is placed in gstrCurrentAnswer. Now, both variables are set to the same value. This example illustrates another way to assign a string to a variable; it uses a property that holds a string—the Text property of a text box. Normally, the preceding procedure would place the value from the Text property of the text box directly into the global variable gstrCurrentAnswer. The extra step is for illustration purposes.

Note

String variables can be set to the return value for a function if the function returns a string. To do so, place the function call after the equal sign, where the quoted string or variable normally goes.

There may be times when you need to include quotation marks within a string. Two quotation marks in a row within a string are treated as a single quotation mark that should be included in the string. For example, the following line of code places two embedded quotation marks into the string variable:

```
strQuote = "He said, ""Give me the report."""
```

EXAMPLES

1. To declare a local **string** variable in a procedure, use the **Dim** statement, such as the following:

   ```
   Dim strLocalVariable As String
   ```

2. To declare a module-level variable, use the **Private** statement, such as the following:

   ```
   Private mstrModuleLevelVariable As String
   ```

3. To declare a global variable, use the **Public** statement, such as the following:

   ```
   Public gstrGlobalVariable As String
   ```

4. To assign a value to a **string** variable, enclose the characters within quotation marks, such as the following:

   ```
   strExample = "Teach Yourself Visual Basic"
   ```

EXERCISES

1. Are all **string** variables exactly the same type?

2. Do different types of strings hold a different amount of data?

3. How would you declare a local **string** variable to hold the value of a license number?

4. How would you assign a license number of MPR274 to the variable declared in the previous exercise?

5. How would you assign the license number if it were in a text box named txtLicenseNumber?

4.2 CONVERTING STRINGS

Strings can be converted *from* other data types and can be converted *to* other data types. The ASCII character set is sometimes used during this conversion. ASCII goes from 0 to 127. Each number represents a character, including backspace, tab, linefeed, and carriage return. For a complete list of the ASCII character set, refer to the Visual Basic help file.

ASCII (American Standard Code for Information Interchange) is a subset of ANSI (American National Standards Institute), which represents the same characters with numbers 0 through 127 and adds characters represented by the numbers 128 to 255.

The following sections discuss functions that can be used to convert strings to ASCII character codes and vice versa. They also show how numeric and other data types are converted to strings.

USING THE ASC FUNCTION

The **Asc** function returns the character code—from 0 to 255—for the first letter in the string that is supplied to the function. This function returns an **integer** value. You might use this function to search for a particular character or a formatting character, such as a linefeed or carriage return. To find out the character code for the question mark character, you would do the following:

```
Dim intCharCode As Integer

intCharCode = Asc("?")
```

This code sets the variable intCharCode equal to 63, which is the ASCII character code for the question mark. Characters after the first one make no difference. The following line of code would also set the variable equal to 63:

```
intCharCode = Asc("?ABC")
```

*If no characters are supplied to the **Asc** function, a run-time error occurs.*

USING THE CHR FUNCTION

The **Chr** function takes a character code and converts it to its corresponding character. This function returns a string value. You could use the **Chr** function to insert special characters. To turn the character code for the uppercase letter Z into the character Z, you would use the following code:

```
Dim strChar As String
strChar = Chr(90)
```

This code places an uppercase letter Z into the variable strChar.

USING THE STR FUNCTION

The **Str** function takes a numeric value with a data type of **Long** and converts it into a **string**. When converting the value, this function always leaves a space at the beginning of the string for the sign of the number. If a number is positive, the leading space is added without a positive sign—the positive sign is implied. The following are examples of numbers being converted into a string:

```
Dim strConvertedNumber As String
strConvertedNumber = Str(500)
```

This returns a value of " 500".

```
Dim strConvertedNumber As String
strConvertedNumber = Str(-3.14)
```

This returns a value of "-3.14".

```
Dim strConvertedNumber As String
strConvertedNumber = Str(724.675)
```

This returns a value of " 724.675".

Note *Only a period can be used to represent a decimal point when using the **Str** function. If any other symbol might be used to represent a decimal point, use the **CStr** function.*

USING THE CSTR FUNCTION

The **CStr** function accepts several different data types as arguments. Depending on the data type supplied as an argument, **CStr** returns different values—although it always returns a string value. Table 4-1 outlines the possible argument data types and the values that **CStr** returns for each.

Note — *The CStr function does not add any leading spaces to numeric values.*

EXAMPLES

1. To obtain the character code for the capital letter A, use the following line of code:

```
intCode = Asc("A")
```

2. To find out what character the character code 45 represents, use the following line of code:

```
strCharacter = Chr(45)
```

3. To convert the number -212.075 to a string, use either of the following lines of code:

```
strNumber = Str(-212.075)
strNumber = CStr(-212.075)
```

Argument Data Type	CStr Return Value
Boolean	String with value of "True" or "False"
Date	String with date in short date format
Null	Causes a run-time error
Empty	An empty string ("")
Error	String with value "Error " followed by the error number
Numeric	String with the number in it

TABLE 4-1 *Possible Return Values for CStr* ▼

EXERCISES

1. What is the character code for an uppercase and lowercase P?

2. What is the difference in the return value when a positive number is converted using both the **Str** and **CStr** functions?

3. What does **CStr** return when supplied a **Boolean** argument?

4. How do you find out the character code for the first letter in a **string** variable?

4.3   *C*ONCATENATING STRINGS

At times, you may need to form several strings into a single string. This process is called *concatenation*. Concatenating strings can be helpful when preparing messages to display or preparing data to be stored in a database. For example, you could have a user enter their name in a text box and then use their name in a sentence by concatenating their name into a predefined sentence structure. Regardless of how you use the concatenation operators, they are discussed in the following two sections.

USING THE & OPERATOR

The **&** operator joins two expressions to create a single string. An expression can be any constant, variable, operator, keyword, or quoted string. If either expression is not a string, it is converted to the String data type. The following lines of code show several examples of using the **&** operator:

```
Dim strExample As String
strExample = "Hi, " & "how are you?"
```

The variable strExample now has a value of "Hi, how are you?"

```
strExample = "The answer is " & 245
```

The variable strExample now has a value of "The answer is 245".

```
strExample = "Bang "
strExample = strExample & strExample
```

The variable strExample now has a value of "Bang Bang ".

*The **&** operator can be used more than once for a line of code. It can be used as many times as you need. So if you have four variables that you need to concatenate together into a single string, do it with one line of code using three **&** operators*

There may be times when you are creating a very long string. To make your code more readable, use the underscore line-continuation character to spread your code out over several lines. The following is an example:

```
strReallyLong = "If you find that you have a really long " _
& "string, you might want to use the underscore " _
& "line-continuation character to make it easier to " _
& "read your code and make it easier to keep track " _
& "of the long string that you are building."
```

There must be a space before the line-continuation character for it to work properly.

The preceding code is treated by Visual Basic as a single line of code. The underscore character is replaced with the following line of code when Visual Basic interprets the line. This can be done for any long line of code, even if it does not involve string concatenation. However, if it does involve building a string, be sure to use the *&* concatenation operator at the beginning of each continued line.

USING THE + OPERATOR

The + operator can also be used to concatenate strings, but it should mainly be used when adding numbers together to obtain a numeric value. When using this operator, if a numeric value is supplied as either expression, then the result must be numeric. For example, the following returns a numeric value of 45.15:

```
".15" + 45
```

But the following returns a string value of "98.6":

```
"98" + ".6"
```

If one of the expressions is a string that does not contain a number and the other expression is numeric, using the + operator causes a type mismatch error.

EXAMPLES

1. Use the following code to build a string with a user name, which was supplied from a text box named txtUserName:

```
Dim strGreetings As String
strGreetings = "Hi " & txtUserName & ", how are you?"
```

2. To build a string that is so long it takes up more than one line of code, use the underscore line-continuation character, like the following:

```
Dim strLongSentence As String
strLongSentence = "For demonstration purposes, this " _
& "sentence is very long and is intended to take up " _
& "several lines of code."
```

3. To build a string with the + operator, be sure that both expressions are strings. The following is an example:

```
Dim strStringValue As String
strStringValue = "When using the + operator, " + "both
expressions must be strings."
```

EXERCISES

1. Which operator should be used when concatenating strings?

2. How would you join the string values stored in variables strValue1 and strValue2 into a single string stored in the variable strNewValue?

3. What is the result of the following:

   ```
   "What does " & "this do?"
   ```

4. What is the result of the following:

   ```
   "10" + 10
   ```

5. What is the result of the following:

   ```
   "10" + ".10"
   ```

4.4   FORMATTING STRINGS

Strings usually store characters that form sentences or phrases. These phrases are most likely displayed to a user. Before displaying a string, you may want to perform some type of formatting on it. For example, you might want to make the first letter in each word capitalized or align all of the text on one side of the string. These types of formatting options are discussed in the following sections.

CHANGING THE CASE OF STRINGS

There are several reasons you might want to change the case of the letters in a string. You might want to make a string all uppercase to emphasize a point or maintain consistency with a formatting standard you must follow. If an all-uppercase string needs to be lowercase, then you definitely need to change the case. The "Using the StrConv Function" section contains more information on changing the case of strings.

Using the LCase Function

To convert a string to all lowercase letters, use the **LCase** function. Syntax for the **LCase** function is very simple. The following is an example:

```
Dim strLowerCase As String
Dim strUpperCase As String
strUpperCase = "LOWERCASE"
strLowerCase = LCase(strUpperCase)
```

The **LCase** function returns a string value. In this example, strLowerCase is set to "lowercase". This function only affects uppercase letters. All lowercase letters and non-letter characters are not affected.

Tip

*If a variable is being passed as the argument to the **LCase** or **UCase** function, that same variable can also accept the return value.*

Using the UCase Function

The **UCase** function converts a string to all uppercase letters. This function takes a string argument and returns a string value. To convert a string to all uppercase, use the following as an example:

```
Dim strUpperCase As String
Dim strLowerCase As String
strLowerCase = "uppercase"
strUpperCase = UCase(strLowerCase)
```

In this case, strUpperCase is now set to "UPPERCASE". Only lowercase letters are changed by this function. All other characters remain the same.

CHANGING THE JUSTIFICATION OF STRINGS

Changing the justification of a string does not mean coming up with a new reason for having the string. It refers to the alignment of the text within the string. The text may be aligned to the left of the string or to the right.

Using the LSet Function

The **LSet** function aligns text to the left side of a string variable. Syntax for this function is a little different than you are used to. A statement is placed after the function call:

```
LSet string_variable = string
```

The string in this expression can be either a string variable or a string in quotes. It is placed into the string variable and aligned to the left side, as in the following example:

```
Dim strExample As String
strExample = "0123456789"
LSet strExample = "LSet"
```

The variable strExample now holds the value "LSet   ". This variable was set to an initial value just to make it large enough to illustrate the use of this variable. While any variable used needs to be of a size at least as large as the string it will hold, it does not need to be initialized exactly as strExample was.

After left aligning the value into the variable, **LSet** fills the rest of the variable with spaces. If the value being placed into the variable is longer than the variable, only the leftmost characters that fit into the variable are added.

Using the RSet Function

The **RSet** function aligns a string to the right side of a variable. Its syntax is the same as the **LSet** function, but it right-aligns text within a string variable. The following is an example:

```
Dim strExample As String
strExample = "0123456789"
RSet strExample = "RSet"
```

The variable strExample is now set to "   RSet". **Rset** fills the rest of the variable with spaces.

USING THE STRCONV FUNCTION

The **StrConv** function can be used to change the case of a string. It has the ability to make a string all uppercase, all lowercase, or *proper case*. Proper case, or title case, means that the first letter of each word is capitalized. The syntax for **StrConv** is as follows:

```
StrConv(string, conversion)
```

Conversion indicates the type of conversion to be performed. This value can be a number or you can use a constant. Table 4-2 lists the constants, their values, and a description of each.

The following example converts a string to proper case:

```
Dim strProperCase As String
strProperCase = "this is proper case"
strProperCase = StrConv(strProperCase, vbProperCase)
```

Constant	Value	Description
vbUpperCase	1	Converts string to uppercase letters.
vbLowerCase	2	Converts string to lowercase letters.
vbProperCase	3	Converts first letter of each word in string to uppercase–initial capital letters.

TABLE 4-2 *Constants for StrConv Function* ▼

After this code executes, the value in strProperCase is "This Is Proper Case".

USING THE FORMAT FUNCTION

The **Format** function is very versatile. It can be used to format strings that hold number, date, time, and text values. The syntax for this function is as follows:

```
Format(expression[, format])
```

Expression is a required argument that can be any date, time, number, or string. Format is an optional argument that specifies how to format the expression argument. There are two more optional arguments (firstdayofweek, firstweekofyear) that are not discussed here.

If no format is supplied, the expression is returned as a string. The following statement formats a number into a string:

```
Dim strNumber As String
strNumber = Format(52)
```

Note **Format** *does not add a leading space to positive numbers like the* **Str** *function does.*

The Format argument can be a predefined format or a user-defined format. The following are examples of using a predefined or system format:

```
Dim strExample As String
strExample = Format(Time, "Long Time")
```

This returns the current time in the long time format.

```
strExample = Format(Date, "Long Date")
```

This returns the current date in the long date format.

```
strExample = Format(#10:11:42#, hh:mm:ss AM/PM)
```

This returns "10:11:42 AM".

```
strExample = Format(#JUN-24-97#, "dddd, mmm d yyyy")
```

This returns "Tuesday, Jun 24 1997".

*The actual output of the **Format** function depends upon the settings of your particular system.*

The following are examples of user-defined formats:

```
Dim strExample As string
strExample = Format(5999.9, "##,##0.00")
```

This returns "5,999.90".

```
strExample = Format(8, "0.00%")
```

This returns "800.00%".

```
strExample = Format("LOWERCASE", "<")
```

This returns "lowercase".

```
strExample = Format("uppercase", ">")
```

This returns "UPPERCASE".

EXAMPLES

1. To convert a string to all uppercase letters, use the **UCase** function. The following is an example:

   ```
   strUpperCase = UCase("All Capital Letters")
   ```

2. Strings can be aligned within a **string** variable using the **LSet** and **RSet** functions. The following is an example of a string that is right aligned within a **string** variable:

```
RSet strExample = "right alignment"
```

3. **StrConv** can change the case of an entire string or just the first letter of each word in the string. The following example capitalizes the first letter of every word of a string:

```
strExample = StrConv("all initial capital letters",
vbProperCase)
```

4. The following example changes a string to all uppercase letters using the **Format** function:

```
strUpperCase = Format("All Capital Letters", ">")
```

EXERCISES

1. What function(s) can be used to convert a string to all uppercase letters?

2. What function(s) can be used to convert a string to all lowercase letters?

3. What function(s) can be used to convert a string to initial capital letters?

4. What function(s) can be used to format dates and times?

5. Write a function called Converter that accepts a string as an argument. The function should convert the string to uppercase, proper case, and lowercase. Concatenate the three different cases of the string together, separated by commas, and make that the return value for the function.

4.5 *MANIPULATING STRINGS*

Strings can be manipulated in many ways. Parts of the string can be trimmed off to eliminate unwanted characters. Functions can extract portions of a string or add a series of characters to a string. The following sections address each of these possibilities.

USING THE LEN FUNCTION

Many of the functions discussed in this section take an argument that deals with the length of a string or a position within the string. For example, you might only want the last three characters of a string. The **Len** function can be helpful when using functions that require this argument. Its syntax is very simple:

```
Len(string)
```

String can be any string expression. This function returns a **long** containing the number of characters in a string. For example, the following would return a size of 5:

```
Len("12345")
```

*If a non-string variable is supplied to the **Len** function, it returns the number of bytes needed to store the value. Passing a non-string value that is not contained in a variable to the **Len** function causes an error.*

USING THE SPACE AND STRING FUNCTIONS

To add a number of spaces to a string or repeat a character many times, use the **Space** and **String** functions. The **Space** function accepts a numeric argument and returns a string value with the number of spaces specified in the argument. The following example sets the variable strSpacedOut equal to 20 spaces:

```
strSpacedOut = Space(20)
```

To repeat a character in a string many times, use the **String** function. It takes an argument that specifies the number of times a character should be repeated and an argument that specifies which character should be used. The following shows an example of building a string that holds a credit card number, but only shows the last four digits:

```
strSecureCardNumber = String(12, "X") & intLastFourDigits
```

If intLastFourDigits is equal to 9999, strSecureCardNumber holds the value "XXXXXXXXXXXX9999". You can supply either a string or a character code for the character argument of the **String** function. Character codes cannot exceed 255 and if a string has more than one character, only the first character is used.

*If a numeric value is concatenated to a string using the **&** operator, the number is automatically converted to a string value.*

USING THE TRIM, LTRIM, AND RTRIM FUNCTIONS

Some strings may have too many spaces in them in already. If so, use one of the trimming functions—**Trim**, **LTrim**, or **RTrim**—to remove the unwanted spaces. Each function takes a string and removes the spaces from the beginning (**LTrim**), end (**RTrim**), or beginning and end (**Trim**) of the string. No spaces are removed within the text of a string; only from the beginning or end. The following example removes the spaces from the beginning of strExample:

```
strExample = LTrim(strExample)
```

Spaces at the beginning of a string are called leading spaces, and spaces at the end of a string are called trailing spaces.

USING THE LEFT, RIGHT, AND MID FUNCTIONS

The **Left**, **Right**, and **Mid** functions accept a string as an argument and return a specified portion of that string. **Left** and **Right** both accept a numeric argument for the length of the string to be returned from either the left side of the string or the right, depending on which function is used. For example, the following statement sets strExample equal to the value "Go":

```
strExample = Left("Go Back Home", 2)
```

The following example sets strExample equal to "Home":

```
strExample = Right("Go Back Home", 4)
```

As you can see, these two functions are very useful if you need text from the left or right side of the string, but they cannot extract text from the middle of a string. In our example, for instance, the word "Back" cannot be extracted using either of these functions, but it can be extracted using the **Mid** function. **Mid** accepts a string and two numeric arguments. The first numeric argument tells **Mid** where to start extracting characters from the string, and the second tells it how many to take. Only the start position is required. If the length is omitted, all of the characters from the start position on are returned. The following example sets strExample equal to "Back":

```
strExample = Mid("Go Back Home", 4, 4)
```

*If the length argument of the **Mid** function specifies more characters than are contained in the string from the start point, the characters from the start point to the end of the string are returned.*

EXAMPLES

1. The following line of code sets intStringLength equal to 9:

   ```
   intStringLength = Len("Good Job!")
   ```

2. To add 10 spaces to a string, use the **Space** function as follows:

   ```
   Space(10)
   ```

3. Trim the spaces from the beginning and end of a string by using the **Trim** function. The following is an example:

   ```
   strTrimmed = Trim("   Trim Me    ")
   ```

4. Use the **Left** function to extract the leftmost characters in a string. The following example sets strExample equal to "That":

   ```
   strExample = Left("That's Right", 4)
   ```

1. How do you find the length of a string?

2. Build the string "XXXOOOXXX", using the **String** function.

3. What function removes trailing spaces?

4. Can you remove the spaces from the middle of a string using the **Trim** function?

5. How could you obtain the text from a **string** variable removing the first two characters and the last two characters?

4.6 *C*OMPARING STRINGS

Searching for a letter, phrase, or pattern in a string can be difficult. However, Visual Basic has several functions and operators that make this task a little easier. Use these when you need to find a particular string or a particular word within a string.

USING THE INSTR FUNCTION

The **InStr** function searches a string for the occurrence of a particular string. Syntax for this function is as follows:

```
InStr([start, ]string1, string2[, compare])
```

This function searches string1 for an occurrence of string2. If found, it returns the position of the first character that matches. If a match is not found, **InStr** returns a value of 0. For example, the following returns a value of 10 because the first occurrence of the word "copy" starts at the 10th position in the string:

```
InStr("Send one copy of your final copy to us.", "copy")
```

Notice that **InStr** only finds the first occurrence. After that, it disregards the rest of the string. To find other occurrences, you could use the start argument to start the search later in the string. The following example returns a value of 29 because it finds the first occurrence of the word "copy" at the 29th position in the string, starting the search at the 11th position in the string:

InStr(11, "Send one copy of your final copy to us.", "copy")

Because this search started after the first character of the first occurrence of the word "copy", **InStr** found the second occurrence. This function can also be case sensitive. If you specify 0 for the compare argument, an exact match (including case) of string2 must be found in string1. The following example returns a value of 8:

InStr(1, "HAPPY, Happy, happy", "Happy", 0)

Specify 1 for the compare argument to make the search non-case sensitive. The following example returns a value of 1:

InStr(1, "HAPPY, Happy, happy", "happy", 1)

*Specify 2 for the compare argument of the **InStr** function when working with Microsoft Access data.*

USING THE STRCOMP FUNCTION

The **StrComp** function compares two strings. The syntax for this function has two required arguments and one optional argument. Table 4-3 shows the possible return values, and the following is the syntax:

StrComp(string1, string2[, compare])

Return Value	Condition
-1	string1 is less than string2
0	string1 is equal to string2
1	string1 is greater than string2
NULL	string1 or string2 is NULL

TABLE 4-3   *StrComp Return Values* ▼

The Compare argument for this function works just as it did in the **InStr** function. If Compare is omitted, the **Option Compare** setting determines the type of comparison that is used.

The following example returns a value of 0:

```
StrComp("ABCD", "abcd", 1)
```

The following example returns a value of -1:

```
StrComp("ABCD", "abcd", 0)
```

The following example assumes the default **Option Compare** setting, and it returns a value of 1:

```
StrComp("abcd", "ABCD")
```

USING THE OPTION COMPARE STATEMENT

The **Option Compare** statement determines how strings are compared within a module. Its syntax is as follows:

```
Option Compare {Binary | Text | Database}
```

This statement must appear before any procedures. If it is not used, the default comparison method is binary. The following statement would set the comparison method to textual or non-case sensitive:

```
Option Compare Text
```

Note

Option Compare Database can only be used within Microsoft Access.

USING THE LIKE OPERATOR

The **Like** operator compares two strings and returns a True or False value indicating if they matched or not. Wildcards and other special characters can be used to match a string to a pattern. This doesn't require an exact match; only the *pattern* must match. Following is the syntax for this operator:

```
result = string Like pattern
```

If the string or pattern is **NULL**, the result will be **NULL** as well.

*The behavior of the **Like** operator depends on the **Option Compare** statement.*

Allowing strings to be matched with patterns makes the **Like** operator very powerful and versatile. Patterns can be identified in strings and matches can be found that might have otherwise been impossible to identify. Table 4-4 lists the pattern-matching characters that can be used with the **Like** operator.

To match the special characters ([, ?, #, *), enclose them in parentheses. Use a hyphen to specify a range of characters in a character list. Ranges must be specified in ascending order—from lowest to highest. More than one range of characters can be specified and no delimiters are needed to separate multiple ranges.

*The right bracket ( ]) can't be used within a character list to match itself using the **Like** operator.*

The following statements all return a value of True:

```
"1on1" Like "#on#"
"B12" Like "[A-E]1#"
"ABC" Like "A?C"
"ABCDEGHIJK" Like "A*"
```

Character	Matches	Example
?	Any single character	"b?d"
*	Zero or more characters	"b*d"
#	Any single digit (0–9)	"9#"
[charlist]	Any single character in charlist	[abcd], [a-d], [A-D]
[!charlist]	Any single character not in charlist	[!abcd], [!a-d], [!A-D]

TABLE 4-4   *Pattern-Matching Characters for the Like Operator* ▼

The following statements all return a value of False:

```
"L" Like "[!A-Z]"
"GIFT" Like "L?FT"
"220" Like "#2"
```

EXAMPLES

1. To find the first occurrence of a string within a string, use the **InStr** function. The following statement returns the position of the first character in the word "help", where it appears in the string:

   ```
   InStr("Please help me.", "help")
   ```

2. Use the **StrComp** function to determine if one string is less than, equal to, or greater than another string. The following example performs a non-case sensitive comparison that returns a value of 0, which indicates that the strings are equal:

   ```
   StrComp("HELLO", "hello", 1)
   ```

3. Placing the following statement at the beginning of a module causes comparisons within the module to default to binary or case sensitive:

   ```
   Option Compare Binary
   ```

4. The following example would return a value of True, indicating that the letter M doesn't occur in the string:

   ```
   "That's all folks" Like "*[!m]*"
   ```

EXERCISES

1. How could you find the second occurrence of a string within a string?

2. What function compares two strings?

3. How do you make comparisons default to a text comparison?

4. How could you find out if a string contains the letters A, F, or G?

**Mastery
Skills Check**

1. Declare a fixed-length string with a size of 5 characters.

2. How would you find the character code for the letter Q?

3. Which concatenation operator should be used when working with strings?

4. What function would you use to make the first letter of each word in a string capitalized?

5. How do you remove the leading and/or trailing spaces from a string?

6. What is the statement that affects the default comparison method for a module?

5

Working with Numbers

Chapter objectives

5.1 Using Numeric Values

5.2 Using Numeric Operators

5.3 Using Math Functions

5.4 Using Random Numbers

Visual Basic uses numeric values for many tasks, including *counters*. Counters keep track of how many times an event occurs or a condition is met. They are also used to perform a specific task a predetermined number of times.

There are different *numeric data types* to handle the different types of numbers. Each data type is best at handling a certain type and range of numbers. Using the proper data type can increase the speed and efficiency of your applications, while using the wrong data type can lead to calculation errors.

Visual Basic has many operators and functions that can be used to manipulate numbers. These do everything from add two numbers together to find the logarithm of a number. One numeric function that is very useful is the **Rnd** function. It generates random numbers that can be used in many different ways, including testing calculations in your application.

Review
Skills Check

You should be able to correctly answer the following questions before beginning this chapter:

1. Can strings be declared to hold a specific number of characters?

2. What character set is ASCII a subset of?

3. Which operator should always be used when concatenating strings?

4. What function can be used to capitalize the first letter of each word in a string?

5. Which functions allow you to isolate and use only a portion of a string?

6. What is the default compare method and what statement is used to change it?

5.1 ▮ USING NUMERIC VALUES

Visual Basic has several different data types that can store numeric values. These data types differ in the amount of resources they consume and the size of number they can hold. The data type for numeric variables is set in the declaration for each variable.

DECLARING NUMERIC VARIABLES

Before going into the details of declaring variables for storing numeric values, let's review the different numeric data types. The following are the numeric data types available in Visual Basic:

▼ **Byte**

▼ **Integer**

▼ **Long**

▼ **Single**

▼ **Double**

▼ **Currency**

Note — *Variables for storing decimal values must be of the **Variant** data type. Then, use the **CDec** function to give the **Variant** variable a decimal subtype.*

Integer variables can range in value from –32,768 to 32,767. They require 2 bytes of storage space each. This data type can only store whole numbers—no fractions or decimals. *Enumerated* values, such as vbProperCase, are constants that represent integer values. *Long* variables store long integer values ranging from –2,147,483,648 to 2,147,483,647 and require 4 bytes of storage space. When working with values that do not contain fractions, use the **Integer** data type. **Integer** uses the least amount of storage space, but still holds the largest value possible in your application. The following are example declarations of local **Integer** and **Long** variables:

```
Dim intFirstChoice As Integer
Dim intFirstChoice, Second Choice As Integer
Dim lngPopulation As Long
Dim lngPopulation As Long, intFirstChoice As Integer
Dim intFirstChoice, intSecondChoice As Integer, lgnPopulation As Long
```

All numeric variables are automatically initialized to a value of 0.

Variables declared with the ***Single*** data type are also referred to as single-precision Floating-point variables. This type uses 4 bytes to store each variable, which can hold values from –3.402823E38 to –1.401298E-45 for negative values and from 1.401298E-45 to 3.402823E38 for positive values. For even larger values (–1.79769313486232E308 to –4.94065645841247E-324 for negative values and from 4.94065645841247E-324 to 1.79769313486232E308 for positive values), the ***Double*** data type is used. Double-precision Floating-point variables use 8 bytes of storage space.

Floating-point variables are subject to rounding errors when working with very large values.

When working with values that contain fractions, use the Floating-point data type that uses the least amount of storage space, but still holds the largest value possible in your application. The following are examples of declarations for local **Single** and **Double** variables:

```
Dim sngRadius As Single
Dim dblLength As Double
Dim sngRadius, sngDiameter As Single, dblLength, dblWidth As Double
```

The ***Currency*** data type holds numbers that represent monetary values. This data type uses 8 bytes of storage space and can hold values from –922,337,203,685,477.5808 to 922,337,203,685,477.5807. Currency values always have 15 numbers to the left of the decimal point and 4 to the right—even if they are not all displayed. Calculations performed with the **Currency** data type are completely accurate; there are no rounding errors. This is absolutely necessary when dealing with calculations that involve money. The following are examples of declarations for local **Currency** variables:

```
Dim curAccountBalance As Currency
Dim curAmountOverdue As Currency
```

Note — *The **Currency** data type can be used for values that have nothing to do with money. This can be especially useful if it is imperative that no rounding errors occur, such as scientific research applications.*

ASSIGNING VALUES TO NUMERIC VARIABLES

Values are assigned to numeric variables in essentially the same way that values are assigned to strings, using the = operator. The obvious difference is that the value must be numeric. Any of the following assignment statements sets the **Integer** variable intExample equal to a numeric value:

```
intExample = 1
intExample = ReturnTwo
intExample = "3"
```

Note — *Variables can also contain a **NULL** value, which means that they have no value at all. **NULL** values behave differently from other values, so be sure you understand the implications of setting a **NULL** value if there is a chance that you might encounter one.*

The first preceding example sets intExample equal to a value of 1. It does not use any quotation marks for the value because they are not necessary when working with numbers. Only strings should be surrounded by quotations. In the next statement, the variable is set using a function that returns an integer value. Finally, intExample is set to 3 using a string.

That's right; you can set a numeric variable using a string. However, this is possible only if the string holds a numeric value. Visual Basic provides a couple of ways to verify that a string holds a numeric value. These functions can be combined with some of the control statements discussed in Chapter 6 to set a numeric variable equal to a string if the string holds a number. The following **IsNumeric**(expression) functions check for number values in strings. A string value is passed in the expression argument:

```
IsNumeric("100")
IsNumeric("A 100")
```

The **IsNumeric** function returns a **Boolean** value of True if the expression passed to it is a number and False if it is not a number. The first preceding example returns a value of True and the second returns a value of False.

Note — *Some numeric values might contain characters or symbols, for example: thousands separators, decimals, and symbols for monetary values. These types of symbols vary from one country to another, so your regional settings could affect the results of the **IsNumeric** function.*

UNDERSTANDING NUMBERING SYSTEMS

You will generally use the decimal numbering system when working in Visual Basic. This is the system that people use every day, and you don't need any special training to use it in Visual Basic. However, there are other numbering systems that can be used in Visual Basic. Although these alternative numbering systems are infrequently used, this section prepares you for any encounter that you might have with them. There are three different numbering systems that are commonly used in Visual Basic:

▼ Decimal

▼ Hexadecimal

▼ Octal

Decimal (or base 10) numbers are based on 10 numbers: 0, 1, 2, 3, 4, 5, 6, 7, 8, 9. By default, Visual Basic recognizes all numbers as based on the decimal numbering system. When 9 is reached in the decimal numbering system, the next number is 0 and 1 is added to the left of the number. For example, after 9 comes 10 and after 239 comes 240. This is obvious to you because you have worked with decimal numbers all of your life. Now, what number comes after 7 in the Octal numbering system? This answer is probably not as obvious, but as you will see, it is just as easy for you to come up with.

Octal (or base 8) numbers are based on 8 numbers: 0, 1, 2, 3, 4, 5, 6, 7. The total numbers available is the only difference between decimal and octal numbers; the method used to increment numbers is exactly the same. The number that comes after 7 in the octal system is 10, 17 is followed by 20, 27 is followed by 30, and so on. When octal numbers are used in Visual Basic, they are preceded with the characters &O. That's how Visual Basic knows that the numbers are based on the octal numbering system.

Hexadecimal (or base 16) numbers are based on 16 numbers: 0, 1, 2, 3, 4, 5, 6, 7, 8, 9, A, B, C, D, E, F. The numbers used for the hexadecimal system are notably different—some of them are letters. Again, the method used to count out hexadecimal numbers is the same. Number 9 is followed by A, F is followed by 10, 19 is followed by 1A, 1F is followed by 20, and so on. In Visual Basic, hexadecimal numbers are preceded by the characters &H.

EXAMPLES

1. The following are declarations for numeric variables that hold varying data types:

```
Dim intWholeNumber As Integer
Dim lngLargeWholeNumber As Long
Dim sngFraction As Single
Dim dblLargeFraction As Double
Dim curPreciseValue As Currency
```

2. The following statements assign values to the variables declared in the previous example:

```
intWholeNumber = 1
lngLargeWholeNumber = 2,000,000,000
sngFraction = 1.1
dblLargeFraction = 1,000,000,000,000,000,000,000.001
curPreciseValue = 500.1275
```

3. To use octal numbers, prefix the number with &O.

4. To use hexadecimal numbers, prefix the number with &H.

EXERCISES

1. What numeric data type should be used for numbers less than 100 that have no fractions?
2. What numeric data type should be used if you want positively no rounding errors?
3. Can numeric variables be set equal to a string?
4. What function determines if a string holds a numeric value?
5. What characters must precede a hexadecimal number?

5.2 USING NUMERIC OPERATORS

The values of numeric variables are often manipulated to derive new values. These variables are manipulated using operators, such as + and -. This allows applications to dynamically determine numeric values. For example, the amount someone should be paid for a week's work can be determined by multiplying (*) the number of hours worked by the amount paid for each hour of work. Further operations could be performed to determine the amount of taxes to be taken out of a paycheck.

USING ARITHMETIC OPERATORS

The following sections discuss the arithmetic operators available in Visual Basic. Trigonometric functions are discussed later in this chapter in the section "Using Trigonometric Functions."

Using the + Operator

The + operator is used to sum two numbers. This operator is commonly used to increment a counter. Counters keep track of the number of times a piece of code executes or a certain condition occurs. For example, the following code increments a counter by 1:

```
intCounter = intCounter + 1
```

After this line of code executes, the value of the counter has increased by 1. If the counter had a value of 3 before this line executed, it would have a value of 4 after the line executed.

*Numbers contained in strings can be summed using the **+** operator, but strings should only be concatenated using the **&** operator.*

Using the – Operator

The **-** operator serves two purposes. It is used to find the difference between two numbers or to indicate that a number has a negative value. To indicate that a value is negative, simply place the **-** operator directly before the value. When finding the difference between two numbers, the syntax is as follows:

```
result = number1 - number2
```

This operator can also be used with a counter variable. In this case the counter would be decremented. For example, if you created a video game in Visual Basic and wanted to reduce a player's score, you might use the following statement:

```
glngScore(gintPlayer) = glngScore(gintPlayer) - mintPenalty
```

This statement reduces the score of the current player by the value in the module-level variable mintPenalty. The score is kept in the global array variable glngScore, and the index of the array variable corresponds to a player's number—player one's score is held in glngScore(1), player two's in glngScore(2), and so on.

Using the * Operator

The * operator is used to multiply two numbers. This operator can be used to find the percentage of a value. For example, the following statement determines what twenty-five percent of a value is:

```
sngOneQuarter = sngValue * .25
```

*Be sure that you use appropriate data types when performing operations on numeric variables. For example, don't try to place the result of multiplying two variables with a **Double** data type into a variable with an **Integer** data type.*

Using the ^ Operator

The ^ operator raises a number to the power of an exponent. This operator is useful when working with statistics and charts. The syntax for using the ^ operator is as follows:

```
result = number^exponent
```

If more than one ^ operator is used in a statement, they are evaluated in order from left to right.

Using the / Operator

The / operator is used to divide one number by another. This operator could also be used to determine percentages. For example, you might create an application that tests an individual's knowledge on a certain subject. To determine the percentage of questions the individual answered correctly, you must divide the number of correct answers by the total number of questions. If the number of correct answers is in the variable intCorrect and the total number of questions is in the variable intPossible, you would use the following statement to place the percentage of correctly answered questions into the variable sngPercentageCorrect:

```
sngPercentageCorrect = intCorrect/intPossible
```

Notice that the result of this statement is placed in a single-precision Floating-point variable. The / operator always returns a Floating-point variable.

Using the \ Operator

The \ operator is also used to divide one number by another, but this operator always returns an integer value. It converts both numbers to whole numbers before performing the division operation and truncates any fractional value after performing the division. So, the following statement sets intExample equal to 2:

```
intExample = 5.1\2.04
```

When 5.1 is divided by 2.04, the result is 2.5. But this example has a result of 2 because the \ operator converts both numbers to whole numbers and truncates any fractional value. This operator is most useful when performing operations that disregard the fractional portion of an equation.

Using the MOD Operator

The **MOD** operator divides two numbers, but only returns the remainder—also known as *modulus*. Before dividing the numbers, they are both turned into integers by rounding them—unless they are already integers. For example, the following statement sets intExample equal to 3:

```
intExample = 15.2 MOD 6
```

MOD rounds 15.2 to 15 and then divides 6 into it twice. The remainder of 3 (15 – 12) is the result of the operation.

UNDERSTANDING OPERATOR PRECEDENCE

More than one operator can appear in the same expression. In fact, the same operator might appear several times in a single equation. When more than one operator appears in an expression, the rules of operator precedence are followed. According to these rules, certain operators are recognized—and their function carried out—before others. When any of the same operators appear in the same expression, their operation is performed from left to right as they appear in the expression. The following lists the operators from first recognized to last recognized:

1. ^ operator
2. - operator (indicating a negative value)
3. * and / operator
4. \ operator
5. **MOD** operator
6. + and - operator

If multiplication and division appear in the same statement, they are processed in order from left to right as they appear. The same goes for addition and subtraction.

Enclosing an expression within parentheses forces the enclosed expression to be performed first. If you wanted to add two numbers together and then multiply the sum by another number, you would have to place the addition expression within parentheses, like the following:

```
intExample = (2 + 2) * 2
```

This statement sets intExample to a value of 8, because 2 + 2 equals 4 and 4 * 2 equals 8. Without the parentheses, the result would have been 6 because the * operator has a higher precedence than the + operator. Therefore, the operation 2 * 2 would have been performed first and then the product (4) would have been added to 2, resulting in a value of 6.

Note — *Expressions enclosed in parentheses can be part of other expressions enclosed in parentheses. The expression from the innermost set of parentheses is always performed first, then the next innermost, and so on.*

EXAMPLES

1. Use the + operator to add two numbers together, such as the following:

   ```
   intExample = 2 + 2
   ```

2. Use the * operator to multiply two numbers together, such as the following:

   ```
   sngExample = 5 * 5
   ```

3. Use parentheses to override operator precedence and force part of an expression to be evaluated before the rest of the expression, such as the following:

   ```
   intExample = (5 + (5 * 5)) \ (4 + 3)
   ```

EXERCISES

1. Write an expression that adds two negative numbers together.
2. Write an expression that multiplies two numbers together.
3. Write an expression that determines the remainder of dividing one number by another.
4. In what order are the arithmetic operators evaluated within an expression?
5. Is there a way to override operator precedence?

5.3 USING MATH FUNCTIONS

The math functions in Visual Basic help perform common mathematical tasks to determine values that might otherwise be difficult to determine. As you build applications, some of these functions will be more useful to you than others. For example, if you don't create applications that perform complex drawing and graphing, you may never use the trigonometric functions.

USING THE ABS FUNCTION

The **Abs** function returns the absolute value of a number. An absolute value is not positive or negative. It is the value of a number without regard to being negative in value. For example, both of the following statements set intExample equal to 10:

```
intExample = Abs(10)
intExample = Abs(-10)
```

The absolute value of 0 is 0.

The data type that **Abs** returns is the same as the data type passed to it as an argument. So if an Integer is passed to **Abs**, an Integer is returned. If a Double is passed to it, a Double is returned. This function is used to determine the magnitude of a number without regard to whether it is positive or negative. **Abs** can be used in applications where the sign of the number doesn't matter or where the number should never be negative.

USING THE EXP AND LOG FUNCTIONS

The **Exp** function returns the value of *e* (approximately 2.718282) raised to the power of the number that is passed as an argument. Syntax for this function is as follows:

```
Exp(number)
```

*The number value passed to the **Exp** function cannot be larger than 709.782712893. If a larger value is passed, an error occurs.*

In this function, *number* can be any valid numeric expression. The **Exp** function is closely associated to the **Log** function and is sometimes referred to as the *antilogarithm*. Logarithms are calculated using the **Log** function, which has the following syntax:

```
Log(number)
```

The **Log** function returns the natural logarithm (logarithm to the base *e*) of the number passed to it. This value is returned as a Double data type.

Calculate base-n logarithms for any number by dividing the natural logarithm of x *by the natural logarithm of the number—**Log**(x) / **Log**(number).*

USING THE FIX AND INT FUNCTIONS

The **Fix** and **Int** functions perform nearly the same action. Both strip the fractional part of a number that is passed to them and return the remaining integer value. But when using negative numbers, **Int** returns the first negative integer that is less than or equal to the number that was passed to it and **Fix** returns the first negative integer greater than or equal to the number that was passed to it. **Fix**(10.3) and **Int**(10.3) both return a value of 10, but **Fix**(-10.3) returns a value of –10 while **Int**(-10.3) returns a value of –11. The syntax for both functions is essentially the same:

```
Fix(number)
Int(number)
```

The *number* that is passed to either argument can be any valid numeric expression. Both functions return a value that is the same data type as the number that was passed to it.

USING THE SGN FUNCTION

The **Sgn** function determines the sign of a number that is passed to it. It returns an integer value that corresponds to one of three possibilities. The syntax for the function is as follows:

```
Sgn(number)
```

If *number* is greater than 0, a 1 is returned; if number is equal to 0, a 0 is returned; if number is less than 0, a –1 is returned. This information can be used to affect the way that a number is processed. For example, an application may need to treat negative numbers differently than positive numbers.

USING THE SQR FUNCTION

Use the **Sqr** function to find the square root of a number. **Sqr** returns the value as a **Double** data type. The syntax for this function is as follows:

```
Sqr(number)
```

Like all of the other math functions, a valid numeric expression must be passed to the **Sqr** function.

USING TRIGONOMETRIC FUNCTIONS

There are several trigonometric functions available in Visual Basic. These functions might be useful when writing a graphing or drawing

Function	Description
Atn(number)	Arctangent of an angle
Cos(number)	Cosine of an angle
Sin(number)	Sine of an angle
Tan(number)	Tangent of an angle

TABLE 5-1 *Trigonometric Functions* ▼

program. Table 5-1 summarizes the trigonometric functions. All of these functions require a valid numeric expression to be passed to them as an argument.

EXAMPLES

1. The following return a value of 10:

```
Abs(10)
Abs(-10)
```

2. The following returns a value of –3:

```
Fix(-3.7)
```

3. The following returns a value of –4:

```
Int(-3.7)
```

4. The following returns a value of 0:

```
Sgn(0)
```

EXERCISES

1. Which function determines the sign of a number?
2. Which function determines the value of a number regardless of the sign?
3. Write a statement that sets dblLogValue equal to the log of 2.7.
4. Write a statement that sets dblSquareRoot equal to the square root of the value contained in the variable dblMyValue.
5. List the trigonometric functions.

5.4 USING RANDOM NUMBERS

Random numbers can serve many purposes in an application. They can be used in computer games to randomly affect behavior and give a new experience each time the game is played. Engineering applications might use them to build statistical models. Many applications can use these numbers to test their own operation. The testing is made more powerful by the fact that the same sequence of random numbers can be generated over and over again, which provides the ability to make changes to the application and then monitor the effects of those changes.

USING THE RND FUNCTION

The **Rnd** function generates a random number that is less than 1 and greater than 0. It returns the value as a **Single** data type, using the following syntax:

```
Rnd[(number)]
```

The *number* argument, which is referred to as the seed, is optional. It determines the number that the **Rnd** function generates. If it is not supplied, **Rnd** returns the next number in its sequence, which is also what it does if a number greater than 0 is given as the seed. Providing a number less than 0 generates the same number each time for that seed. Anytime 0 is specified as the seed, Rnd returns the most recently generated number. After Rnd generates a number, that number is used as the seed the next time the function is called.

Because of this behavior, the same sequence of numbers can be generated over and over. This is a great advantage when testing an application that accepts numbers as input, because the exact same test data can be generated with little effort. If numbers must be completely random, the Randomize statement should be used.

*Although the **Rnd** function only generates numbers less than 1, it can be used to create random numbers that are larger. For example, this formula produces random integers between 1 and 10: Int(10 * **Rnd** + 1).*

USING THE RANDOMIZE STATEMENT

The **Randomize** statement initializes the random-number generator. The syntax for the **Randomize** statement is as follows:

```
Randomize [number]
```

*The number value that is specified when using the **Randomize** statement is not an argument and does not have to be enclosed in parentheses—although it can be.*

Issuing this statement gives the random-number generator (**Rnd**) a new seed value. If a number is not specified after the **Randomize** statement, the new seed value is derived from the system timer. To generate truly random values, the **Randomize** statement should be issued without specifying a seed value.

EXAMPLES

1. The following calls the **Rnd** function with a seed of 3 and sets dblExample equal to the return value:

   ```
   dblExample = Rnd(3)
   ```

2. The following call to the **Rnd** function generates the same number as the last call to the **Rnd** function:

   ```
   dblExample = Rnd(0)
   ```

3. The following code initializes the random-number generator function with a seed value of 1:

   ```
   Randomize 1
   ```

EXERCISES

1. How do you generate the same random number every time you call the **Rnd** function?

2. What seed value does **Rnd** use after the first time that it is called?

3. If no seed value is specified, what value does the **Randomize** statement use for the seed value?

4. Write code that would generate a completely random number each time it was called.

Mastery
Skills Check

1. Which numeric data types can handle numeric values that have fractions?

2. How can you dictate the order in which numeric operators should be used?

3. Which function is sometimes called the antilogarithm?

4. How can you generate the same random number each time you call the **Rnd** function?

6

Using Control Statements

chapter objectives

6.1 Using the If and Ilf Statements

6.2 Using the Select Case Statement

6.3 Using the Do Statement

6.4 Using the For Statement

6.5 Using the Exit Statement

Control statements help determine the behavior of an application. This is usually accomplished by interacting with a user. If a user chooses one option, the application behaves one way, but if the user chooses a different option, the behavior changes to that particular option. Some control statements compare the value of a variable or control property to predetermined values. Any time a match is found the code that is associated with that condition is performed.

Other control statements perform the actions specified by a piece of code several times in a row. The number of times the code is run might be a certain predetermined number of times or it may depend upon a particular condition being met. Code might be run over and over until the user clicks a button, a variable contains a certain value, or the end of a file is reached. These types of control statements are called *loops*.

There may be times when you would want to interrupt the actions of a control statement. Several options are available for stopping the execution of a control statement, depending on the particular situation.

Review

Skills Check

You should be able to correctly answer the following questions before beginning this chapter:

1. Can a string variable be used to assign a value to a numeric variable?

2. When using numeric operators, what does operator precedence determine?

3. Which function returns the absolute value of a number?

4. Which statement is executed before the **Rnd** function to ensure that a truly random number is generated?

6.1　*U*SING THE IF AND IIF STATEMENTS

The *If...Then* statement is used to test for a condition and perform an action if that condition is **True**. There are variations of this statement that allow it to also perform an alternative task if the condition is **False**. It can even test several different conditions. Conditions are usually tested using comparison operators, such as < , = , or > .

The types of conditions that are tested vary from comparing two strings to testing the value of a numeric variable. Strings might be compared to test for a password or find a match to search criteria. Numbers are usually tested to find if they are less than, equal to, or greater than another value. Regardless of what condition is being tested, the result of the condition is always either **True** or **False**. This result determines which code is performed and which is not.

The values being tested can be of any data type, and any condition can be tested as long as the result is True or False.

USING THE IF...THEN STATEMENT

In the **If...Then** statement, the *condition* follows the **If** and the *code* follows the **Then**. The code is executed only if the condition evaluates to **True**. For example, the following code sets the Boolean variable blnCorrectPassword equal to **True** if the **Text** property of the text box control txtPassword is equal to "secret". This code could easily be used in the **Click** event procedure of a button on a login window. Figure 6-1 shows what this window might look like.

```
If txtPassword.Text = "secret" Then blnCorrectPassword = True
```

The Option Compare statement determines if comparisons are case sensitive within a module. The UCase or LCase functions could also be used to ensure that both string values being compared are either uppercase or lowercase.

In this example, the entire statement appears on the same line of code. This works fine for short and simple **If...Then** statements, but is inadequate when statements become longer or more complex. Alternative syntax for handling long or complex **If...Then** statements is discussed in the following sections.

Writing Blocks of Code for the If...Then Statement

Long or complex **If...Then** statements use an alternative syntax, as illustrated in the following example. The following code expands on

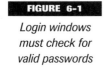

FIGURE 6-1

Login windows must check for valid passwords
▼

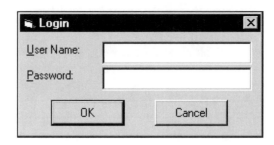

the previous example. It performs the same actions as before and sets a global string variable named gstrUserName equal to the **Text** property of the text box control txtUserName.

```
If txtPassword.Text = "secret" Then
    blnCorrectPassword = True
    gstrUserName = txtUserName.Text
End If
```

Note

The multiple-line syntax for the If...Then statement can be used even if there is only one line of code. This might be done for readability or to conform to coding standards within an organization.

Using this syntax, all of the code from the **Then** to the **End** If is performed if the condition is **True**. This allows more than one line of code—called a *block* of code—to be performed when a condition is met.

Notice that the code blocks are indented. This makes it easier to identify and read the code for the statement, especially if *nested* **If...Then** statements are used. A nested **If...Then** statement is simply an **If...Then** statement inside of another, such as the following:

```
If txtPassword.Text = "secret" Then
    blnCorrectPassword = True
    If txtUserName <> "guest" Then
        gstrUserName = txtUserName.Text
    End If
End If
```

More than one statement can be nested at a time.

The indented code makes it easy to see which code belongs to which statement. This is a necessity as **If...Then** statements become larger, so it is a good practice to get into.

Using Else in the If...Then Statement

You may also want to perform some type of action if the condition is not met. This is done using **Else** in the **If...Then** statement. The syntax for this statement is the same as the multiple-line **If...Then** statement, but only the code between the **Then** and the **Else** is performed if the condition evaluates to **True**. If the condition evaluates to **False**, the code from the **Else** to the **End If** is performed. The following code illustrates the use of this statement by adding on to our previous example. Now when an incorrect password is provided, blnCorrectPassword is set to **False** and gstrUserName is set to "guest".

```
If txtPassword.Text = "secret" Then
    blnCorrectPassword = True
    gstrUserName = txtUserName.Text
Else
    blnCorrectPassword = False
    gstrUserName = "guest"
End If
```

The **Else** may seem unnecessary if it only sets variables equal to values that they already hold, but this redundancy makes code more readable and easier to maintain. For instance, blnCorrectPassword may already be equal to **False** and gstrUserName may already be equal to "guest" before the example statement is executed, which would make it seem unnecessary to set them equal to those values again. But doing so clearly illustrates the logic of this code because it specifically states what values those variables should hold if an incorrect password is provided. This makes it easier for other programmers to understand and work with the code.

You can use more than one expression for the condition of an If...Then statement. For example, you could say If x = 1 and y =2 Then z = 3, If x = 1 or y = 2 Then z = 3, or If (x = 1 and y = 2) or y = 3 Then z = 4. The statement is only concerned with the final result of the condition–True or False.

Using Elself in the If...Then Statement

The **If...Then** statement is also capable of testing for more than one condition at a time. An **ElseIf** makes it possible. It works like an **Else**, but a condition can be specified. Code in an **ElseIf** is only run if the original condition is not met. In the following code, an **ElseIf** has been added to the previous example. If the **Text** property of txtPassword is equal to "guest", gstrUserName is set to "guest".

```
If txtPassword.Text = "secret" Then
    blnCorrectPassword = True
    gstrUserName = txtUserName.Text
ElseIf txtPassword.Text = "guest" Then
    blnCorrectPassword = True
    gstrUserName = "guest"
Else
    blnCorrectPassword = False
    gstrUserName = "guest"
End If
```

An Elself can be used in an If...Then statement without an Else.

Using multiple **ElseIfs** in an **If...Then** statement allows you to test for different conditions. If you are comparing the same variable to several different values, the **Select Case** statement provides a better method. The **Select Case** statement is discussed in more detail in the "Using the Select Case Statement" section of this chapter.

USING THE IIF FUNCTION

The **IIf** function evaluates a condition and returns one value if the condition is **True** and a different value if the condition is **False**. A condition and two possible values are supplied to this function using the following syntax:

```
IIf(condition, TrueValue, FalseValue)
```

The variable gstrUserName, which is used in the previous examples, could be set using this function. In the following code, gstrUserName is set to the **Text** property of txtUserName if the **Text** property of txtPassword is equal to "secret," and is set to "guest" if it is not:

```
gstrUserName = IIf(txtPassword.Text = "secret",
txtUserName.Text, "guest")
```

Both the True value and the False value of the IIf function are always evaluated. This means functions or mathematical formulas used in those sections must not contain errors, such as division by zero.

EXAMPLES

1. To set the variable blnNegativeValue equal to **True** if the value contained in intSomeNumber is negative, you would use the following:

```
If intSomeNumber < 0 Then blnNegativeValue = True
```

2. To set the variable blnNegativeValue equal to **True** if the value contained in intSomeNumber is negative and **False** if it is not, you would use the following:

```
If intSomeNumber < 0 Then
    blnNegativeValue = True
Else
    blnNegativeValue = False
End If
```

3. The work of the previous **If...Then...Else** statement is also accomplished by the following code:

```
blnNegativeValue = IIf(intSomeNumber < 0, True, False)
```

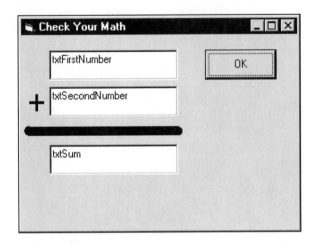

FIGURE 6-2

Check your math
▼

EXERCISES

1. Write a statement that sets y equal to 2 if x equals 1.

2. Write a statement that sets y equal to 2 if x equals 1. If x isn't equal to 1 it sets z equal to 3, but only if y equals 2.

3. Figure 6-2 shows a simple program that checks addition. The names of controls are shown as text on the control. Numeric values are placed in the controls txtFirstNumber, txtSecondNumber, and txtSum. The value in txtSum should be equal to the value in txtFirstNumber added to the value in txtSecondNumber. If the txtSum contains the correct value, lblResult displays "Correct" when the OK button is clicked. Otherwise, it displays "Incorrect". Write the code that should be used for the **Click** event procedure of cmdOK.

6.2 **U**SING THE SELECT CASE STATEMENT

The *Select Case* statement evaluates a single expression. It then compares the value derived from that expression to other values. If a match is found, the code block associated with the matching value is executed. For example, the last code block in the following is executed when this code is run:

```
Select Case 1 + 2
    Case 1
        lblFinish.Caption = "First"
    Case 2
        lblFinish.Caption = "Second"
    Case 3
        lblFinish.Caption = "Third"
End Select
```

If more than one match exists in a Select Case statement, only the first match encountered is used.

This statement is a good alternative to the **If...Then** statement when the same expression needs to be compared to several different values. Comparing an expression to a range of values is also a good use of the **Select Case** statement, which is discussed in the following section.

SPECIFYING RANGES OF VALUES IN THE SELECT STATEMENT

A range of values can be specified in the **Select Case** statement using several different methods. Values can be grouped together using commas to separate them, such as the following:

```
Select Case strCountry
    Case "USA", "Canada", "Germany"
        lblRegion.Caption = "North America"
    Case "England", "France", "Germany"
        lblRegion.Caption = "Europe"
End Select
```

This method is best used when looking for string values or noncontiguous ranges of numbers. Ranges of continuous numbers are specified using the **To** keyword. For example, the following classifies values into three different ranges (1-3, 4-5, 6-10):

```
Select Case intFinishPosition
    Case 1 To 3
        lblFinishGroup.Caption = "Top 3 Finish"
    Case 4 To 5
        lblFinishGroup.Caption = "Top 5 Finish"
    Case 6 To 10
        lblFinishGroup.Caption = "Top 10 Finish"
End Select
```

The second and third cases could have been 1 **To** 5 and 1 **To** 10 because the **Select Case** statement only uses the first match it encounters, but stating the exact ranges makes the code more clear.

Ranges of letters can be used in the Select Case statement, such as "a" To "c", "p" To "x", or "A" To "Z".

USING CASE ELSE IN THE SELECT CASE STATEMENT

The **Select Case** statement also allows you to specify code for the situation when no match is found. This is specified using **Case Else**, similar to the **Else** in the **If...Then** statement. In the following, any time a country does not match one that is specified, it is classified as being in an "Other Region":

```
Select Case strCountry
    Case "USA", "Canada", "Germany"
        lblRegion.Caption = "North America"
    Case "England", "France", "Germany"
        lblRegion.Caption = "Europe"
    Case Else
        lblRegion.Caption = "Other Region"
End Select
```

This syntax should be used when an action must be performed even if no match is found. For example, a shipping program might use a specific code for each US State, but use a generic international code for all packages not being delivered in the US. Each state would have a code block in the **Select Case** statement, and all other destinations would use the code after the **Case Else**.

Case Else can be specified with or without code. Using Case Else without
code makes it clear that an action should not be performed if a specific
match is not found.

EXAMPLES

1. The following code calls a function to ship a package. This
function needs two arguments: the package number and the
region of the country the package is being shipped to. A Select
Case statement determines which region the package is
going to. For this example, only a couple of states are used for
each region:

```
Select Case strDestinationState
    Case "WA", "OR"
        ShipPackage(lngPackageNumber, "Northwest")
    Case "CA", "AZ"
        ShipPackage(lngPackageNumber, "West")
    Case "FL", "GA"
        ShipPackage(lngPackageNumber, "South")
    Case "NY", "CT"
        ShipPackage(lngPackageNumber, "Northeast")
End Select
```

2. To set the **Caption** of a label to "Small", "Medium", or "Large"
based upon the absolute value in the variable intAnyNumber,
where 1 to 100 is small, 101 to 1000 is medium, and anything
greater is large, use the following code:

```
Select Case Abs(intAnyNumber)
    Case 1 To 100
        lblAnyLabel.Caption = "Small"
    Case 101 To 1000
        lblAnyLabel.Caption = "Medium"
    Case Else
        lblAnyLabel.Caption = "Large"
End Select
```

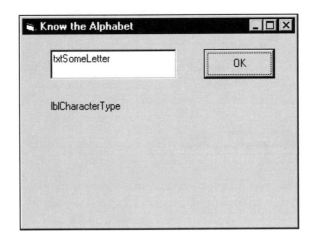

FIGURE 6-3

*Knowing the
alphabet*

▼

EXERCISES

1. What is the syntax for the **Select Case ElseIf** statement?

2. Write a **Select Case** statement that checks the variable intSomeNumber for each of the following values: 1, 2, 3, 4, 5. There doesn't need to be anything in the code blocks.

3. Create a form that looks like Figure 6-3. Write a **Select Case** statement in the **Click** event procedure of the button that evaluates the **Text** property of txtSomeLetter, which holds a single character. If the character is from the first half of the alphabet (a-m), set the **Text** property of lblCharacterType to "first half of alphabet". If the character is from the second half of the alphabet (n-z), set the Text property of lblCharacterType to "second half of alphabet". Otherwise, set lblCharacterType.Text to "not part of alphabet".

6.3 USING THE DO STATEMENT

At times, you may want to perform a task repeatedly until a certain condition is met, for example, reading data from a file until reaching the end of the file. The *Do* statement accomplishes this. Depending on the syntax used, the **Do** statement checks for a particular condition either before or after performing the code contained within the ***Do Loop***. To have your code executed before the **Do** statement checks the condition you specify, use the following syntax:

```
Do
    [code block]
Loop [{While | Until} condition]
```

This statement executes the code block and then evaluates the condition. Use ***While*** in this statement to have the loop continue as long as the condition evaluates to **True**. For example, you could increment a number by 1 while it is less than a specified value, as in the following:

```
Do
    intCounter = intCounter + 1
Loop While intCounter <10
```

The code in this loop executes while the value of intCounter is less than 10. So when intCounter becomes equal to 10, Visual Basic stops executing the code in the loop. In the following code, the exact same results are achieved using the ***Until*** clause:

```
Do
    intCounter = intCounter + 1
Loop Until intCounter = 10
```

Note *Use the Do statement to execute a code block repeatedly until a condition is met, but use the For statement to execute a code block a specific number of times.*

Again, the code within the loop is executed until intCounter = 10. Choosing between the **While** and **Until** clauses is basically a personal preference. This syntax—with the condition being evaluated at the end of the **Do** statement—can cause problems if the code being executed within the loop can cause errors if the condition specified is not met, for instance, reading from an empty file. Testing the condition at the beginning of the **Do** statement would prevent code from trying to read from an empty file because it's at the end of the file as soon as it is opened. To test a condition before code is executed, use the following syntax:

```
Do [{While | Until} condition]
    [code block]
Loop
```

Do statements can be nested—a Do statement within another Do statement.

USING THE WHILE STATEMENT

The **While** statement is another way to execute a block of code repeatedly until a condition is met. This statement is similar to the **Do** statement, but not identical. Preferably, the **Do** statement should be used because it is more flexible in its structure. The syntax for the **While** statement is as follows:

```
While condition
    [code block]
Wend
```

There are no variations of the syntax for this statement. As long as the condition is met at the beginning of the statement, the code block is executed again and again.

EXAMPLES

1. The following code retrieves customer numbers and checks to see if the customer wants to be notified about an upcoming event, which only 100 customers can be invited to. GetNextCustomer, EventCustomer, and AddToMailer are procedures that would have been written especially for this task; they are not built-in Visual Basic procedures.

```
Dim lngCustomer As Long

Do
    lngCustomer = GetNextCustomer
```

```
        If EventCustomer(lngCustomer) Then
            AddToMailer(lngCustomer)
            intCounter = intCounter + 1
        End If
Loop Until intCounter = 100
```

2. The following code opens a file and reads its contents line by line until it reaches the end of the file, printing each line:

```
Dim intCounter As Integer
Dim intFileNumber As Integer
Dim strText As String

intFileNumber = FreeFile
Open "C:\SCANDISK.LOG" For Input As intFileNumber

Do Until EOF(intFileNumber)
    Line Input #intFileNumber, strText
    Printer.Print strText
Loop

Printer.EndDoc
Close intFileNumber
```

3. The previous example could have also been written using the **While** statement:

```
Dim intCounter As Integer
Dim intFileNumber As Integer
Dim strText As String

intFileNumber = FreeFile
Open "C:\SCANDISK.LOG" For Input As intFileNumber

While Not EOF(intFileNumber)
    Line Input #intFileNumber, strText
    Printer.Print strText
Wend

Printer.EndDoc
Close intFileNumber
```

1. Which statement is more flexible: the **Do** statement or the **While** statement?

2. Write a **Do** statement that adds the text "I will learn Visual Basic" to a string variable until the string is greater than 255 characters long.

3. Write a **Do** statement that only executes if the integer variable intNumber is greater than 10. Don't worry about adding any code to the statement.

4. Write a **Do** statement that executes at least once, but then only executes if the integer variable intNumber is greater than 10. Don't worry about adding any code to the statement.

6.4 *U*SING THE FOR STATEMENT

The *For* statement is ideal for repeatedly executing a block of code a specific number of times. For example, if you have five questions to ask users, the **For** statement can execute a code block asking the questions five times. This example is explained more in the following section.

USING FOR...NEXT

In its simplest form, the **For** statement increments a counter variable a specific number of times. It can also use different values to increment the counter variable. The following is the syntax:

```
For counter = start To end [Step step]
    [code block]
Next counter
```

Placing the counter variable after the Next clause of the For statement is optional, but makes code easier to follow, especially when nesting For statements.

Note

Any numeric variable can be used for the counter. You might want to use a single character, such as an *i*, *x*, or *y* when specifying a variable for the counter. This makes it easier to use the counter in the code block without taking up a lot of space and is generally accepted as an exception to normal naming conventions. *Start* and *end* specify the initial and final value of the counter variable. These can be numbers or numeric variables. **Step** indicates the amount that the counter is incremented—or decremented when a negative value—each time the **Next** statement executes. If the step clause is omitted, the value defaults to one. When the counter exceeds the specified end value, the code block of the **For** statement is no longer executed.

Caution

The For statement evaluates the counter after the Next statement increments it. This means the value is at least one more or less than the end value, depending on the step value.

The following code asks five questions, which are stored in a string array, and accepts five answers, also stored in a string array. This code has some *comments* in it. Comments are used to make code more clear, but are not used in the execution of the code. Any line of code with an apostrophe in front of it is a comment. If the apostrophe appears in the middle of a line of code, the text from the apostrophe to the end of the line is treated as a comment. It's a good habit to comment code that might be unclear to other programmers. In this case, the comments explain two functions that readers may not have seen before. This code also uses the **InputBox** function, which is explained in Chapter 7.

Note

Comments affect neither the size of an executable file nor its speed, so use as many comments as you feel necessary.

```
Dim intCounter As Integer
Dim intStart As Integer
Dim intEnd As Integer
Dim strQuestion(1 To 3) As String
Dim strAnswer(1 To 3) As String

strQuestion(1) = "What is your first name?"
strQuestion(2) = "What is your middle initial?"
strQuestion(3) = "What is your last name?"
```

```
intStart = LBound(strQuestion) 'Finds smallest array index
intEnd = UBound(strQuestion)    'Finds largest array index

For intCounter = intStart To intEnd
    strAnswer(intCounter) = _
        InputBox(strQuestion(intCounter), "Q&A")
Next intCounter
```

Use a negative step value to count down instead of increment the counter in the For statement.

To see a practical use of this code, create a new project and add this code plus the following to the **Load** event procedure of the form. As indicated in the following code, a label (lblGreetings), must be placed on the form.

```
lbleGreetings.Text = "Hello"
For intCounter = intStart To intEnd
    lblGreetings.Text = lblGreetings.Text & " "
    lblGreetings.Text = lblGreetings.Text &
strAnswer(intCounter)
Next intCounter
```

Figure 6-4 shows one of the question dialog boxes. They all look the same, except for the question being asked.

Figure 6-5 shows the form after all of the questions have been answered.

Questions collect information from users

▼

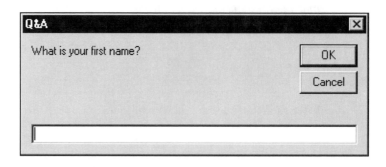

FIGURE 6-5

Responses from users make it possible to customize applications

▼

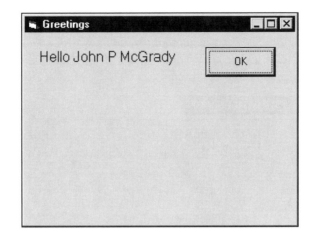

USING FOR EACH...NEXT

In the previous section, a block of code is executed for each element in an array. This is accomplished by determining the beginning and ending index of the array with the **LBound** and **UBound** functions. However, the **For** statement has an alternate syntax that automatically executes a block of code for each element in an array. The following is the syntax for this specialized version of the **For** statement:

```
For Each element In array
    [code block]
Next element
```

The element in this statement must be a **Variant** data type. The code in the previous example that places the user's name in the label could have used the **For Each** statement. It would look like the following:

```
For Each vntAnswer In strAnswer
    lblGreetings.Text = lblGreetings.Text & " "
    lblGreetings.Text = lblGreetings.Text & vntAnswer
Next vntAnswer
```

If you try this code, be sure to declare vntAnswer as a **Variant**. The results of both methods are the same, but this method could prevent you from having to call the **LBound** and **UBound** functions.

The For Each statement can be used with collections as well as arrays. Collections are an ordered set of items, such as the properties of an object.

EXAMPLES

1. The following function uses the **For** statement to raise a number to the power of an integer:

```
Private Function RaiseToPower(dblNumber As Double,
intPower As Integer) As Double

RaiseToPower = dblNumber

For intCounter = 1 To intPower - 1
    RaiseToPower = RaiseToPower * dblNumber
Next intCounter

End Function
```

2. The following function is the same as the previous one, but it uses a negative step value:

```
Private Function RaiseToPower(dblNumber As Double,
intPower As Integer) As Double

RaiseToPower = dblNumber

For intCounter = intPower - 1 To 1 Step -1
    RaiseToPower = RaiseToPower * dblNumber
Next intCounter

End Function
```

3. The following code loops through all of the controls on a form and adds the *type* of each control to a list box, as shown in Figure 6-6:

```
For Each vntControl In frmMain.Controls
    lstControlList.AddItem (TypeName(vntControl))
Next vntControl
```

FIGURE 6-6

The For...Each statement can process a form's controls
▼

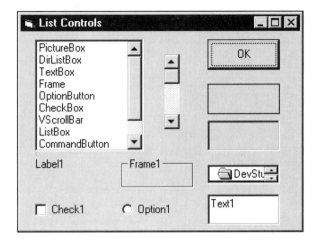

EXERCISES

1. Write a function called MyFiller that accepts a single character and a number. The function should use the **For** statement to build a string containing the character that is repeated the amount of times specified by the number.

2. Write a **For** statement nested within another **For** statement. There does not need to be any other code than the **For** statements.

3. Create a form and add five TextBox controls to it, as shown in Figure 6-7. Add code to the Load event procedure of the form that uses the **For...Each** statement to change the **Text** property of each control to make it look like Figure 6-7.

6.5 USING THE EXIT STATEMENT

Control structures and especially loops are an invaluable tool when creating Visual Basic programs, but there may be situations when you need to immediately exit from a loop. Visual Basic provides a method for accomplishing just that.

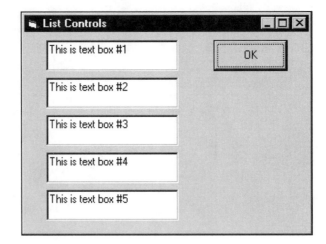

FIGURE 6-7

The Load event procedure and the For…Each statement can customize the behavior of forms

▼

There are two control structures that create a loop: the **Do** statement and the **For** statement. Each of these provides a way to prematurely exit the loop that they create. This allows you to plan for rare circumstances when either the loop doesn't need to run to completion or a condition other than the one being checked by the loop makes it necessary to exit.

USING EXIT DO

The **Do** statement repeatedly executes a code block until a certain condition is met. While several different conditions can be combined using the **And** and **Or** operators, it is still treated as a single condition. To halt the processing of a **Do** loop and continue executing code at the first statement after the loop, use the **Exit Do** statement. In the following example, a **Do** statement executes a code block until a local integer variable is equal to 20:

```
Do
    intCounter = intCounter + 1
    If intCounter = 10 Then
        Exit Do
    End If
Loop Until intCounter = 20
```

Normally, this **Do** statement executes the code block 20 times, which is when the intCounter reaches a value of 20 and the condition is met. However, the **Exit Do** statement that is executed when intCounter equals 10 causes Visual Basic to exit the loop immediately and execute the next line of code after the **Do** statement. This example is very simple, but still illustrates that you would use this feature to exit a loop because of a secondary condition being satisfied.

Note

Many times a nested Do statement might accomplish the same thing as an Exit Do statement, but it may make the code harder to read and understand.

USING EXIT FOR

The **For** statement executes a block of code a set number of times. There may be situations when you want to stop executing the code block contained in the **For** statement and exit the loop before it has been executed the number of times specified. The following example is the **Exit For** equivalent of the previous **Exit Do** example:

```
For intCounter = 1 To 20
    If intCounter = 10 Then
        Exit For
    End If
Loop Until intCounter = 20
```

As you can see, the **Exit For** statement allows the **For** loop to have the comparative ability of the **Do** loop. It executes a block of code a set number of times, but can also exit the loop if a particular condition is met.

EXAMPLES

1. The following example searches a directory specified by the user in a text box and adds the names of the files contained in that directory to a list box. Also, the user can specify a limit to the number of file names that are retrieved.

```
Dim strFile As String
Dim intCounter As Integer
```

```
    strFile = Dir(txtPath)
    Do While strFile <> ""
        intCounter = intCounter + 1
        lstFiles.AddItem (strFile)
        If intCounter = Int(txtLimit.Text) Then
            Exit Do
        End If
        strFile = Dir
    Loop
```

2. The following example collects the scores for a round of golf, which consists of 18 holes. It allows for the possibility that the round may not have been completed by ending the process if nothing is entered for one of the holes.

```
Dim intCounter As Integer
Dim strScore As String
Dim intScore As Integer

For intCounter = 1 To 18
    strScore = InputBox( _
      "Enter your score for hole #" & Str(intCounter) _
      & ".", "Golf Score Calculator")
    If strScore <> "" Then
        intScore = intScore + Int(strScore)
    Else
        Exit For
    End If
Next intCounter
```

EXERCISES

1. What statement immediately halts the execution of a **For** loop, and what is the next line of code executed after that statement?

2. What statement immediately halts the execution of a **Do** loop, and what is the next line of code executed after that statement?

3. Write a procedure that collects names of golfers and then collects scores for those golfers.

Mastery
Skills Check

1. Do all code blocks for an **If** statement require code in their code block area?

2. In a **Select** statement, how many times is the expression that is being compared to the different cases evaluated? (In other words, if the expression is two numbers being added together, how many times are the two numbers added together?)

3. Which syntax of the **Do** statement executes the code block for the statement at least once?

4. Does a start and end value always have to be provided to the **For** statement?

5. Which line of code is executed after an **Exit Do** statement?

7

Using Dialog Boxes

chapter objectives

Dialog boxes are specialized forms that serve two basic purposes. Their primary use is to provide information to users. For example, a dialog box might appear to notify a user that a process has completed successfully—or even unsuccessfully. Some dialog boxes are more sophisticated and interact with the user, accepting input and possibly providing feedback. This type of dialog is used, for example, when opening a file or changing printer properties. In both roles, dialog boxes provide an important tool for Visual Basic programmers.

Two types of dialog boxes exist. All dialog boxes are either *modal* or *modeless*. Modal dialog boxes require user interaction before any other part of an application can be used. Most dialog boxes are modal because a response is usually required for the application to continue processing. Modeless dialog boxes don't prevent users from interacting with other parts of an application while they are open. Visual Basic's Find dialog box is modeless, and the Save dialog box is modal.

Visual Basic provides a number of *predefined* dialog boxes. While these dialog boxes are predefined, they accept parameters used to customize their behavior and appearance. If none of the predefined dialog boxes meets your needs, *custom* dialog boxes are created using forms. The forms are created just like any other form; the difference is in how the form is opened. A parameter is passed to the **Show** method that makes the form modal and the border style is set to fixed dialog, so that the form does not appear in the task list.

Review
Skills Check

You should be able to correctly answer the following questions before beginning this chapter:

1. How do you test for more than one condition when using the If statement?

2. How many times is the expression in the **Select** statement evaluated?

3. How do you ensure that the code block of a **Do** statement is executed at least once?

4. What is the default step value of the **For** statement?

5. What line of code is executed after an **Exit Do** statement?

7.1 *U*SING THE MSGBOX FUNCTION

The *MsgBox* function displays a dialog box that is created using the arguments supplied to the function. This is a simple dialog box that displays a message and accepts feedback from users only through the form of closing the dialog box—no text can be entered by the user.

Many times, this function is used to supply information to users without expecting any feedback. For example, Figure 7-1 shows a Microsoft Word dialog box used to notify the user that it has completed its search and the item was not found.

The user has no choice but to press the OK button to close this dialog box. Because there is only one way to close this dialog box, the choice has no effect on how the program operates. Other dialog boxes present users with more than one choice to close the dialog box, such as Figure 7-2.

Figure 7-2 shows a dialog box that Microsoft Word displays when closing a file that has not been saved. The user is presented with three choices for closing the dialog box. The choice affects the actions of the application. Clicking the Yes button saves the file, while clicking the No button doesn't save the file. Choosing the Cancel button doesn't save the file, but it also doesn't close the file—it cancels the Close command. The following sections discuss the method for both uses of the **MsgBox** function.

FIGURE 7-1

The MsgBox function can create dialog boxes for informational purposes

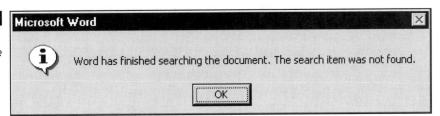

Dialog boxes can affect the processing of an application
▼

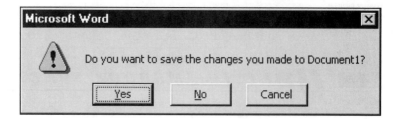

DISPLAYING INFORMATION USING THE MSGBOX FUNCTION

Displaying information is the most basic task for the **MsgBox** function. The following is the syntax for this function:

```
MsgBox(prompt[, buttons] [, title] [, helpfile, context])
```

The prompt is the only argument that is required for the **MsgBox** function. It is a string that is displayed in the message area of the dialog box. In Figure 7-1 the prompt is "Word has finished searching the document. The search item was not found." This argument is limited to approximately 1024 characters, depending on the characters used.

Use the carriage return character (Chr(13)) and the linefeed character (Chr(10)) to separate lines in the message of a dialog box.

No other parameters need to be supplied to create an informational dialog box. When you supply only the prompt, this results in a dialog box that uses the application name in its title bar and contains a single OK button.

To open a **MsgBox** that informs a user their choice is invalid, you could use the following code. Figure 7-3 shows the dialog box that this statement creates.

```
MsgBox("You have made an invalid choice. " _
& "Please make another selection")
```

The **MsgBox** function uses the application name as the default title for the dialog box that it opens (Project1). However, you may

*Display information
to the user with
dialog boxes*
▼

want to customize the appearance of the dialog box. The buttons and
title bar customize the appearance of the dialog box. Many changes
can be made using the buttons parameter, which is discussed in the
following section. Different titles are specified for the dialog box using
the title parameter.

*Two optional MsgBox arguments are available for applications that have a help
file. The helpfile parameter is a string expression that identifies a Windows help
file. If helpfile is supplied, a context must also be supplied. Context is a
numeric expression that indicates the context number for the topic in the help
file that relates to the dialog box. For more information on help files, refer to
the documentation of your help file compiler. If you don't have a help file
compiler, always omit these two parameters.*

INTERACTING USING THE MSGBOX FUNCTION

An application can interact with a user by changing the optional
buttons parameter of the **MsgBox** function. The buttons parameter is a
numeric expression that determines the following items:

▼ Number and type of buttons

▼ Icon displayed

▼ Default button

▼ Modality

Each possibility for the items in the list equates to a numeric value.
Those numeric values are added together to determine how the
individual items are displayed. Table 7-1 summarizes the possibilities.

Item Affected	Constant	Value	Description
Number and type of buttons	vbOKOnly	0	Display OK button only
	vbOKCancel	1	Display OK and Cancel buttons
	vbAbortRetryIgnore	2	Display Abort, Retry, and Ignore buttons
	vbYesNoCancel	3	Display Yes, No, and Cancel buttons
	vbYesNo	4	Display Yes and No buttons
	vbRetryCancel	5	Display Retry and Cancel buttons
Icon displayed	vbCritical	16	Display Critical Message icon
	vbQuestion	32	Display Warning Query icon
	vbExclamation	48	Display Warning Message icon
	vbInformation	64	Display Information Message icon
Default button	vbDefaultButton1	0	First button is default
	vbDefaultButton2	256	Second button is default
	vbDefaultButton3	512	Third button is default
	vbDefaultButton4	768	Fourth button is default
Modality	vbApplicationModal	0	No other part of the application can be used until a response is made
	vbSystemModal	4096	No part of any application can be used until a response is made

TABLE 7-1 *Commonly Used Values for the Buttons Parameter of the MsgBox Function* ▼

Only one value from each group of numbers can be specified. The first column of Table 7-1 displays the items that these values affect. Visual Basic uses the sum of the values supplied for the buttons argument to determine which parameters are specified and what their value is.

Specify values using their constant (including 0 values) to make your code clear. A variable can be used to hold the value. The following code shows the necessary variable declaration. A value is placed in the variable that creates a dialog box with a Yes, No, and Cancel button, where the No button is the default. This dialog box uses the information icon and is application modal.

```
Dim Style As vbMsgBoxStyle

Style = vbYesNoCancel + vbInformation + vbDefaultButton2
```

To create a dialog box using the MsgBox function that doesn't contain an icon, don't include any of the values for that item (16, 32, 48, 64).

The **MsgBox** function returns a value, which can always be ignored. If you need to use the return value, store it in a variable with a data type of **vbMsgBoxResult**. Table 7-2 shows the possible return values.

Variables declared with a **vbMsgBoxResult** data type store the return value for the **MsgBox** function. The following code creates a dialog box with the same appearance as the one in Figure 7-1:

```
Dim strMessage, strTitle As String
Dim Style As vbMsgBoxStyle
Dim Result As vbMsgBoxResult

strMessage = "Word has finished searching the document. "
strMessage = strMessage & "The search item was not found."
strTitle = "Microsoft Word"
Style = vbOKOnly + vbInformation

Result = MsgBox (strMessage, Style, strTitle)
```

In this case, the Result variable is always equal to 1. When more return values are possible, **If** statements or **Select** statements can be used to perform processing according to which button the user clicked.

Constant	Value	Description
VbOK	1	OK
VbCancel	2	Cancel
VbAbort	3	Abort
VbRetry	4	Retry
VbIgnore	5	Ignore
VbYes	6	Yes
VbNo	7	No

TABLE 7-2 *Return Values for the MsgBox Function* ▼

EXAMPLES

1. Create simple dialog boxes that present a message and an OK button using the **MsgBox** function. The following code informs the user that a download is complete by displaying the dialog box shown in Figure 7-4:

```
MsgBox ("Download complete.")
```

2. The appearance of a dialog box can be customized. For example, the following code changes the title of the dialog box in Figure 7-4 and adds an information icon. See Figure 7-5 for the results of the changes.

```
Dim Style As vbMsgBoxStyle
Dim Result As vbMsgBoxResult

Style = vbOKOnly + vbInformation
Result = MsgBox("Download complete.", Style, "Internet")
```

3. If action is only taken for one of the buttons on a dialog box, an **If** statement works great for processing the return value. The following **If** statement only executes its code block if the user clicks the No button on the dialog box created by the **MsgBox** function:

```
If MsgBox (strMessage, vbYesNo, strTitle) = vbNo Then
    'Empty Code Block
End If
```

4. To use an **If** statement that executes a code block for each possibility of a dialog box, the return value must first be stored in a variable. Calling the **MsgBox** function for each possible return value creates a dialog box for each return value. The following code shows an If statement that executes a code block

FIGURE 7-4

*Return Values for
the MsgBox
Function*

▼

Icons give users a visual indication about the type of information a dialog box contains

▼

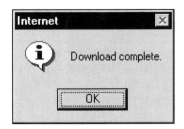

for any return value of a dialog box that has a Yes, No, and Cancel button:

```
Dim strMessage, strTitle As String
Dim Style As vbMsgBoxStyle
Dim Result As vbMsgBoxResult

strMessage = "Click a button to see a confirmation."
strTitle = "Dialog Box Demonstration"
Style = vbYesNoCancel + vbInformation + vbDefaultButton3

Result = MsgBox (strMessage, Style, strTitle)

If Result = vbYes Then
    MsgBox ("You clicked the Yes button.")
ElseIf Result = vbNo Then
    MsgBox ("You clicked the No button.")
ElseIf Result = vbCancel Then
    MsgBox ("You clicked the Cancel button.")
End If
```

EXERCISES

1. Write a **MsgBox** function, supplying only a prompt argument of "Your hard drive is almost full."

2. Change the **MsgBox** function in the previous exercise to add a critical icon to it.

3. Write code that recreates the dialog box in Figure 7-2.

4. Rewrite the code in the fourth example in the previous section, using a **Select** statement instead of an **If** statement.

7.2 USING THE INPUTBOX FUNCTION

The **MsgBox** function creates dialog boxes that convey information to users and can even interact with the users. However, this interaction is restricted to a limited number of predetermined possibilities. To give the user the ability to supply any value they wish, use the *InputBox* function. This function's syntax is as follows:

```
InputBox(prompt[, title] [, default] [, xpos] [, ypos]
[, helpfile, context])
```

The prompt and title arguments have the same effect on dialogs created with **InputBox** as they did using **MsgBox**—as do the helpfile and context arguments. In addition, only the prompt argument is required.

If a default value is supplied to the **InputBox** function, it appears in the text box of the dialog box. Omitting the default value leaves the text box blank. An x and y position for the location of the dialog box on the screen is supplied using the xpos and ypos arguments, which accept the distance of the edge of the dialog box from the left and top of the screen respectively. Leaving out xpos centers the dialog box horizontally, while leaving out ypos places the dialog box about one-third of the way from the top of the screen.

Note *Include only the comma in the argument list to omit a value, when values after it in the argument list are included. For example, to use the default title and still specify a default value, use the following argument list (strMessage, , strDefault).*

The **InputBox** returns a string value. If the user clicks the OK button or presses the ENTER key, the string contained in the text box is returned. But if the user clicks the Cancel button or presses the ESC key, an empty string is returned, regardless of what the text box contains.

EXAMPLES

1. To allow a user to change the title of a window named frmMain, place a button on the form and add the following code to the **Click** event procedure of the button:

```
Dim strMessage, strTitle, strDefault, strReturn As string

strMessage = "Please provide a new title for the main window."
strTitle = "Rename Window"
strDefault = "New Name"

strReturn = InputBox (strMessage, strTitle, strDefault)
If strReturn <> "" Then
    ReturnfrmMain.Caption = strReturn
End If
```

Figure 7-6 shows the dialog box that this code creates.

2. Use a **Do** statement to prevent the user from entering an empty string, as in the following code:

```
Dim strMessage, strTitle, strResponse As string

strMessage = "You must enter a value in the text box to continue."
strTitle = "No Empty Strings"

Do
    strResponse = InputBox (strMessage, strTitle)
Loop While strResponse = ""
```

FIGURE 7-6

The InputBox function collects string data from users

Rename Window

Please provide a new title for the main window.

OK

Cancel

New Name

EXERCISES

1. Write a block of code that creates a dialog box using the **InputBox** function until the user enters the text "stop".

2. Write a block of code that uses the **InputBox** function to ask for two numbers to add together and then displays the results in a dialog box.

7.3 *U*SING THE COMMONDIALOG CONTROL

The Windows operating system contains a set of dialog boxes that are used to complete frequently used tasks, such as the following:

▼ Open a file

▼ Save a file

▼ Select a color

▼ Select a font

▼ Print or change print options

▼ Show help

These dialog boxes are defined in COMDLG32.OCX, which must be present in the Windows system directory. Visual Basic's CommonDialog control provides access to the dialog boxes defined in this file. Calling a different method of the CommonDialog control opens each type of dialog box.

There are many advantages to using these common dialog controls across all applications. The greatest advantage to programmers is the ability to use the same code each time one of these common tasks is necessary. This cuts down on programming time and helps prevent errors. Users reap the greatest benefits from a common interface being used across applications that are created by different programmers and different companies. They require less training and learn to use programs more quickly because they don't have to learn how to use a new set of dialog boxes for each application.

ADDING THE COMMONDIALOG CONTROL TO A FORM

By default, the CommonDialog control is not included in the standard Toolbox. You must install it using the Components dialog box. Figure 7-7 shows this control being added to a project.

Note ——— *Open the Components dialog box by selecting Components from the Project menu or pressing CTRL-T. You can also open the Components dialog box by right-clicking on the Toolbox and selecting Components from the shortcut menu.*

The CommonDialog control is a non-visual object, meaning that it is never visible at run time. Because of this, it can be placed anywhere on a form without regard to the way it looks or how it interacts with users; it is never seen and has no direct interaction with users.

FIGURE 7-7

Add the CommonDialog control to each project that needs to use it
▼

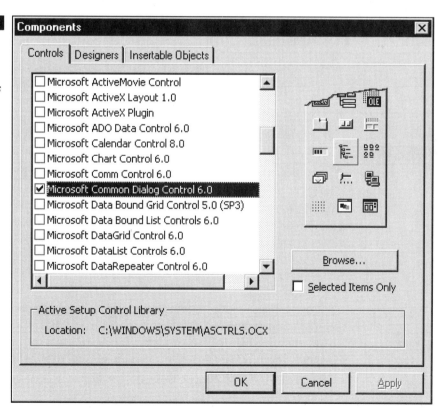

After placing the control on a form, set properties as with any other control, with one exception. The CommonDialog control has no size properties. This prevents the size of the control from being changed, which really isn't necessary because it is a non-visual object. In the following sections, you learn which properties to set for different dialog boxes and the methods used to open them.

EXAMPLES

1. To add the CommonDialog control to a project, open the Components dialog box and select the control in the list.

2. To add the CommonDialog control to a form, open the form in the Forms window and double-click on the control in the Toolbox. Place the control near any other non-visual objects on the form to make future maintenance of the project easier.

EXERCISES

1. Can any project use the CommonDialog control?

2. What is the optimum size for a CommonDialog control?

7.4   USING THE COMMONDIALOG CONTROL OPEN AND SAVE AS DIALOG BOXES

Any application that deals with opening and saving files needs a mechanism for doing so. The CommonDialog control offers a solution for both: the Open and Save As dialog box. These dialog boxes are discussed together because they are so similar. The only difference between them is the default dialog title and the caption on the action button.

Figure 7-8 shows the Open dialog box. This dialog box is opened using the **ShowOpen** method of the CommonDialog control. The Open button sets the **FileName** property of the control to the currently selected file, and the Cancel button closes the dialog box without changing the **FileName** property

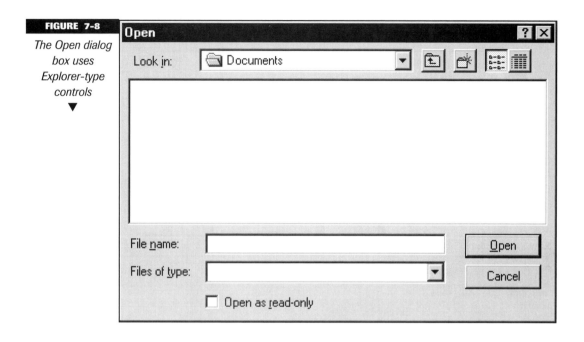

FIGURE 7-8

The Open dialog box uses Explorer-type controls ▼

Caution

When a user clicks the Cancel button, the FileName property remains unchanged. So if the FileName was set prior to the Open dialog box being opened, that value remains unchanged.

Figure 7-9 shows the Save As dialog box. Use the CommonDialog control's **ShowSave** method to open this dialog box. The Save button works like the Open button of the Open dialog box, and the Cancel button is the same.

These dialog boxes have no methods to actually manipulate any files. They only present a common interface for selecting a path and filename to open and save. Then, their **FileName** property is used to perform actions that either open a file or save a file. See Chapter 10 for more information on using files.

SETTING THE PROPERTIES OF THE OPEN AND SAVE AS DIALOG BOXES

The Open and Save As dialog boxes are affected by the same properties of the CommonDialog control. At design time, these properties are set

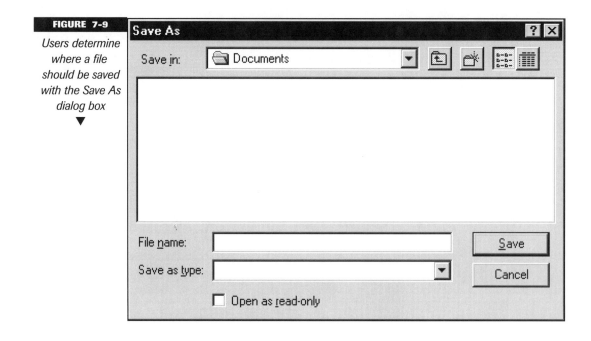

FIGURE 7-9

Users determine where a file should be saved with the Save As dialog box
▼

either in the Properties window or in the property page of the CommonDialog control, which is shown in Figure 7-10. Double-click the Custom property in the Properties window to open the property page.

At run time these properties are set using dot notation. Table 7-3 briefly describes each of the properties used with the Open and Save As dialog boxes of the CommonDialog control.

The **Flags** property can affect the appearance and behavior of the dialog boxes. It is an advanced option that is generally beyond the scope of this book. However, several of the dialog boxes depend on this property containing a particular value. For those dialog boxes, the value is supplied, but no additional information is provided. For more on this property, refer to the Visual Basic documentation.

FIGURE 7-10

The Open and Save As dialog boxes share the same property page

▼

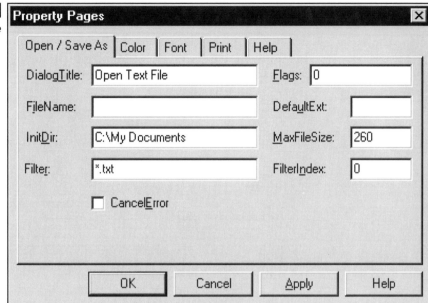

Property	Description
DialogTitle	Text displayed in the title bar of the dialog box
Flags	Options that affect the behavior of the dialog box
FileName	Path and filename
DefaultExt	Default filename extension when using SaveAs dialog box
InitDir	Initial file directory
MaxFileSize	Maximum size of filename
Filter	Filters used to limit the types of files being displayed
FilterIndex	Default filter; the first defined filter's index is 1
CancelError	Determines if error is generated when user clicks Cancel button

TABLE 7-3 *Properties for Open and Save As Dialog Boxes* ▼

EXAMPLES

1. The following block of code opens an Open dialog box. If a text file is selected, it opens the file in Notepad using the **Shell** command. This code does not check the return value of the **Shell** function for errors.

```
Dim dblTaskID As Double

'Prompt user for file to open
dlgFileOpen.Filter = "Text (*.txt)|*.txt|" _
  & "Graphics (*.bmp;*.gif)|*.bmp;*.gif"
dlgFileOpen.FilterIndex = 1
dlgFileOpen.InitDir = "C:\My Documents"
dlgFileOpen.ShowOpen

'Open selected file in Notepad only if it is a text file
If UCase(Right(dlgFileOpen.filename, 3)) = "TXT" Then
    dblTaskID = Shell("Notepad " _
        & dlgFileOpen.filename, vbNormalFocus)
End If
```

2. The following code uses the **ShowSave** method of the CommonDialog control to obtain what filename should be used to save a file. More code is required to actually save the file.

```
dlgFileSave.DefaultExt = "txt"
dlgFileSave.Filter = "Text (*.txt)|*.txt|" _
  & "Graphics (*.bmp;*.gif)|*.bmp;*.gif"
dlgFileSave.FilterIndex = 1
dlgFileSave.InitDir = "C:\My Documents"
dlgFileSave.ShowSave
```

EXERCISES

1. Write a code block that uses a CommonDialog control named dlgFileOpen. It should allow users to select from any files (*.*) and the following Microsoft Office files:

   ▼ Word documents (*.doc)—make this the default

   ▼ Excel workbooks (*.xls;*.xlb)

▼ Access databases (*.mdb)

2. Write a code block that gives the user the ability to choose a filename in the SaveAs dialog box, using the same filters as in the previous exercise. Make the default extension *.doc.

7.5 *USING THE COMMONDIALOG CONTROL COLOR DIALOG BOX*

Applications dealing with formatted text or graphics normally give users the ability to change colors. A text editor might allow the color of the text to be changed to emphasize a word or phrase, and varying colors are nearly a requirement for graphical presentations. Although very specialized programs might require very specialized input to make these types of adjustments in color, most applications benefit from using the CommonDialog control Color dialog box. Figure 7-11 shows the Color dialog box, which is opened by calling the CommonDialog control's **ShowColor** method.

Using this control presents a consistent interface to users needing to affect changes in color. Just as in the other uses of the CommonDialog control, this cuts down on the learning curve for the application, which lowers training costs. In addition, programmers have access to a complicated interface that is already tested and proven. It even offers the advanced feature of allowing users to choose custom colors, as shown in Figure 7-12.

The number of properties that affect the Color dialog box are limited. In fact, **Color**, **Flags**, and **CancelError** are the only properties that control the display of this dialog box. Open the property page for the CommonDialog by double-clicking the Custom property. Then, click the Color tab to view the properties of the Color dialog box, as shown in Figure 7-13.

The **Color** property stores color information as a long value that represents an RGB color. Several methods are available for setting this property.

Note

RGB specifies how a color should be displayed by stating the relative intensity of red, green, and blue to be used.

Choose a color
from the Color
dialog box's palette

▼

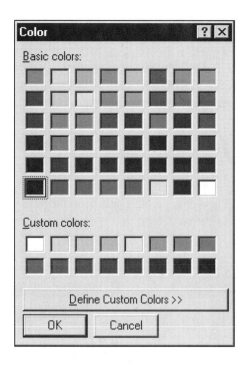

FIGURE 7-12

Create custom
colors with the
Color dialog box

▼

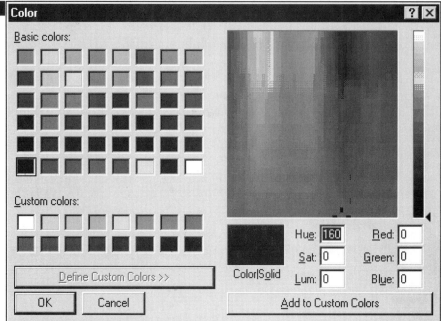

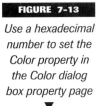

FIGURE 7-13

Use a hexadecimal number to set the Color property in the Color dialog box property page
▼

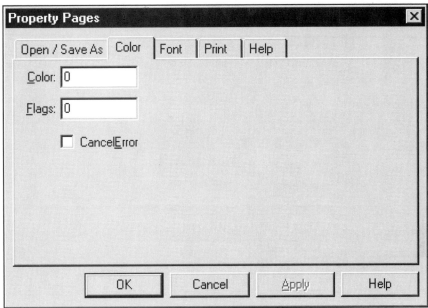

The **QBColor** function returns an RGB color code. This function is left over from earlier versions of Visual Basic, but can still be used to set color values. **QBColor** accepts a number from 0 to 15, which it converts to a corresponding RGB color code. Table 7-4 shows the colors that each number represents.

The **RGB** function also returns an RGB color code. This function accepts three arguments: one each for red, green, and blue. Syntax for this function is as follows:

```
RGB(red, green, blue)
```

Each argument, which can range from 0 to 255, specifies the intensity of its corresponding color. This provides much greater flexibility for specifying colors over the **QBColor** function. Table 7-5 shows some commonly used colors and the red, green, and blue values required to create them using the **RGB** function.

Any argument passed to the RGB function that exceeds 255 is assumed to be equal to 255.

Number	Color
0	Black
1	Blue
2	Green
3	Cyan
4	Red
5	Magenta
6	Yellow
7	White
8	Gray
9	Light Blue
10	Light Green
11	Light Cyan
12	Light Red
13	Light Magenta
14	Light Yellow
15	Bright White

TABLE 7-4 *QBColor Function Color Codes* ▼

Color	Red	Green	Blue
Black	0	0	0
Blue	0	0	255
Green	0	255	0
Cyan	0	255	255
Red	255	0	0
Magenta	255	0	255
Yellow	255	255	0
White	255	255	255

TABLE 7-5 *RGB Function Arguments for Common Colors* ▼

As you become more familiar with some of the RGB values, you may wish to directly enter the hexadecimal number for a desired color. In addition, Visual Basic provides constants that also can be used to specify some of the most frequently used colors, as described in Table 7-6.

Another common task in Windows programming is to match the colors of applications with those being used in the Windows environment. This is especially challenging because of the ease with which Windows color schemes are changed and customized. To help programmers match application colors with the colors users might have set on their machines, Visual Basic provides constants that evaluate to the colors of specific controls in the Windows environment. These constants are normally applied at design time when you set the properties of controls, but can also be used in code. For a complete list of these constants, refer to the Color Constants help topic of the Visual Basic help file.

In the Properties window, the Color property has a dropdown list box that allows you to choose from either a color palette or a list of system colors.

Constant	Value	Description
vbBlack	&H0	Black
vbRed	&HFF	Red
vbGreen	&HFF00	Green
vbYellow	&HFFFF	Yellow
vbBlue	&HFF0000	Blue
vbMagenta	&HFF00FF	Magenta
vbCyan	&HFFFF00	Cyan
vbWhite	&HFFFFFF	White

TABLE 7-6 *Constants for Frequently Used Colors* ▼

EXAMPLES

1. The following code block prompts the user to select a color and then uses that color to set the **BackColor** property of a picture control. If the user clicks the Cancel button, the color is still changed to the default color selection of the Color dialog box—black.

```
dlgColor.ShowColor
picWaterColor.BackColor = dlgColor.Color
```

2. The following code block prompts the user to select a color, but won't accept black or white as an answer:

```
Do
    dlgColor.ShowColor
    picWaterColor.BackColor = dlgColor.Color
Loop While dlgColor.Color = vbBlack Or dlgColor.Color =
vbWhite
```

EXERCISES

1. Write a code block that prompts the user for a color and then changes the **BackColor** property of a list box to that color.

2. Write a code block that repeats the action performed in the previous exercise, except make the title of the dialog box "Select a Color".

7.6 # USING THE COMMONDIALOG CONTROL FONT DIALOG BOX

The Font dialog box allows users to make choices about how text is displayed. This dialog box offers choices based upon the fonts that are installed on the user's machine. These fonts are divided into two categories: *screen fonts* and *printer fonts*. Screen fonts determine how text is displayed on your monitor, and printer fonts control the appearance of printed text.

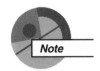

Fonts can be both a screen font and a printer font at the same time.

Note

The **Flags** property of the CommonDialog control must be set to a value specifying the fonts to be used before the **ShowFont** method is called to display the Font dialog box. If the **Flags** property is not set to one of the values described in Table 7-7, a run-time error occurs, which complains that no fonts are installed.

Open the CommonDialog control's property pages and click on the Font tab to view the other properties relating to fonts. Figure 7-14 shows that a font name and size can be specified. Also, font size can be limited to a minimum or maximum value. Styling (bold, italic, underline, and strikethrough) is indicated using checkboxes. A selected checkbox means that the style should be used.

Call the **ShowFont** method of the CommonDialog control to open the Font dialog box. Figure 7-15 shows the Font dialog box that appears—with **Flags** set to **cdlCFBoth**.

The Font dialog box in Figure 7-15 doesn't contain the underline and strikethrough options that were available in the property page. To include these options on the dialog box, the **Flags** property needs the **cdlCFEffects** value added to it. This is done using either of the following methods:

```
dlgFont.Flags = cdlCFBoth + cdlCFEffects
dlgFont.Flags = cdlCFBoth Or cdlCFEffects
```

The **cdlCFEffect** flag also makes it possible for users to select a color for fonts. The Font dialog box sets the color and the other font properties of the CommonDialog control, which are then used to effect changes for displaying or printing text.

Constant	Value	Description
cdlCFScreenFonts	&H1	Screen fonts
cdlCFPrinterFonts	&H2	Printer fonts
cdlCFBoth	&H3	Screen and printer fonts

TABLE 7-7 *Flags for Installing Fonts* ▼

FIGURE 7-14

*Property page for
the Font
dialog box*

▼

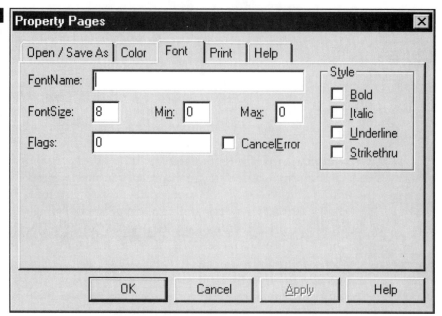

FIGURE 7-15

*The Font dialog
box does not
contain all style
options by default*

▼

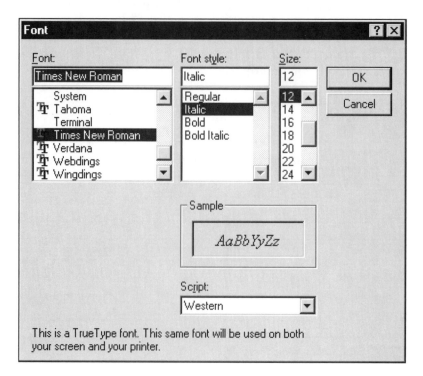

USING THE FONT OBJECT

Many objects that use fonts do not have separate properties for each aspect of their fonts. Rather, they combine all of the font properties into a single object and make that font object one of their properties. Font properties stored this way can be set in two ways. First, dot notation can directly set the different properties. For example, the size of a font object is accessed in the following manner:

```
txtText.Font.Size
```

This method gives you the ability to directly manipulate font properties, but it doesn't take advantage of the power provided by encapsulating all the font properties into an object. To take advantage of this second method for setting font properties, you must use a font object to manipulate font properties. The following is a simple example of using a font object to change font properties:

```
Dim f As New StdFont

f.Name = "Courier"
f.Size = 12
f.Bold = True
Set txtText.Font = f
```

Font objects are created using the **StdFont** object. When declaring a font object, the **New** keyword must be included in the declaration. Also, when setting the font property equal to a font object, the **Set** keyword must appear before the assignment.

EXAMPLES

1. The following code block prompts the user for font properties and then uses the response to set the font properties of a text box:

```
dlgFont.Flags = cdlCFBoth + cdlCFEffects
dlgFont.ShowFont

txtText.Font.Name = dlgFont.Name
txtText.Font.Size = dlgFont.FontSize
txtText.Font.Bold = dlgFont.FontBold
txtText.Font.Italic = dlgFont.FontItalic
txtText.Font.Underline = dlgFont.FontUnderline
```

```
txtText.Font.Strikethrough = dlgFont.FontStrikethru
txtText.ForeColor = dlgFont.Color
```

2. The following code block sets a text box's font object using the **GetFont** function, which is explained after this code block:

```
dlgFont.Flags = cdlCFBoth
Set txtText.Font = GetFont(dlgFont)
```

The following function accepts a CommonDialog control as its only argument. It assumes that any properties that need to be set for the control, such as the **Flags** property, have been taken care of. Then, it uses the choices in the Font dialog box to return a font object.

```
Public Function GetFont(dlgFont As CommonDialog) As
StdFont
Dim f As New StdFont

dlgFont.ShowFont
f.Name = dlgFont.FontName
f.Size = dlgFont.FontSize
f.Bold = dlgFont.FontBold
f.Italic = dlgFont.FontItalic
f.Underline = dlgFont.FontUnderline
f.Strikethrough = dlgFont.FontStrikethru

Set GetFont = f

End Function
```

EXERCISES

1. Write a code block that shows a Font dialog box without the underline, strikethrough, and color options. Then, write a code block that shows the Font dialog box with them.

2. Write code that prompts the user for font properties and then uses those properties to create a new font object and set its properties.

7.7 **U**SING THE COMMONDIALOG CONTROL PRINT DIALOG BOX

Display the Print dialog box by calling the **ShowPrinter** method of the CommonDialog control. This dialog box (see Figure 7-16) allows users to make changes to the way output should be printed, but it doesn't do any actual printing. For more information on printing in Visual Basic, see Chapter 9.

Figure 7-16 shows that you can select which printer output should be sent to and even change the properties for that printer by clicking the Properties button. You can also change the range of pages that are printed, how many copies are printed, and whether or not multiple copies should be collated. Figure 7-17 shows that the property page for the Print dialog box contains about the same properties as the dialog box.

All of the CommonDialog control properties that pertain to the Print dialog box are summarized in Table 7-8. Most of the time, these properties are set in code because of the dynamic nature of print jobs—you rarely know the exact number of pages an application will print each time.

FIGURE 7-16

The Print dialog box presents users with many printing options
▼

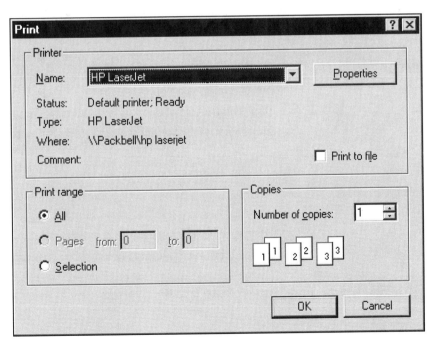

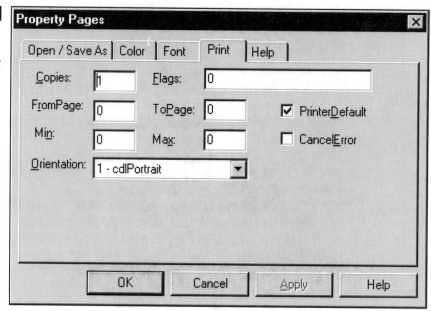

FIGURE 7-17

The property page for the Print dialog box is a convenient way to set properties at design time
▼

Property	Description
Copies	Number of copies to be printed
Min	Minimum number allowed in range of pages to be printed
Max	Maximum number allowed in range of pages to be printed
FromPage	Page number that printing should begin on
ToPage	Page number that printing should end on
PrintDefault	Determines if properties set in Print dialog box affect the default printer
Orientation	Specifies the orientation to be used when printing
Flags	Options that affect the behavior of the dialog box
CancelError	Determines if error is generated when user clicks Cancel button

TABLE 7-8 *Properties That Affect Print Dialog Box* ▼

In order for a range of pages to be specified, the **Min** and **Max** properties must be assigned values—**Max** must be greater than **Min**. Also, a default value must be specified for the **FromPage** and **ToPage** properties. These values need to be within the range specified by the **Min** and **Max** properties.

Note

To make the Pages option the default option for the print range, specify cdlPDPageNums for the Flags property. Set the Flags property to cdlPDSelection to make Selection the default choice.

EXAMPLES

1. To open a Print dialog box, you use the **ShowPrinter** method of the CommonDialog control. The following statement does so, using a control named dlgPrint. This statement shows the same dialog box shown in Figure 7-16.

```
dlgPrint.ShowPrinter
```

2. The following code sets properties of the same control used in the previous example, so that the user can also choose a print range. Figure 7-18 shows how this dialog box differs in appearance.

```
dlgPrint.Min = 1
dlgPrint.Max = 125
dlgPrint.FromPage = 1
dlgPrint.ToPage = 125
```

EXERCISES

1. Write a code block that opens a Print dialog box that defaults to printing 3 copies.

2. Write a code block that opens a Print dialog box that defaults to printing 1 copy, has a possible print range of 5 to 25, and does not affect the default printer.

FIGURE 7-18

The Print dialog box allows users to specify a range of pages to print
▼

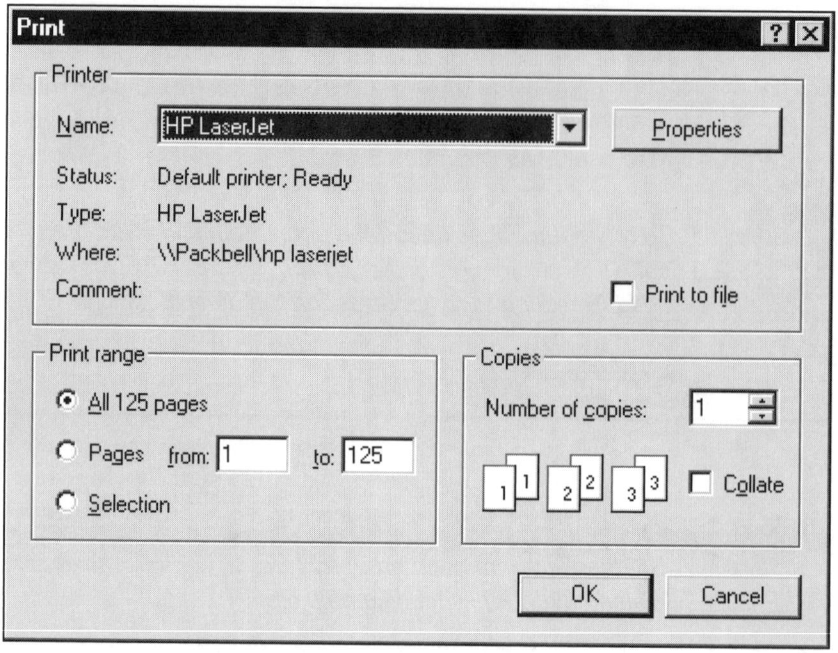

7.8

USING THE COMMONDIALOG CONTROL SHOWHELP METHOD

As applications become more complex, they need to be explained in more detail. This translates into more training and more documentation. Windows help files are a very effective tool that allows users to quickly locate answers to their questions from within the application.

The CommonDialog control contains an interface into this help system with its **ShowHelp** method, which runs WINHLP32.EXE—the Windows help engine. If you are writing a program that complements another application, such as Microsoft Office or Internet Explorer, you may want to provide access to the help files for those applications using the **ShowHelp** method. Also, many tools are available to create your own help files. Either way, the CommonDialog control provides a convenient way to activate these help files. Table 7-9 describes the properties that control the results of the **ShowHelp** method call.

Property	Description
HelpFile	Path and filename of help file
HelpKey	Keyword that identifies requested help topic
HelpContext	Specifies context ID of requested help topic
HelpCommand	Options for the behavior of this method—similar to the Flags property—described in Table 7-10

TABLE 7-9 *Properties That Affect the ShowHelp Method* ▼

The **HelpCommand** property has several different possible values. Depending on the value assigned to this property, the **ShowHelp** method produces different results. Table 7-10 describes the different outcomes of the possible values for the **HelpCommand** property.

Tip

Set the HelpCommand property to &HB to display the Contents tab of the Help dialog box for the specified help file.

Figure 7-19 shows the property page that contains the properties listed in Table 7-9. Due to the relatively static nature of help file names and locations, using this property page is a convenient way of setting up the properties for showing a help file.

EXAMPLES

1. The following code block displays the topics found in the Windows help file pertaining to the Start menu, as shown in Figure 7-20:

```
dlgHelp.HelpFile = "C:\WINDOWS\HELP\WINDOWS.HLP"
dlgHelp.HelpKey = "Start menu"
dlgHelp.HelpCommand = cdlHelpKey
dlgHelp.ShowHelp
```

2. The following code block opens the help file on how to use the Windows help file:

```
dlgHelp.HelpCommand = cdlHelpHelpOnHelp
dlgHelp.ShowHelp
```

Constant	Value	Description
CdlHelpCommand	&H102	Executes a Help macro
CdlHelpContents	&H3	Displays the Help contents topic as defined by the Contents option in the [OPTION] section of the .hpj file
CdlHelpContext	&H1	Displays Help specified in the HelpContext property
CdlHelpContextPopup	&H8	Displays Help topic identified by context number defined in the [MAP] section of the .hpj file
CdlHelpForceFile	&H9	Ensures WinHelp displays the correct Help file
CdlHelpHelpOnHelp	&H4	Displays Help for using the Help application itself
CdlHelpIndex	&H3	Displays the index of the specified Help file
CdlHelpKey	&H101	Displays Help for the keyword specified in the HelpKey property
CdlHelpPartialKey	&H105	Displays topic(s) found in the keyword list
CdlHelpQuit	&H2	Notifies the Help application that the specified Help file is no longer in use
CdlHelpSetContents	&H5	Determines which contents topic is displayed when a user presses the F1 key
CdlHelpSetIndex	&H5	Sets the context specified by the HelpContext property as the current index

TABLE 7-10 *Constants and Values for HelpCommand Property* ▼

EXERCISES

1. Write a code block that displays the contents of the Windows help file that goes directly to all of the information that has to do with starting something.

2. Write a code block that displays the Windows help file.

FIGURE 7-19

Property page for showing help files
▼

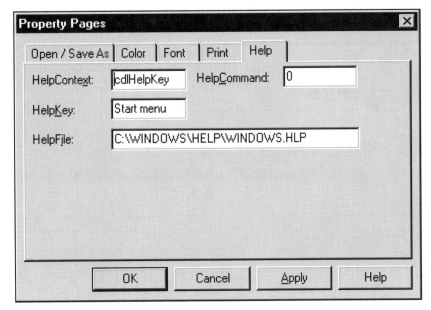

FIGURE 7-20

ShowHelp displays the Topics Found dialog box
▼

Mastery
Skills Check

1. Which data type stores the results of the **MsgBox** function?

2. What is the data type of the return value for the **InputBox** function?

3. What are the steps for adding a CommonDialog control to a form?

4. How do you specify a default extension for filenames obtained using the CommonDialog control's Save As dialog box?

5. How are colors specified in Visual Basic?

6. Which property of the CommonDialog control must be set to open a Font dialog box?

7. What is the effect of the **PrintDefault** property being set to **True** when opening a Print dialog box?

8. How do you show help on how to use a help file?

8

Using Menus in Visual Basic Applications

chapter objectives

8.1 Creating Menus

8.2 Adding Code to Menus

8.3 Creating Shortcut Menus

Menus offer a logical, visual interface to commands available in an application. They group commands into categories, which describe the type of commands a menu contains. For example, commands contained within the File menu of an application perform actions pertaining to files—open, save, and close.

An application can present menus in two ways. Menus are most commonly displayed using a *menu bar*. A menu bar normally appears directly beneath the title bar of a window and lists the titles of the menus. The commands of each menu in the menu bar display below the menu title when it is selected. An alternative way to present a menu is a single list of commands displayed as a *pop-up* menu. Pop-up menus appear at the current position of the mouse pointer, usually in reaction to the right mouse button being clicked.

Within a menu, *separator bars* group similar commands together. The cut, copy, and paste commands are commonly enclosed within separator bars because they are so closely related. *Submenus* provide another way for commands performing similar functions to be grouped together. A menu item with a right-pointing arrow is not a command, but a submenu title. Selecting the item opens the submenu. Then, commands—or other submenus—can be chosen from that submenu.

Regardless of the structure or intended use of a menu, it is created using the *Menu Editor*. The Menu Editor enables you to create menus, submenus, separator bars, and accelerator keys. After you create a menu in the Menu Editor, it is integrated into an application as a menu bar or a pop-up menu.

Review

Skills Check

You should be able to correctly answer the following questions before beginning this chapter:

1. How many different types of buttons can the **MsgBox** function display on a dialog box?

2. What is the return value of the **InputBox** function if the user clicks the Cancel button or presses the ESC key?

3. How do you resize the CommonDialog control?

4. What is the index of the first filter defined for the CommonDialog control's Save As dialog box?

5. What do the letters in RGB stand for?

6. What are the two types of fonts that the CommonDialog control supports?

7. How do you force changes made in the Print dialog box of the CommonDialog control to immediately affect the default printer?

8. Which property of the CommonDialog control determines the behavior of the **ShowHelp** method?

8.1 *C*REATING MENUS

Menus are created using the Menu Editor, which is a dialog box. Submenus and separator bars are also created with the Menu Editor. Most properties of menus can be set using the Menu Editor, but all menu properties can be set in the Properties window.

Properties of objects contained on a form can be viewed or modified using the Properties window. Each item in a menu is an object, which means that the properties of all menu items can be set using the Properties window. While this method gives you access to all of the properties for a menu, the Menu Editor provides a convenient interface for setting and viewing the most commonly used menu properties.

Note — *The Menu Editor must be used to establish and maintain the structure of menus. No other method is currently available for creating a menu in Visual Basic.*

CREATING A MENU IN THE MENU EDITOR

To open the Menu Editor, open a form in the Form window. Then, choose Menu Editor from the Tools menu or press CTRL-E. Figure 8-1 shows the Menu Editor with no entries. Changes made in the Menu Editor create or change the menu for the form that you selected in the Form window.

FIGURE 8-1

When the Menu Editor has no entries, the form does not have a menu bar

▼

Adding Menu Bar Titles

The top level of a menu is the title displayed in the menu bar. File, Edit, View, Window, and Help are some of the most commonly used menu titles. To add these to your own menu, follow these steps:

1. Open the Menu Editor.

2. Enter "**&File**" into the Caption text box. Adding an ampersand (&) before a letter makes that letter the *access key* for the item. Like command buttons, the access key makes it possible to quickly select menu items using the keyboard.

3. Enter "**mnuFile**" into the Name text box. Combining the prefix for the menu control with the caption of a menu provides a consistent and easy-to-follow naming convention. The Menu Editor should now look like Figure 8-2.

4. Click the Next button.

5. Repeat steps 1 through 4, replacing "File" with "Edit" (&Edit; mnuEdit), "View" (&View; mnuView), and so on.

FIGURE 8-2

The caption appears immediately as the title of a menu item
▼

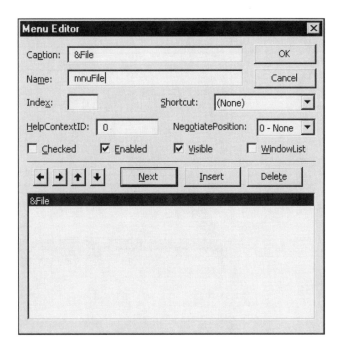

When you are finished adding these titles, your Menu Editor should look like Figure 8-3.

Click the OK button to accept the menu structure that you have created and return to the Form window. Figure 8-4 shows the menu bar created from the definition in Figure 8-3, as it appears in the Form window.

Adding Menu Commands

The first level of a menu provides only the titles to be displayed in the menu bar. At this stage, nothing would happen if you ran the application and clicked on one of the menus. Menu items must be added to the next level of the menu structure. These items appear as commands in the menu of the title in the level immediately above them.

To add commands to the File menu, complete the following steps:

1. Open the form from the previous section in the Form window.

2. Open the Menu Editor.

3. Select the Edit menu from the list box at the bottom of the dialog box.

FIGURE 8-3

The ampersand indicating the access key only appears in the Menu Editor
▼

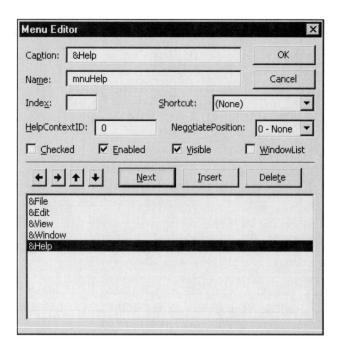

FIGURE 8-4

Menu bars appear in the Form window while designing your form
▼

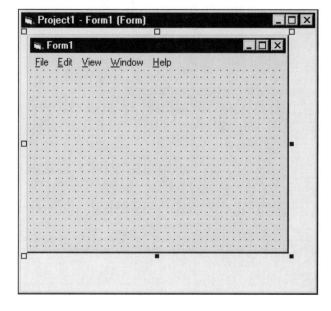

4. Click the Insert button. This inserts a menu item before the one that is currently selected, as shown in Figure 8-5.

5. Click the right arrow button to make this item one level below the menu item above it, which is shown in Figure 8-6.

Note *The left arrow button in the Menu Editor moves menu items up one level in the menu structure.*

6. Add the command that you wish to display when the highest-level menu item is selected in the menu bar. Name the menu objects by adding their caption to the name of their parent item. For example, the New command on the File menu would be named mnuFileNew.

Note *Ending a menu item with an ellipsis (...) indicates that selecting that item opens some type of form that the user must interact with to complete the command. This could be a form you created or a standard dialog box.*

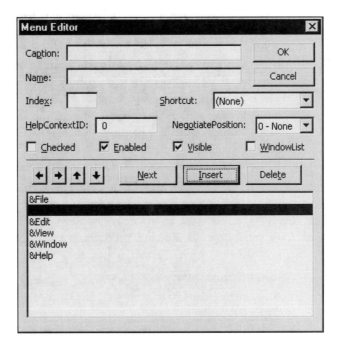

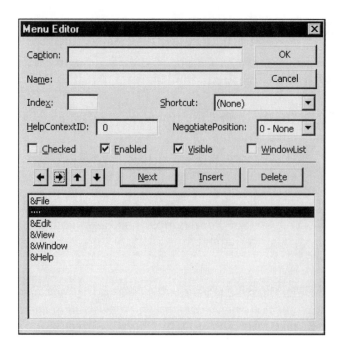

Repeat these steps for each item you need to add to a menu. Figure 8-7 shows the group of commands that you could add to the File menu. In addition to using access keys, you can designate a *shortcut key* combination in the Shortcut dropdown list box that, when selected, has the same effect as selecting that menu item. That gives users the ability to issue a command contained in a menu without opening that menu. For example, CTRL-P causes most applications to print.

Click the OK button to return to the Form window and see how the menu looks now. Figure 8-8 shows the effect that this change has on the File menu. This same procedure can be used to create the structure of the other menus in the menu bar.

Note

Selecting a menu command in the Form window opens the Code Editor to the Click event procedure of that menu object.

Adding Submenus

Visual Basic allows you to create up to five levels of submenus for each menu title. Submenus group commands that either are similar or have a relationship with a particular object. For example, the New command

FIGURE 8-7

*Access keys
should be different
for each item in
the same level of a
menu*

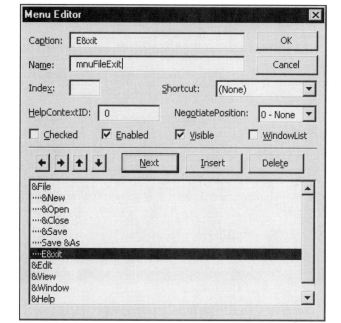

FIGURE 8-8

*You can view
menus in the
Form window*

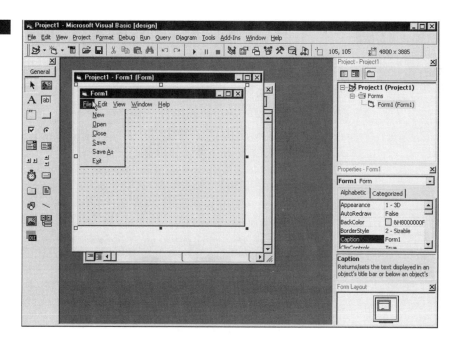

of the File menu could have a submenu that specifies what type of new file should be created (for example, a text file or a graphics file). Complete the following steps to add such a submenu:

1. Open the form from the previous section in the Form window.

2. Open the Menu Editor.

3. Select the Open menu from the list box at the bottom of the dialog box.

4. Click the Insert button.

5. Click the right arrow button to make this item one level below the menu item above it (two levels from the menu titles).

6. Make the first item in the submenu Text File and name it mnuFileNewTextFile.

7. Use the same process to make the second item in the submenu Graphics File, as shown in Figure 8-9.

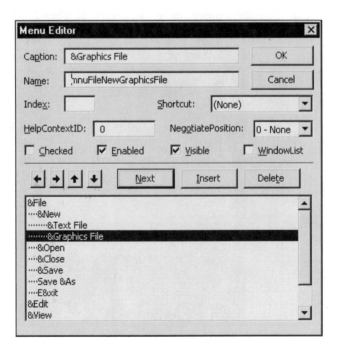

Now, the New command of the File menu is the New submenu, which is indicated by the right-facing arrow next to mnuFileNew. Figure 8-10 shows the two commands of the newly created submenu.

Adding Separator Bars

Separator bars have only one function: to separate menu items. Generally, separator bars are used to group menu items by function. Visual Basic's Debug menu contains separator bars that group commands, for example, for stepping through code, watching variables, using breakpoints, and setting the next statement.

Complete the following steps to add separator bars to the File menu of the example being used in this section:

1. Open the form from the previous section in the Form window.

2. Open the Menu Editor.

3. Select the Save menu from the list box at the bottom of the dialog box.

4. Click the Insert button.

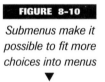

FIGURE 8-10

Submenus make it possible to fit more choices into menus
▼

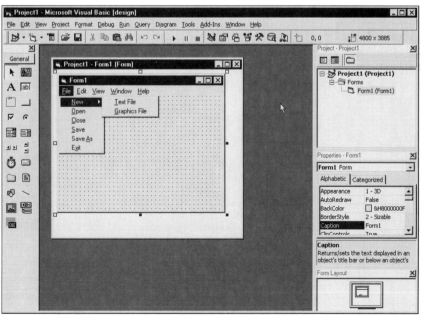

5. Enter a single dash (-) as the caption and name the menu mnuFileSeparatorBar1.

6. Select the Exit menu from the list box at the bottom of the dialog box.

7. Click the Insert button.

8. Enter a single dash (-) as the caption and name the menu mnuFileSeparatorBar2, as shown in Figure 8-11.

You can shorten the name that you give to separator bars. For example, you could just use Bar1, Bar2, and so on in the menu name instead of using SeparatorBar1, SeparatorBar2, and so on.

Visual Basic interprets the single dash as a separator bar that runs across the width of the menu, so that's all there is to adding a separator bar. Figure 8-12 shows the result that this change has on the appearance of the menu.

FIGURE 8-11

Give separator bars unique names

▼

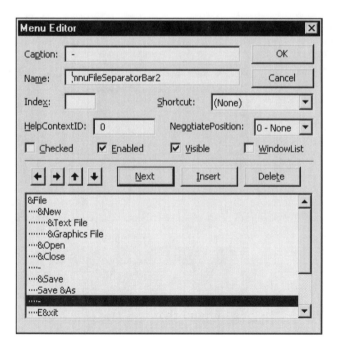

Separator bars make menus more readable

▼

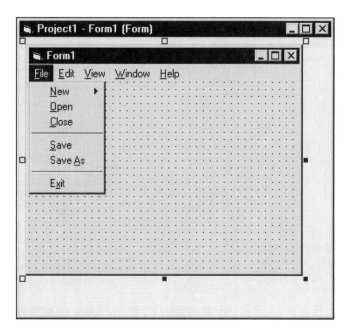

EXAMPLES

1. Figure 8-13 shows the Menu Editor with a definition that would recreate Visual Basic's Tools menu—without any icons. Notice that the CTRL-E shortcut is defined for the Menu Editor.

2. Figure 8-14 shows a menu structure with a submenu that is two levels deep. The appearance of this menu is shown in Figure 8-15.

EXERCISES

1. Use the Menu Editor to create a menu structure that resembles Visual Basic's Run menu.

2. Use the Menu Editor to create a menu structure that resembles Visual Basic's Add-Ins menu.

3. Create a series of submenus, naming them according to the level of submenu that they are.

FIGURE 8-13

*Structure of Visual
Basic's Tools menu*
▼

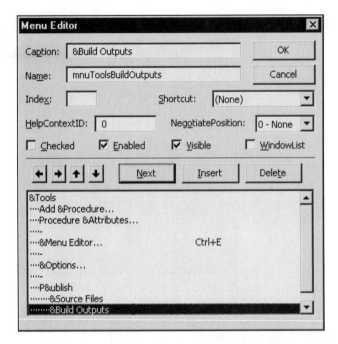

FIGURE 8-14

*Submenus can go
up to five
levels deep*
▼

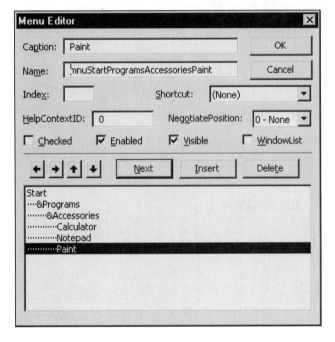

FIGURE 8-15

*Multiple submenus
take up more
screen space*
▼

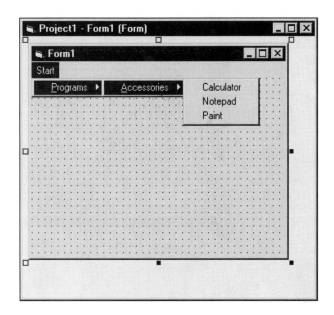

8.2 *A*DDING CODE TO MENUS

The Menu Editor creates a menu structure: menu titles, menu commands, submenus, separator bars, access keys, and shortcut keys. These menu items work together to present users with a series of commands in a logical manner. However, the Menu Editor only creates the structure of the menu. The commands that the menu items perform must be added using the *Code Editor*.

Create a new form to be used for coding menu commands. Name it frmText and make its **Caption** "Text". Create a menu for this form using the structure shown in Figure 8-16. Be sure to select the Black menu item's **Checked** property, as shown in Figure 8-16.

After creating the menu, add a text box to the form and name it txtText. Set its **MultiLine** property to **True** and delete the default text. Then, size the text box so that it takes up the entire form. Now, you should have a form that looks like the one in Figure 8-17.

Adding code to a menu command is easy. In the Form window, simply select the menu command. The Code Editor opens and defines the **Click** event procedure for that menu item. Select the Black command from the Text Color submenu. When the Code Editor

FIGURE 8-16

Structure for an editing menu
▼

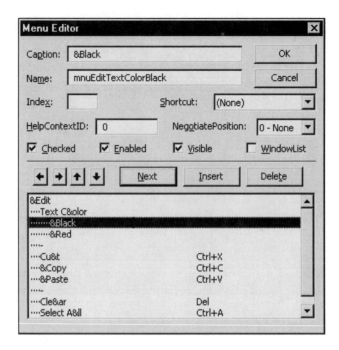

FIGURE 8-17

A very basic text editor form with only an Edit menu
▼

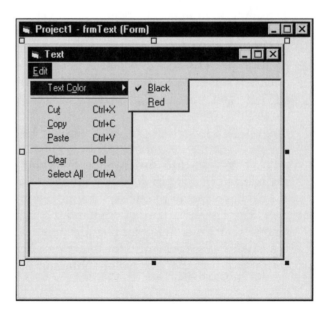

appears, enter the following code (the **Sub** declaration is created by Visual Basic):

```
Private Sub mnuEditTextColorBlack_Click()

'Set text color to black
txtText.ForeColor = RGB(0, 0, 0)
mnuEditTextColorRed.Checked = False
mnuEditTextColorBlack.Checked = True

End Sub
```

Use the following code for the Red command of the Text Color submenu:

```
Private Sub mnuEditTextColorRed_Click()

'Set text color to red
txtText.ForeColor = RGB(255, 0, 0)
mnuEditTextColorBlack.Checked = False
mnuEditTextColorRed.Checked = True

End Sub
```

The previous two procedures must manage the checked status of the Text Color submenu. Checked menu items are not automatically mutually exclusive, like option buttons—more than one menu item can be checked at one time.

Checked menu items are best used for options that are toggled on and off, such as displaying a ruler onscreen or displaying a toolbar.

Add the following code to the **Click** event procedure of the Cut and Copy commands, respectively:

```
Private Sub mnuEditCut_Click()

'Verify that text is selected
If txtText.SelLength > 0 Then
    'Place selected text on clipboard
    Clipboard.Clear
    Clipboard.SetText txtText.SelText
```

```
        'Clear selected text
        txtText.SelText = ""
    End If

End Sub

Private Sub mnuEditCopy_Click()

'Verify that text is selected
If txtText.SelLength > 0 Then
    'Place selected text on clipboard
    Clipboard.Clear
    Clipboard.SetText txtText.SelText
End If

End Sub
```

These procedures verify that text is selected before placing the selection on the clipboard. The Cut command also deletes the selected text from the text box. If no text is selected, these commands do nothing.

The Paste command replaces the selected text with text from the clipboard. This procedure only works if the clipboard contains text. If no text is selected in the text box, the text from the clipboard is inserted at the current position of the cursor. To create this procedure, select the Paste command in the Form window and enter the following code:

```
Private Sub mnuEditPaste_Click()

'Verify that clipboard contains text
If Clipboard.GetText <> "" Then
    'Replace selected text with clipboard text
    txtText.SelText = Clipboard.GetText
End If

End Sub
```

To finish adding code for the menu commands, select the Clear and Select All commands and add the appropriate code listed here:

```
Private Sub mnuEditClear_Click()
```

```
'Clear selected text
txtText.SelText = ""

End Sub

Private Sub mnuEditSelectAll_Click()

txtText.SelStart = 0
txtText.SelLength = Len(txtText.Text)

End Sub
```

In addition to menu commands, you may also wish to add code to menu or submenu titles, possibly to cause a sound to play when a menu opens. To do this, write the procedure in the Code Editor in the same way that the other menu procedures were written. Although it cannot be accessed from the Form window, the Edit menu title still has a **Click** event. The following code uses the **Click** event of the Edit menu title to enable or disable the Cut, Copy, and Paste commands. Cut and Copy are enabled only if text is selected, because that is the only time that these commands are useful. Paste is enabled only if the clipboard contains text. Otherwise this command has no way to add new text.

```
Private Sub mnuEdit_Click()

'Enable Cut and Copy if text is selected
If txtText.SelLength = 0 Then
    mnuEditCut.Enabled = False
    mnuEditCopy.Enabled = False
Else
    mnuEditCut.Enabled = True
    mnuEditCopy.Enabled = True
End If

'Enable Paste if clipboard contains text
If Clipboard.GetText = "" Then
    mnuEditPaste.Enabled = False
Else
    mnuEditPaste.Enabled = True
End If

End Sub
```

Adding this code to the **Click** event of mnuEdit customizes its behavior so that the appearance and abilities of the menu change according to the amount of text selected and the amount of text on the clipboard. For example, Figure 8-18 shows the Edit menu when no text is selected.

If text is added to the form and selected, the Cut and Copy commands are enabled, as shown in Figure 8-19.

EXAMPLES

1. To create a File menu with an Exit command that closes the form, create a File menu with a single command, Exit. Then, select the Exit command in the Form window and add the **Unload** statement, as in the following:

```
Unload Me
```

2. The following code toggles a menu item between being checked and unchecked:

```
mnuItem.Checked = Not (mnuItem.Checked)
```

FIGURE 8-18

Disabling menu commands limits the ability of an application

▼

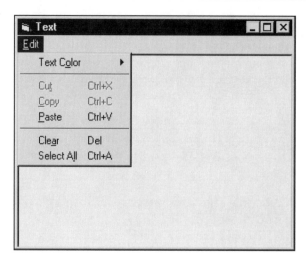

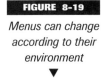

FIGURE 8-19

Menus can change according to their environment

▼

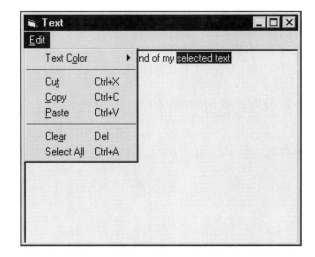

EXERCISES

1. What is the quickest way to create a **Click** event procedure for a menu command?

2. Using the text editor example from this chapter, add code to mnuEdit's **Click** event that makes the Text Color submenu invisible if the **ForeColor** of the text box is not black or red.

8.3 *CREATING SHORTCUT MENUS*

Many Windows applications provide shortcut menus to make users more productive. These menus appear when users click the right mouse button. The content of the shortcut menu depends upon the context in which it was opened. For example, right-clicking on a text box should open a shortcut menu that deals with text, but the same menu doesn't make sense to appear if right-clicking on a graphics display.

USING THE POPUPMENU METHOD

Visual Basic provides a method for opening these shortcut menus—**PopupMenu**. The **PopupMenu** method opens a menu directly under the mouse pointer, unless specified otherwise. Only one pop-up menu can be open at any one time. Syntax for this method is as follows:

```
object.PopupMenu menuname, flags, x, y, boldcommand
```

The code following a call to the PopupMenu method is not executed until either a menu item is selected or the user presses the ESC key.

The object argument is optional for this method. It refers to a form, but if omitted, Visual Basic just uses the form that has the focus at the time. This is almost always the desired result, so this argument is usually left off.

Menuname can be any menu item that has at least one submenu item in the level directly below it. *Flags* is a parameter that affects appearance, as described in Table 8-1, and behavior, as described in Table 8-2. If provided, the x and y arguments specify the location at

Constant	Value	Description
VbPopupMenuLeftAlign	0	X specifies left side of menu
VbPopupMenuCenterAlign	4	X specifies center of menu
VbPopupMenuRightAlign	8	X specifies right side of menu

TABLE 8-1 *PopupMenu Flags That Affect Location* ▼

Constant	Value	Description
vbPopupMenuLeftButton	0	Menu items respond to left mouse button only
vbPopupMenuRightButton	2	Menu items respond to left or right mouse button

TABLE 8-2 *PopupMenu Flags That Affect Behavior* ▼

which the menu displays. The boldcommand argument specifies a menu item to appear in bold. Only one item can appear in bold at any one time.

DETERMINING THE MOUSE BUTTON

Different processing may need to occur depending upon which mouse button was pressed. If the **PopupMenu** method is called from the **MouseDown** event, the Button parameter specifies the mouse button that caused the event. Table 8-3 lists the constants for the different mouse buttons.

With this information, a program could only make a shortcut menu appear when a particular mouse button is clicked or cause a different menu to appear depending on the mouse button clicked.

Constant	Value	Description
vbLeftButton	1	Left mouse button
vbRightButton	2	Right mouse button
vbMiddleButton	4	Middle mouse button

TABLE 8-3 *Mouse Button Constants* ▼

EXAMPLES

1. The menu structure defined in Figure 8-20 contains a single top-level menu item, which has its **Visible** property set to **False**. That prevents it from appearing on the form. The following code causes the items contained within the top-level menu to appear at the mouse pointer when the right mouse button is clicked:

```
Private Sub Form_MouseDown(Button As Integer, _
Shift As Integer, X As Single, Y As Single)

If Button = vbRightButton Then
    PopupMenu mnuFile
End If

End Sub
```

2. The following code performs the same operation as the previous example, but it causes the menu to appear near the middle of the screen and the Close command to be selected:

```
Private Sub Form_MouseDown(Button As Integer, _
Shift As Integer, X As Single, Y As Single)
Dim intX As Integer

intX = Screen.Width / 2

If Button = vbRightButton Then
    PopupMenu mnuFile, vbPopupMenuCenterAlign, intX, Y,
mnuClose
End If

End Sub
```

EXERCISES

1. Using the menu structure defined in Figure 8-21, write code that makes the Form submenu appear when a user clicks the middle mouse button.

2. Rewrite the **PopupMenu** method call from the previous exercise so that the menu appears when the left mouse button is clicked and the Text item appears bold.

FIGURE 8-20

*Menu structure
with invisible
top level*
▼

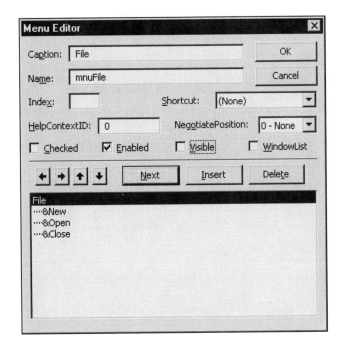

FIGURE 8-21

*Menu structure
that has several
levels of submenus*
▼

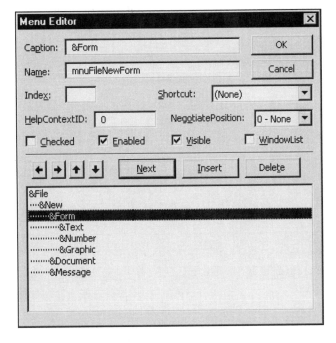

Mastery
Skills Check

1. How do you move a menu item around within the Menu Editor?

2. How do you create the **Click** event procedure for menu titles and submenu titles?

3. What is the default location and behavior of a popup, or shortcut, menu?

9

Printing in Visual Basic Applications

chapter objectives

9.1 Using the PrintForm Method

9.2 Using the Printers Collection

9.3 Using the Printer Object

9.4 Placing Text and Graphics on the Printer Object

Printing provides a way to supply a user with output. The output could be many things: text from an editor, status of a program, report on data collected by a program, or many more. Users can then distribute the printed output to others or keep it as a written record.

Visual Basic handles printing differently than most other actions. Normally, you place a control on a form and manipulate its properties and methods to accomplish specific tasks. But Visual Basic does not have a printer control. Instead, it has created several objects that deal directly with Windows' printing system.

Using the Windows printing system has several advantages. The greatest advantage is that all of the code for talking with the printer has already been written and tested for you. So, you use one set of commands to deal with printers and let the Windows printing system send the proper commands to any individual printer.

Review

Skills Check

You should be able to correctly answer the following questions before beginning this chapter:

1. How do you add a separator bar to a menu?

2. What is the fastest way to add code to a menu item?

3. How do you determine which mouse button caused a **MouseDown** event?

9.1 USING THE PRINTFORM METHOD

The **PrintForm** method is the easiest way to create printed output from Visual Basic. As this method's name implies, it prints the contents of a form. Form images are sent to the printer using the following syntax:

```
formName.PrintForm
```

The form name is optional—leaving it out prints the current form. This method also prints the entire form, regardless of which part of the form is visible onscreen. Print quality will vary when using this method because it depends upon the resolution of the user's screen. Normally, this results in less-than-spectacular results, which is why the **Printer** object is most often used for printing in Visual Basic.

EXAMPLES

1. To create a form that prints itself when its **DoubleClick** event is triggered, add the following code:

```
Private Sub frmImage_DblClick()
PrintForm
End Sub
```

2. To print the image of a particular form, qualify the method call with the name of the form, as shown in the following:

```
frmName.PrintForm
```

3. To print all of the loaded forms in an application when a form's **DoubleClick** event is triggered, use the following code:

```
Private Sub frmImage_DblClick()
Dim F As Form

For Each F In Forms
    F.PrintForm
Next F
End Sub
```

EXERCISES

1. Create a new application with a single form. Then, add a button to the form that causes the image of the form to be printed when the button is clicked.

2. Create a new application with several forms. On the main form add a button that loads all of the other forms and then prints the image of any form with the number 4 in its title bar.

9.2 USING THE PRINTERS COLLECTION

The **Printers** collection allows you to reference each of the printers installed on a particular computer. It contains the same printers you would see if you opened the Windows Printers folder. Each printer within the collection is a **Printer** object, which is discussed in the "Using the Printer Object" section of this chapter. The following is the syntax for using the **Printers** collection:

```
Printers(index)
```

Printer objects are referenced using the **Printers** collection in the same way that values are referenced in array variables. The Index of the **Printers** collection ranges from zero to the number of printers minus one. So if the **Printers** collection contains four printers, the index would go from zero to three.

Note *The properties of **Printer** objects can be referenced using the **Printers** collection and the index of the particular printer, but the properties will be read only. To change properties, you must use the **Printer** object.*

As with other arrays, you can use the **For Each** statement to loop through the **Printer** objects in the **Printers** collection. Use the following syntax to accomplish this:

```
Dim P As Printer
For Each P In Printers
    'Your code here
    'Reference printer properties as P.Property
Next P
```

EXAMPLES

1. To address the first printer in the **Printers** collection, use the following:

   ```
   Printers(0)
   ```

2. To address the last printer in the **Printers** collection, use the following:

   ```
   Printers(Printers.Count - 1)
   ```

EXERCISES

1. How would you address the second printer in the **Printers** collection?

2. Write a **For** statement that steps through each of the printers in the **Printers** collection.

3. How would you address the next-to-last printer in the **Printers** collection?

9.3 USING THE PRINTER OBJECT

The **PrintForm** method provides a quick and easy way to create printed output, but doesn't produce very high quality output. Visual Basic also provides you with a space that is used specifically for drawing text and graphics to be sent to the printer. This drawing space is the **Printer** object, and it produces the best quality output for the printer. Methods of the Printer object place text and graphics on its drawing space—as designated by the properties of the **Printer** object.

The **Printer** object is device-independent. It simply provides a drawing surface. When the contents of the **Printer** object's drawing surface are sent to the printer, Windows translates the contents to match the language and capabilities of the associated printer. This provides high quality output without concern for the printer device being used. However, more code is required to use the **Printer** object than the **PrintForm** method. Using the **Printer** object also uses more resources and takes longer than **PrintForm** to send similar print jobs.

SETTING THE DEFAULT PRINTER

Only one **Printer** object exists in Visual Basic. However, this single **Printer** object can be used with any installed printer. Initially, it refers to the default printer as specified in the Windows Control Panel. Changes made to properties of the **Printer** object are made to the current default printer. To change the default printer, use the **Printers** collection as follows:

```
Set Printer = Printers(index)
```

This statement sets the default printer. To do this, it uses the printer specified by the Index of the **Printers** collection. Any changes to the **Printer** object's properties after this statement affect the newly selected default printer only.

*If you are using the **For Each** statement to loop through the **Printers** collection, you set the **Printer** object equal to the **Printer** variable being used in the loop to change the default printer.*

SETTING PROPERTIES FOR THE PRINTER OBJECT

The **Printer** object has many properties that control how output is produced. Some of these properties control how text and graphics are placed on the **Printer** object and some control how the contents of the **Printer** object are sent to the current printer. Table 9-1 lists these properties with a brief description for each. For more information on a particular property, refer to Visual Basic's online documentation.

Property	Description
ColorMode	Specifies if output should be color or monochrome for color printers
Copies	Number of copies to be printed
CurrentX	Horizontal position for the next drawing method
CurrentY	Vertical position for the next drawing method
DeviceName	Name of device being used to print output
DrawMode	Controls appearance of text and graphics drawn on Printer object
DrawStyle	Specifies the style used to draw lines
DrawWidth	Width of lines drawn
DriverName	Software driver used by a Printer object
Duplex	Specifies if page is printed on both sides
FillColor	Color used to fill in shapes
FillStyle	Pattern used to fill in shapes
Font	Font object for current printer

TABLE 9-1 *Printer Object Properties* ▼

Property	Description
FontBold	Boolean value that specifies if font should be bold
FontCount	Number of fonts available for active printer
FontItalic	Boolean value that specifies if font should be italic
FontName	Font to be used when drawing text
Fonts	Fonts available for active printer
FontSize	Font size in points
FontStrikethru	Boolean value that specifies if font should be strikethru
FontTransparent	Controls how background text and graphics are treated
FontUnderline	Boolean value that specifies if font should be underline
HDC	Value used by Windows to control the printer
Height	Height of the printer paper in twips
Orientation	Specifies if documents are printed in portrait or landscape mode
Page	Current page number
PaperBin	Default paper bin
PaperSize	Size of paper being used in current printer
Port	Port being used to control printer
PrintQuality	Resolution of current printer
RightToLeft	Boolean value that specifies the direction text should be displayed
ScaleHeight	Number of units for vertical measurement
ScaleLeft	Horizontal position of left and top edges of an object
ScaleMode	Unit of measure for specifying positions
ScaleTop	Vertical position of left and top edges of an object
ScaleWidth	Number of units for horizontal measurement
TrackDefault	Boolean value that specifies if the Printer object should change its default printer if the default printer is changed in the Control Panel
TwipsPerPixelX	Twips per pixel horizontally for an object
TwipsPerPixelY	Twips per pixel vertically for an object
Width	Width of the printer paper in twips
Zoom	Percentage printed output should be scaled

TABLE 9-1 *Printer Object Properties* (continued) ▼

Printer driver software doesn't always allow all printer properties to be changed. Drivers can also limit the values that can be specified for some properties. Refer to the documentation of a particular driver for specific information on its limitations.

EXAMPLES

1. To set the default printer to the first printer in the **Printers** collection, use the following statement:

```
Set Printer = Printers(0)
```

2. To determine the number of fonts available for a printer, use the following code:

```
Dim intFontCount
intFontCount = Printer.FontCount
```

3. To cause text to be italicized, use the following statement:

```
Printer.FontItalic = True
```

4. Use the following statements to change the quality of printed output:

```
'Use Draft Print Quality
Printer.PrintQuality = vbPRPQDraft
'Use Low Print Quality
Printer.PrintQuality = vbPRPQLow
'Use Medium Print Quality
Printer.PrintQuality = vbPRPQMedium
'Use High Print Quality
Printer.PrintQuality = vbPRPQHigh
```

EXERCISES

1. Set the default printer to the last printer in the **Printers** collection.

2. Change the properties of the **Printer** object so that its default printer always matches the Windows default printer.

3. Set the properties of the **Printer** object so that it will print three copies of everything.

4. Set the Font property of the **Printer** object to 8 point bold Courier.

9.4 *P*LACING TEXT AND GRAPHICS ON THE PRINTER OBJECT

The **Printer** object has several methods that allow you to place text and graphics on its drawing surface. Setting the properties of the **Printer** object is an integral part of using these methods. Many of the properties control the appearance of the output produced by the methods discussed in the following sections.

*The drawing methods used with the **Printer** object work with other objects as well, such as forms and picture controls.*

USING THE CIRCLE METHOD

Circles, ellipses, and arcs are all drawn using the **Circle** method. This method takes several arguments, which control the size, shape, and color of the drawing. The following is the syntax for the **Circle** method, and Table 9-2 describes each argument:

```
Printer.Circle [step] (x, y), radius [,color, start, end, aspect]
```

***Step** is a keyword in drawing methods, not an argument that requires you to provide a value. In other words, you actually include the word "step" in the method call statement.*

USING THE LINE METHOD

Lines and rectangles are drawn using the **Line** method. Drawing four separate lines at positions that form a rectangle creates a rectangle, but the **Line** method provides a way to draw a rectangle with a single

Argument	Description
Step	Optional keyword that indicates the center of the circle, ellipse, or arc is relative to CurrentX and CurrentY
(x, y)	Coordinates for center of circle, ellipse, or arc
Radius	Radius of circle, ellipse, or arc
Color	Optional argument that specifies the color used to draw the lines for the circle, ellipse, or arc (defaults to ForeColor)
start, end	Optional arguments that control where a circle, ellipse, or arc starts and ends by specifying the positions in radians (range of –2 pi radians to 2 pi radians; default is 0 radians for start and 2 pi radians for end)
Aspect	Optional argument that specifies the aspect ratio of circle (default of 1.0 produces perfect circle)

TABLE 9-2   *Circle Method Arguments* ▼

statement. The following is the syntax for the **Line** method, and Table 9-3 describes each argument:

```
Printer.Line [step] (x1, y1) [step] - (x2, y2) [,color] [,B[F]]
```

Argument	Description
Step	Optional keyword that indicates the start of the line or rectangle is relative to CurrentX and CurrentY
(x1, y1)	Optional coordinates for start of line or rectangle (defaults to CurrentX, CurrentY)
Step	Optional keyword that indicates the end of the line is relative to the beginning of the line
(x2, y2)	Coordinates for end of line or opposite corner of rectangle
Color	Optional argument that specifies the color used to draw the line or rectangle (defaults to ForeColor)
B	Optional parameter that forces the Line method to create a rectangle instead of a line
F	Optional parameter that causes a rectangle to fill with the same color used to draw it (must be used with the B argument)

TABLE 9-3   *Line Method Arguments* ▼

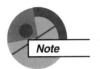

*After the **Line** method is called, the CurrentX and CurrentY properties are set to the ending point of the line or rectangle.*

USING THE PAINTPICTURE METHOD

Pictures contained in graphics files are drawn on the Printer object with the **PaintPicture** method. This method supports the following file formats:

▼ Bitmap (.bmp)

▼ Windows Metafile (.wmf)

▼ Windows Enhanced Metafile (.emf)

▼ Cursor (.cur)

▼ Icon (.ico)

▼ Device-independent Bitmap (.dib)

The following is the syntax for the **PaintPicture** method, and Table 9-4 describes each argument:

```
Printer.PaintPicture picture, x1, y1, width1, height1,
x2, y2, width2, height2, opcode
```

If the width or height of the picture differs from the values in width1 and height1, the picture is stretched or compressed to fit into the dimensions specified for the destination.

If any optional arguments are supplied, all arguments that appear before it must also be specified.

USING THE PRINT METHOD

Text is placed in the **Printer** object's drawing area with the **Print** method. Each **Print** method statement produces a new line of text, or the carriage return character (**Chr** (13)) can be used in the expression

Parameter	Description
Picture	Picture property of a Form or GraphicBox control
x1, y1	Coordinates of destination where picture is to be drawn
Width1	Optional argument that specifies width of picture in destination (defaults to the width of the picture)
Height1	Optional argument that specifies height of picture in destination (defaults to the height of the picture)
x2, y2	Optional coordinates that specify a clipping region within the picture
Width2	Optional argument that specifies width of a clipping region within the picture (defaults to the width of the picture)
Height2	Optional argument that specifies height of a clipping region within the picture (defaults to the height of the picture)
Opcode	Optional argument that defines bit-wise operations for bitmaps only

TABLE 9-4 *PaintPicture Method Arguments* ▼

list of a single **Print** method statement to produce several lines of text. The following is the syntax for this method:

```
Printer.Print [outputlist]
```

The output list can include one or more expressions. An expression can include quoted strings, variables, and properties. If more than one expression is listed, separate them with semicolons. A blank line is printed if no expression is provided. Don't worry about formatting numbers and dates; they are formatted using the regional settings of the computer the program runs on.

Use a fixed-width font, such as Courier, to know exactly how many characters fit across a printed page.

USING OTHER GRAPHICS METHODS

The methods discussed in the previous sections provide the ability to complete most printing tasks. For some more advanced tasks, you may need to use one of the following graphics methods:

▼ **Cls**   This method clears the drawing surface. While this can be very useful, keep in mind that it eliminates all text and graphics from the entire drawing area.

▼ **Point**   This method determines the color of a specific point on a drawing surface. This can be very useful if you are trying to match a color from a bitmap or other graphics file.

▼ **Pset**   This method sets a specific point to the color you specify. When used in combination with the Point method, you can create coordinated color schemes on the fly for printed material.

USING THE NEWPAGE METHOD

Some output may be too large to fit on a single page or it may make more sense to group data on different pages—especially for reports. To start a new page on the **Printer** object, use the appropriately named **NewPage** method, which uses the following syntax:

```
Printer.NewPage
```

*After calling the **NewPage** method, you cannot go back and make modifications to the previous page.*

USING THE ENDDOC METHOD

After placing text and graphics on the **Printer** object, it just sits there. All you've done is draw it. Now, you must send the contents of the **Printer** object's drawing surface to the current printer device. Calling the **EndDoc** method does this, as in the following:

```
Printer.EndDoc
```

This method is automatically called when using the **PrintForm** method, but must be called manually when using other graphics methods to create the printed output on the **Printer** object's drawing area. If you don't call the **EndDoc** method after placing text or graphics on the **Printer** object, the output is not sent to the printer until the application is closed.

USING THE KILLDOC METHOD

At times, you may not want to print the contents of the **Printer** object or the user may wish to cancel a print job. In either case, call the **KillDoc** method to prevent or stop the **Printer** object's contents from being sent to the printer device, as shown in the following:

```
Printer.KillDoc
```

*The **KillDoc** method can be called after the **EndDoc** method to stop a print job, but depending on the printer device and the settings for it, some of the contents may have already been sent to the printer.*

EXAMPLES

1. Add a command button to a form and then add the following code. Start the application and click the button to create a homemade Valentines Day card. The **EndDoc** method forces the drawings to print.

```
Private Sub cmdPrint_Click()
Printer.Circle (1000, 1000), 1000, , 6.28, 3.89
Printer.Circle (3000, 1000), 1000, , 5.53, 3.14
Printer.Line (175, 1575)-(2000, 3500)
Printer.Line (3825, 1575)-(2000, 3500)
Printer.CurrentX = 1250
Printer.CurrentY = 1500
Printer.Print "Happy Valentines Day"
Printer.EndDoc
End Sub
```

2. Use the following code to print a picture contained in a picture control:

```
Printer.PaintPicture frmImage.Picture
```

3. Use the following to create a separate page for each printer that lists the printer's device name and its driver's name:

```
Private Sub Form_DblClick()
Dim i, intIndexMax As Integer

intIndexMax = Printers.Count - 1
For i = 0 To intIndexMax
    Printer.Print "Printer: "; Printers(i).DeviceName
    Printer.Print "Driver: "; Printers(i).DriverName
    If i < intIndexMax Then
        Printer.NewPage
    End If
Next

Printer.EndDoc
End Sub
```

EXERCISES

1. Use the **Circle** method to draw several ellipses and circles so that they have the appearance of a pair of eyes.

2. Use the **Line** method to draw a triangle.

3. Use the **Print** method to print a numbered list of the names of all the controls on a form.

4. Create a subroutine that prints a separate page for each control on a form, which lists the type of control and the control's name.

Mastery Skills Check

1. What is printed when you call the **PrintForm** method?

2. What is the index of the first printer in the **Printers** collection?

3. What statement is used to set the default printer?

4. How do you terminate a print job?

10

Using Files and Databases

chapter objectives

10.1 Opening, Closing, and Deleting Files

10.2 Reading and Writing to Files

10.3 Using the ADO Data Control

10.4 Using the DataGrid Control

10.5 Using the Data Form Wizard

M

ost applications interact with data of some sort. It might be a simple text file that contains only a few lines of text, or it might be a large database with millions of records. Regardless of the amount of data, Visual Basic provides a way to access these types of data.

Text files have many uses. You could store text for a document, a log file, or even comma-delimited records. The **FileSystemObject** (FSO) object supplies you with methods to easily open and manipulate text files. Databases have become invaluable in today's computing environment. They provide an extremely fast way to store, categorize, and retrieve large amounts of data. To work with all types of databases, Visual Basic now uses the ADO Data Control (ADO is an acronym for **ActiveX Data Objects**).

Review
Skills Check

You should be able to correctly answer the following questions before beginning this chapter:

1. What is the index of the first printer in the **Printers** collection?

2. What statement is used to change the default printer?

3. What method sends the contents of the **Printer** object to the current printer device?

10.1 *O*PENING, CLOSING, AND DELETING FILES

Visual Basic provides several methods for working with files. This book demonstrates the manipulation of text files using the **FileSystemObject** object. The FSO object is an ActiveX object and provides all of the versatility and ease-of-use that you find in most ActiveX objects.

Before learning about the FSO object, you must understand how to create an ActiveX object in code. The **CreateObject** function creates and returns a reference to an ActiveX object. This function has one required parameter (class) and one optional parameter (servername), as shown in the following:

```
CreateObject(class, [servername])
```

The class argument is the name of an ActiveX object class, and the servername is the name of a remote server. If servername is provided, the object is created on that remote server. This book doesn't go into that much detail, but you can find more information on it at the MSDN Web site or in the online documentation.

Caution

The class argument of the CreateObject function must be a string, so remember to always enclose it in quotes.

The class argument has two parts: application and class. Application is the name of the application that is providing the object. For example, you could create a Microsoft Word document with the following syntax:

```
CreateObject("Word.Document")
```

To make it possible to manipulate the object, it must be assigned to an object variable. After that, the object variable makes the properties and methods of the new object available. So, the previous code would become:

```
Set doc = CreateObject("Word.Document")
```

When finished with the object, it should be released, which means the resources used by that object are freed up. To release an object, set the object variable that points to it equal to **Nothing**, as in the following:

```
Set doc = Nothing
```

The FSO object is part of the Microsoft Scripting Runtime, which is referred to as Scripting. FSO is a class within the Scripting application. To create an object that provides access to a computer's file system, use the following code:

```
Set fso = CreateObject("Scripting.FileSystemObject")
```

If you always declare your variables, you can declare variables that hold references to FSO objects as type **Object**, as in the following:

```
Dim fso As Object

Set fso = CreateObject("Scripting.FileSystemObject")
```

For faster performance, declare variables that will reference FSO objects as the type Scripting.FileSystemObject. This specifically designates that the variable will reference an FSO object.

The following sections discuss some of the uses for the FSO object. After using the properties and methods of the FSO object to manipulate files, release the object using a statement similar to the following:

```
Set fso = Nothing
```

OPENING FILES

Before you can work with any text file, you need a reference to the file. Obtaining this reference is commonly known as *opening the file*. The FSO object uses the **OpenTextFile** method to do this, as in the following:

```
Set fso = CreateObject("Scripting.FileSystemObject")
Set ts = fso.OpenTextFile("C:\TYVB.TXT", 8, True, -2)
```

The first line of code creates the FSO object. Then, the **OpenTextFile** method creates a **TextStream** object and assigns it to the variable ts. Text is read from or written to the file using the **TextStream** object.

Several arguments are supplied to the **OpenTextFile** method. Only the Filename argument is required. In this example, "C:\TYVB.TXT" is the filename, which includes the full path to the file. By default, **OpenTextFile** opens files for read only. To be able to write text to the file, the second argument (Iomode) must be set to 8. Omitting this argument or specifying a 1 opens the file as readonly. The third argument (Create) determines if **OpenTextFile** creates the file if it doesn't exist. A **True** Create argument causes **OpenTextFile** to create the file if it doesn't exist. A **False** Create argument, which is the default, doesn't allow it to create the file.

Use constants for the arguments of the OpenTextFile method to make it easier to use.

A fourth argument exists that affects the format used to store text in a file. Passing 0 as the Format argument or omitting the argument opens the file using ASCII. A value of -1 opens the file using Unicode, and -2 opens the file using the default on the system being used. If you don't know which is best, use ASCII. It is widely used and is compatible with almost every text editor. Table 10-1 summarizes the arguments for the **OpenTextFile** method of the **TextStream** object, which has the following syntax:

```
Set ts = fso.OpenTextFile(Filename, IOMode, Create, Format)
```

CLOSING FILES

After opening a file, you most likely perform several actions on the file. For example, you might write several new lines of text to the file. When finished with the file, you should close the file, which is done using the **Close** method of the **TextStream** object. The following expands upon the previous example by closing the file immediately after opening it:

```
Set fso = CreateObject("Scripting.FileSystemObject")
Set ts = fso.OpenTextFile("C:\TYVB.TXT", 8, True, -2)
ts.Close
```

Argument	Description
Filename	The string value that gives the path and filename of the file to open.
Iomode	The input/output mode used with the file.
Create	Controls if non-existent files are created.
Format	The format that the file is opened in.

TABLE 10-1 *OpenTextFile Arguments* ▼

Calling the TextStream object's Close method does not affect the FSO object. To free the resources being used by the FSO object, its object variable must be set equal to Nothing.

DELETING FILES

Certain files have a limited time span in which they are useful. For whatever reason a file is no longer needed, the file is usually deleted to free up storage space. The **DeleteFile** method of the FSO object deletes a file that you specify using the following syntax:

```
fso.DeleteFile filespec [, force]
```

If wildcard characters are used in the Filespec argument, several files can be deleted at once. The Force argument is optional. Specifying True for force causes all files matching the Filespec argument to be deleted, even if they are read-only files. If force is **False** or omitted, read-only files are not deleted, even if they match the Filespec argument.

An error occurs if no files match the Filespec argument of the DeleteFile method.

EXAMPLES

1. The following creates an FSO object and then releases it:

```
Dim fso As Object

Set fso = CreateObject("Scripting.FileSystemObject")
Set fso = Nothing
```

2. The following opens and closes a file using the FSO object:

```
Dim fso As Object
Dim ts As Object

Set fso = CreateObject("Scripting.FileSystemObject")
Set ts = fso.OpenTextFile("C:\EXAMPLE.TXT", , True)
```

```
ts.Close
Set fso = Nothing
```

3. The following deletes the text file created in the previous example:

```
Dim fso As Object

Set fso = CreateObject("Scripting.FileSystemObject")
fso.DeleteFile "C:\EXAMPLE.TXT", True
Set fso = Nothing
```

4. The following deletes all files on the root of the C: drive with the .txt extension:

```
Dim fso As Object

Set fso = CreateObject("Scripting.FileSystemObject")
fso.DeleteFile "C:\*.TXT", True
Set fso = Nothing
```

EXERCISES

1. Create a **TextStream** object.
2. Create a text file named EXERCISE.TXT on the root of your C: drive.
3. Open the text file named EXERCISE.TXT on the root of your C: drive.
4. Delete the text file named EXERCISE.TXT on the root of your C: drive.

10.2 *R EADING AND WRITING TO FILES*

After you are familiar with creating the FSO object and using its **OpenTextFile** method to return a **TextStream** object, you can begin to manipulate the files that the **TextStream** object is associated with. The following sections discuss the different methods available for reading from and writing to files.

READING FROM FILES

Text could be retrieved from a file for a number of reasons. The methods used to retrieve the text can be just as varied. This section discusses the different methods used to retrieve text from a file. To read from a file, it must be opened for reading, as in the following example:

```
Dim fso As Object
Dim ts As Object

Set fso = CreateObject("Scripting.FileSystemObject")
Set ts = fso.OpenTextFile("C:\EXAMPLE.TXT")
```

Reading Characters

At a minimum, you will read at least one character from a file. In fact, you might want to read a file a single character at a time. The **Read** method of the **TextStream** object makes this possible. It returns one or more characters at a time, using the following syntax:

```
TextStream.Read(characters)
```

The Characters argument is a numeric value that specifies how many characters to read from the file. If the **Read** method is called again before other changes to the file, it returns the character(s) after the last character read in the file. This method returns the characters as a string value.

You may not want some of the characters. If this is the case, use the **Skip** method to avoid reading certain characters. In the following syntax for the **Skip** method, the Characters argument is a numeric value that controls how many characters are skipped:

```
TextStream.Skip(characters)
```

Reading Lines

Some situations might be well suited to reading an entire line of text at a time. For this, you use the **TextStream** object's **ReadLine** method. **ReadLine** takes no arguments and returns one line of text each time that it is called. The following is the syntax for this method:

```
TextStream.ReadLine
```

Skipping Lines

In the same way that you might not want to read all of the characters in a file, you also may not want to read all of the lines in a file. The **SkipLine** method skips the next line of text in the file. The following is the syntax for this method:

```
TextStream.SkipLine
```

The amount of actual text skipped using this method varies. When the **SkipLine** method is called, it moves to the first character after the next new line character. A line of text could have a couple of characters and then a new line character, or it could have a hundred words before it has a new line character.

Reading Entire Files

If you have little interest in individual characters or lines of text and want all of the text contained in the file, use the **ReadAll** method. As the name implies, this method reads the entire contents of the file and then returns it as a string value. The following is the syntax for this method:

```
TextStream.ReadAll
```

When reading all of a large file, read it line by line if at all possible. This conserves resources and makes your application faster.

WRITING TO FILES

Writing text to a file is a little simpler than reading it. Either you want to add characters to the current line of text or you want to create a new line of text. In some cases, you might want to do both. For these purposes, the **TextStream** object has the **Write** method and the **WriteLine** method.

To write to a file, it must be opened for appending. Specify an 8 for the Iomode argument of the OpenTextFile method to do this.

Add to the current line of text with the **Write** method. This method adds the string argument passed to it to the current line of text. It does not add any characters or spaces that you do not specify. The following is the syntax for the **Write** method:

```
TextStream.Write(string)
```

However, if this is the only method you use to add text to files, all of your text files will contain only one line of text. To add a new line character, which signals the end of a line of text, use the **WriteLine** method. The following is the syntax for the **WriteLine** method:

```
TextStream.WriteLine([string])
```

If you supply the optional string argument to the **WriteLine** method, it adds that string to the current line of text and then adds the new line character. To add several new line characters at once, use the **WriteBlankLines** method. The following is the syntax for the **WriteBlankLines** method, which inserts the number of new line characters specified in the Lines argument:

```
TextStream.WriteBlankLines(lines)
```

USING THE PROPERTIES OF THE TEXTSTREAM OBJECT

When navigating through a file using a **TextStream** object, a file pointer is used. The file pointer indicates where you are currently in the file. The **TextStream** object has several properties that describe the location of this pointer to make it easier to process the contents of a file. Table 10-2 describes these properties, which are all read-only.

Property	Description
AtEndOfLine	Returns True if the pointer is immediately before a new line character and False if it is not.
AtEndOfStream	Returns True if the pointer is at the end of the file and False if it is not.
Column	Returns the column number of the current character; each new line starts with column number 1.
Line	Returns the current line number; each file starts with line number 1.

TABLE 10-2   *TextStream Object Properties* ▼

EXAMPLES

1. The following code creates five text files. It adds the name of the text file to the first line and some additional text and blank lines in the rest of the file.

```
Dim fso As Object
Dim ts As Object
Dim s As String
Dim strDir As String
Dim strFiles(1 To 5) As String

strDir = "C:\"
strFiles(1) = "01FILE.TXT"
strFiles(2) = "02FILE.TXT"
strFiles(3) = "03FILE.TXT"
strFiles(4) = "04FILE.TXT"
strFiles(5) = "05FILE.TXT"

Set fso = CreateObject("Scripting.FileSystemObject")

For Each s In strFiles
    Set ts = fso.OpenTextFile(strDir & s, 8, True)
    ts.WriteLine (s)
    ts.WriteBlankLines (2)
    ts.WriteLine ("Beginning Of File")
    ts.WriteLine
    ts.WriteLine ("End Of File")
    ts.Close
Next

Set fso = Nothing
```

2. The following code uses the files created in the previous example to demonstrate the use of the read method. This example assumes that the file always begins with the filename and that the name always begins with a two-digit number. It reads that number from the file and appends each number to the caption of the parent control, which will most likely be a form that you are using to test this.

```
Dim fso As Object
Dim ts As Object
Dim s As String
Dim strDir As String
Dim strFiles(1 To 5) As String
```

```
Dim intFileNumber As Integer

strDir = "C:\"
strFiles(1) = "01FILE.TXT"
strFiles(2) = "02FILE.TXT"
strFiles(3) = "03FILE.TXT"
strFiles(4) = "04FILE.TXT"
strFiles(5) = "05FILE.TXT"

Set fso = CreateObject("Scripting.FileSystemObject")

For Each s In strFiles
    Set ts = fso.OpenTextFile(strDir & s)
    intFileNumber = ts.Read(2)
    Caption = Caption & intFileNumber
    ts.Close
Next

Set fso = Nothing
```

3. The following example uses the same assumption as the previous example that the file it is opening contains the filename on the first line. It also assumes that the filename always contains eight characters, a period, and a three-letter extension. It skips straight to the extension and reads it into a string variable. FILENAME.TXT can be replaced with any filename that contains this type of information.

```
Dim fso As Object
Dim ts As Object
Dim strExtension As String

Set fso = CreateObject("Scripting.FileSystemObject")
Set ts = fso.OpenTextFile("C:\FILENAME.TXT")
ts.Skip (9)
strExtension = ts.Read(3)
ts.Close
Set fso = Nothing
```

4. The following code opens a file and reads the first line character by character. When it gets to the end of the first line, it stops. Normally, you would do something with each character, but this is for demonstration purposes only.

```
Dim fso As Object
Dim ts As Object
```

```
Set fso = CreateObject("Scripting.FileSystemObject")
Set ts = fso.OpenTextFile("C:\FILENAME.TXT")

Do While Not ts.AtEndOfLine
    ts.Read(1)
Loop

ts.Close
Set fso = Nothing
```

5. The following code opens a file and reads it line by line. When it gets to the end of the file, it stops. Normally, you would do something with each line of text, but this is for demonstration purposes only.

```
Dim fso As Object
Dim ts As Object

Set fso = CreateObject("Scripting.FileSystemObject")
Set ts = fso.OpenTextFile("C:\01FILE.TXT")

Do While Not ts.AtEndOfStream
    ts.ReadLine
Loop

ts.Close
Set fso = Nothing
```

EXERCISES

1. Create a new text file named NEW.TXT on the root of the C: drive.

2. Open NEW.TXT and add several lines of text to it.

3. Open NEW.TXT and read every other line of text starting with the first one.

4. Open NEW.TXT and read the entire file one character at a time.

| 10.3 | # *U*SING THE ADO DATA CONTROL |

Many applications access information contained in databases. Because of the variety of database systems, it would be difficult to implement a separate mechanism for accessing each type of database. Instead, an interface has been established that can interact with the different types of databases. This interface is called OLE DB. While OLE DB is designed to interact with databases, it is not ideal for use in applications, which leads to the need for something to connect the capabilities of OLE DB to your applications.

Microsoft **ActiveX Data Objects** (ADO) act as that connection. ADO is compatible with any OLE DB data source and can be used to bind controls to that data source. Binding a control to a data source basically means that the control displays the data contained in one of the fields in a database. This can be done for display purposes only, or the user could also use the control to make changes to the data that is displayed.

You could create an application that deals directly with ADO, but Microsoft has supplied an easier and quicker way to take advantage of the features of ADO. While the ADO Data Control makes it very easy to use the power of ADO in your applications, it does not give you access to all of the features of ADO. You must use ADO directly to have access to all of its features, but most programs do not require this level of sophistication.

The ADO Data Control is a graphical control that has basic navigation features built into it. This means that very little extra programming will be required for many applications that use the ADO Data Control. The following are some of the controls that can be bound to a database using the ADO Data Control:

▼ CheckBox

▼ ComboBox

▼ Image

▼ Label

▼ ListBox

▼ PictureBox

▼ TextBox

Visual Basic contains several other data controls beyond the ADO Data Control. These are provided for backward compatibility purposes only. All new database applications should use ADO.

ADDING THE ADO DATA CONTROL TO A FORM

By default, the Toolbox does not contain the ADO Data Control. You must add the ADO Data Control component to each project that needs to use it. To add the ADO Data Control to a project, open the Components dialog box and select the Microsoft ADO Data Control (OLEDB), as shown in Figure 10-1

After the ADO Data Control is added to the Toolbox, it is placed on a form in the same manner that all other controls are. Figure 10-2 shows a form with an ADO Data Control on it.

Several properties must be set in order to use the ADO Data Control. As usual, these can all be modified using the Properties window. The

FIGURE 10-1

The Components dialog box adds the ADO Data Control to a project
▼

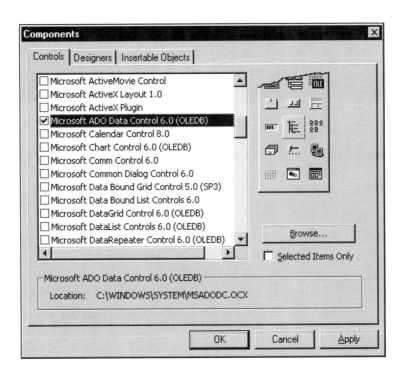

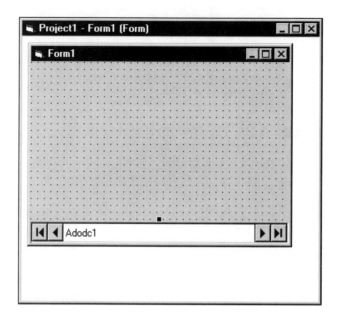

ADO Data Control also provides property pages that can be used to set the most important properties. To open the property pages, click the button with an ellipsis on it for the property labeled (Custom) at the top of the properties listed in the Properties window.

The ADO Data Control property pages open to the General page, which includes the Data Source Name (DSN). DSNs describe a data source that has been defined on a computer. This chapter uses a DSN that points to the Northwind database that is included as a sample with Visual Basic, but any DSN works. Select the Use ODBC Data Source Name option button and choose and existing DSN from the dropdown list box, as shown in Figure 10-3. You can create new DSNs by clicking the New button or using the ODBC Administrator in the Control Panel.

Click the Authentication tab if you need to supply a user name and password for a database. Figure 10-4 shows the Authentication page.

Caution

Depending on how sensitive data is, you may not want to supply the user name and password for a database in your application. In that case, you could prompt the user for the information and supply it to the ADO Data Control in your code.

General page of the ADO Data Control property pages
▼

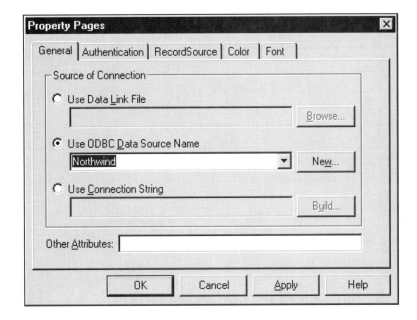

Authentication page of the ADO Data Control property pages
▼

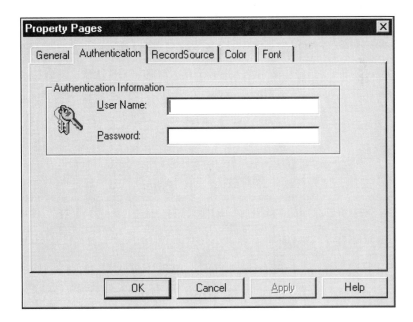

Click the RecordSource tab to specify where the records will come from in the database. First, you must specify what type of object is supplying the data. In most cases, you will be using a table. So, select 2-adCmdTable from the Command Type dropdown list box. Then, select the Categories table from the Table or Stored Procedure Name dropdown list box, as shown in Figure 10-5.

Note   *If a table name contains spaces, you must place quotation marks around the name. Otherwise, only the first part of the name is used when trying to locate fields in the table.*

In addition to the previous property pages, two more are available that affect the appearance of the ADO Data Control: Color and Font. Use these to make changes to the way that the control is displayed.

LINKING CONTROLS TO THE ADO DATA CONTROL

You should now have a form with a single control on it, the ADO Data Control. This control should be set to connect to the Categories table of

FIGURE 10-5

RecordSource page of the ADO Data Control property pages
▼

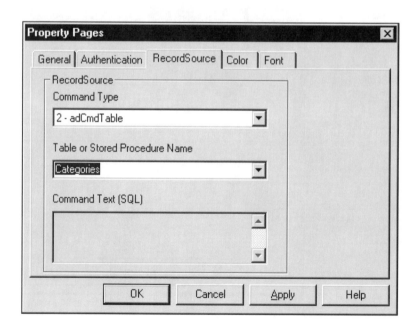

the Northwind sample database. Now, add three text boxes and three labels to the form so that it looks similar to Figure 10-6.

Select each of the text boxes and set its **DataSource** property to Adodc1. Selecting the value from the dropdown list box does this easily. Adodc1 is the only choice because it is the only data source on the form. Forms can have multiple data sources, but too many can seriously degrade the performance of the application.

Tip

When assigning several controls the same DataSource property, select all of the controls at once and then set the property. This sets the property for all of them at the same time, without having to select each one of them individually and modify the property.

Select the first text box and set its **DataField** property to CategoryID. Then, double-click on the field for the **DataFormat** property. Set the Format Type to Number, as shown in Figure 10-7.

Set the **DataField** of the other two fields to CategoryName and Description. You don't need to set the **DataFormat** property for these controls because the textual data doesn't require any special format. If you like, though, you can signify this by setting the Format Type

FIGURE 10-6

Main project form with ADO Data Control and text boxes

▼

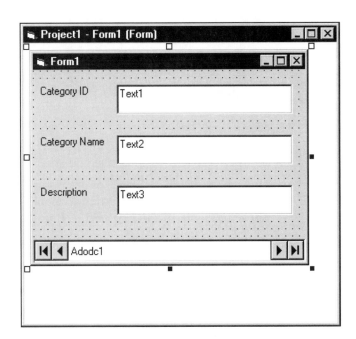

*The Format
property page
formats displayed
data*

▼

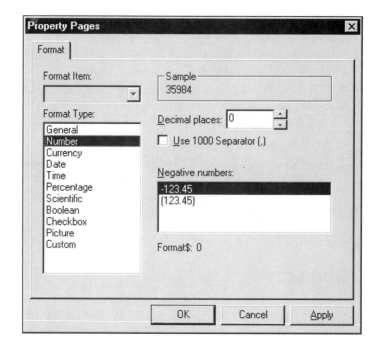

property to General. If you run the project, the form appears as shown
in Figure 10-8. Use the arrow button on the ADO Data Control to move
around in the records of the table.

EXAMPLES

1. Figure 10-9 shows a form that displays all of the fields for the
   Customers table of the Northwind sample database.

2. Figure 10-10 shows a form that displays all of the fields for the
   Employees table of the Northwind sample database.

3. Figure 10-11 shows a form that displays all of the fields for the
   Suppliers table of the Northwind sample database.

*The ADO Data
Control takes care
of the logic for
navigating between
records*
▼

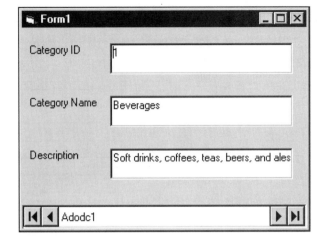

*Customers form
using the ADO
Data Control*
▼

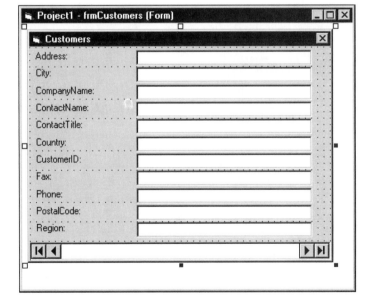

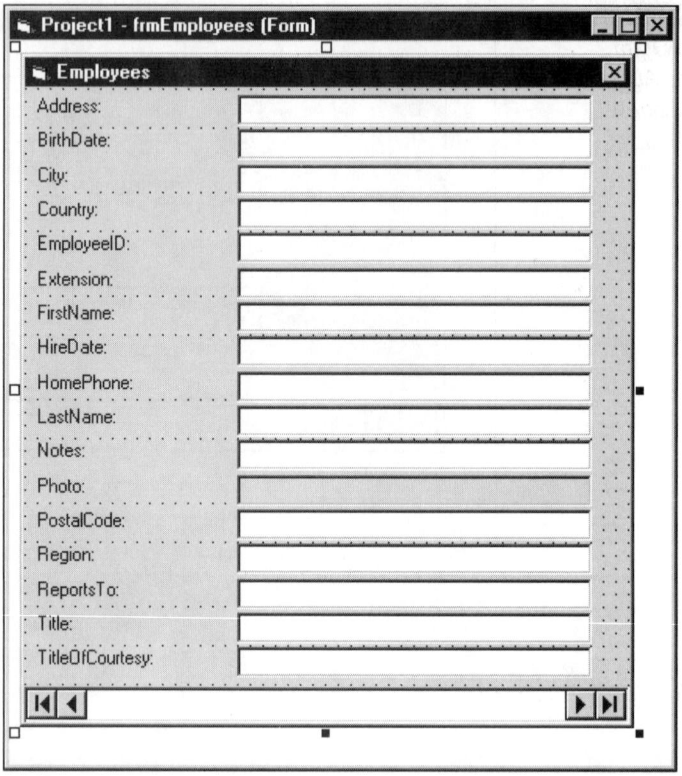

FIGURE 10-10

*Employees form
using the ADO
Data Control*
▼

EXERCISES

1. Add to the form built in this section that lists the fields from the Categories table by adding an Image control to display the picture for a category.

2. Create a form that displays the data from the Shippers table of the Northwind sample database.

3. Create a form that displays the ProductID, ProductName, and Discontinued fields from the Products table of the Northwind sample database.

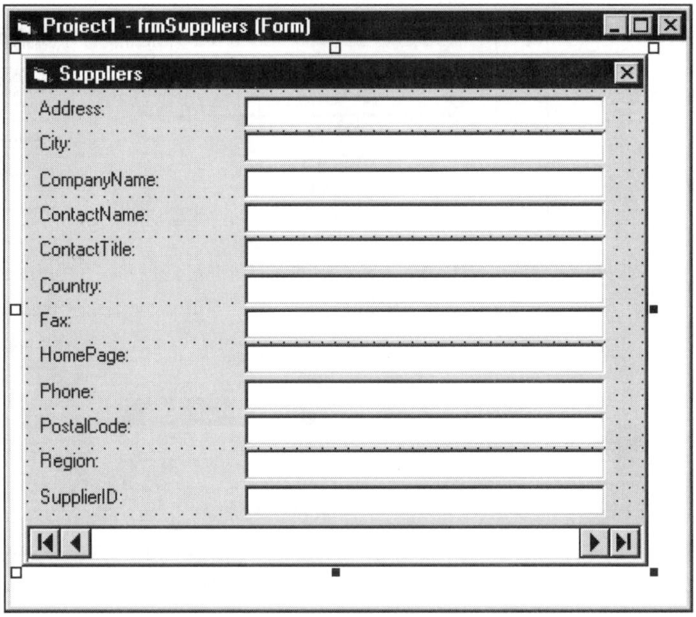

FIGURE 10-11

*Suppliers form
using the ADO
Data Control*
▼

10.4 USING THE DATAGRID CONTROL

Display data using specific controls when the quality of the display is most important. However, if you just need to display the data and the formatting of the display is not important, use the DataGrid control. The DataGrid control is quick and easy to use. In fact, the combination of the ADO Data Control and the DataGrid control could be used to create a data maintenance form without writing a single line of code. Data maintenance forms are used to keep database tables up to date.

ADDING THE DATAGRID CONTROL TO A FORM

Like the ADO Data Control, the DataGrid is not a standard item in the Toolbox. Use the Components dialog box to add the Microsoft DataGrid Control 6.0 (OLEDB) to a project, as shown in Figure 10-12.

After adding the DataGrid to the Toolbox, place it on the form that already has an ADO Data Control on it. For example, Figure 10-13

*Add the DataGrid
Control using the
Components
dialog box*
▼

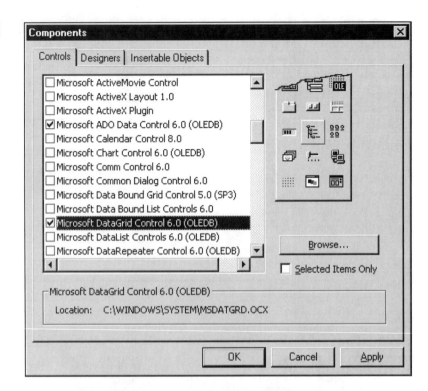

*Shippers form with
DataGrid Control*
▼

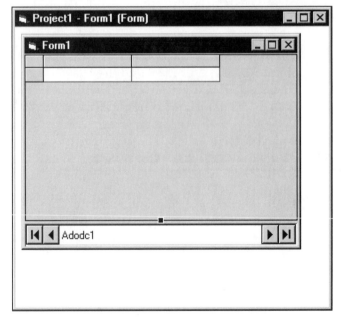

shows a form with an ADO Data Control that points to the Shippers table in the Northwind sample database and a DataGrid on it.

Right-click on the DataGrid control and choose Retrieve fields from the shortcut menu. As shown in Figure 10-14, you are asked if you want to replace the existing grid layout.

Click the Yes button. The DataGrid control automatically formats itself to have the same number of columns as there are fields in the table it is associated with. It also places the field names in the headers of the columns that display them. Figure 10-15 shows the form after retrieving the fields from the Shippers table. At this point, you have a fully functioning database form without having written any code.

CUSTOMIZING THE DATAGRID CONTROL

A fast and easy way to set up the columns and column headers of the DataGrid Control is to use the layout of the underlying table. However, you may not always want to use all of the fields in the table, or you may want to use column headers that are different from the field names.

Right-click on the DataGrid and choose Edit from the shortcut menu. The control is now in edit mode, which allows you to change the layout of the columns. You can delete, insert, or append columns by right-clicking on the DataGrid Control and choosing the appropriate command from the shortcut menu.

Tip

Right-click on a DataGrid Control and choose Clear fields from the shortcut menu to delete all of the columns at once. Then, the control immediately adds two blank columns.

Assuming that you have the correct number of columns, you might now want to make some changes to the appearance of the DataGrid.

FIGURE 10-14

The DataGrid verifies your actions

▼

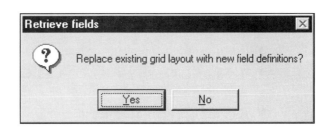

Retrieve fields

? Replace existing grid layout with new field definitions?

Yes   No

*Shippers form after
retrieving fields
from the database*

▼

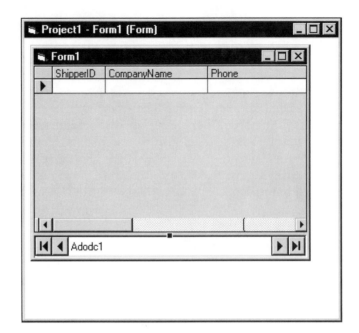

Right-click on the control and choose Properties from the shortcut
menu. Figure 10-16 shows the General page of the DataGrid Control
property pages.

Most of the properties on the General page deal with the appearance
of the DataGrid. If you don't want the user to be able to add new
records or delete existing records, make sure that the AllowAddNew
and AllowDelete options are unchecked. For this example, add a
caption of Shippers and change the Headlines property to 2. Then,
click the Columns tab to display the Columns page, which Figure
10-17 displays.

Use the Columns page to control which fields' columns display. You
can also specify captions for the columns. Specify the following
captions by selecting the column in the Column dropdown list box and
changing the caption:

▼ Column 0 (ShipperID)— Shipper ID Number

▼ Column 1 (CompanyName)—Company or Parent
Company Name

▼ Column 2 (Phone)—Direct Phone Number

FIGURE 10-16

*General page of
the DataGrid
Control property
pages*

▼

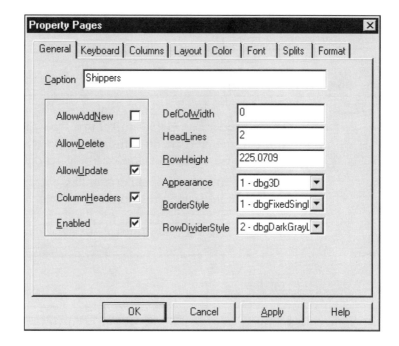

FIGURE 10-17

*Columns page of
the DataGrid
Control property
pages*

▼

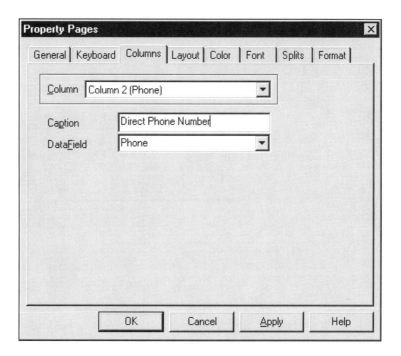

Run the project when finished. The run-time form should look similar to Figure 10-18.

EXAMPLES

1. Figure 10-19 shows a form created by adding an ADO Data Control and a DataGrid Control to a form. The ADO Data Control points to the Northwind sample database Categories table and the DataGrid uses the DataControl as its data source.

2. Figure 10-20 shows a form created by adding an ADO Data Control and a DataGrid Control to a form. The ADO Data Control points to the Northwind sample database Products table and the DataGrid uses the DataControl as its data source.

EXERCISES

1. Create a form that allows the user to view the records of the Northwind sample database Customers table.

2. Change the sample form created in this section that uses the Categories table so that the user can add and delete records.

FIGURE 10-18

Categories table displayed in a DataGrid Control

▼

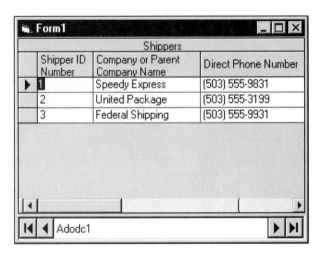

Categories table displayed in a DataGrid
▼

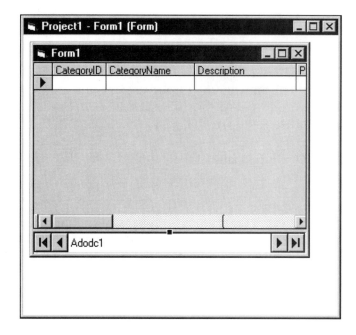

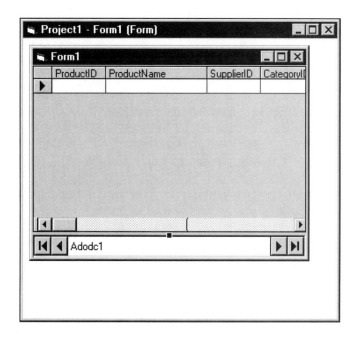

10.5 USING THE DATA FORM WIZARD

In this section, you will create database forms using the Data Wizard. If you are struggling with some of the concepts in this chapter, analyzing the forms that the Wizard creates can help you learn how to create your own data forms. Inspect all of the procedures that the Wizard creates and note all of the database properties that it sets.

You may already have a good understanding of the controls in this chapter, but find the creation of data forms boring and tedious. In that case, this chapter is still for you because you can learn how to use the Data Form Wizard to quickly create data forms with very little action on your part.

As a practical matter, you may want to use the Data Form Wizard to quickly create prototype forms or even an entire prototype application. Using the Wizard in this way allows you to create many forms in a short period of time. Then, you can have the users of the application test the forms and make any suggested changes directly to the Wizard-generated forms.

Using the Data Form Wizard can have a nice effect on your application. It generates forms in a very similar manner, which helps give your applications a standardized, professional look.

GETTING STARTED WITH DATA FORM WIZARD

The first step to using the Wizard is to add a form to your project. Either select Add Form from the Project menu or click the Add Form button on the toolbar. Select the VB Data Form Wizard in the Add Form dialog box, as shown in Figure 10-21, and click the Open button.

The first step in the Data Form Wizard allows you to choose a profile for the Wizard to use. Profiles are created by running the Wizard and saving the settings you chose into a Wizard profile file (.rwp). This feature makes it easy to standardize on a group of settings for your data forms. If you don't want to use a profile, select (None). Click the Next button to continue on to the Database Type step, shown in Figure 10-22.

The number of database types available will vary from system to system, depending upon which database drivers are installed. In general, the selections will most likely be Access, SQL Server, or

FIGURE 10-21

*The VB Data Form
Wizard is a choice
in the Add Form
dialog box*
▼

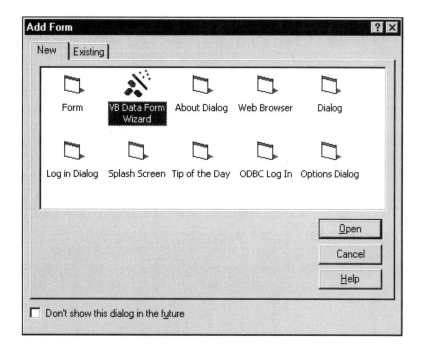

FIGURE 10-22

*The Data Form
Wizard must know
what type of
database the form
uses*
▼

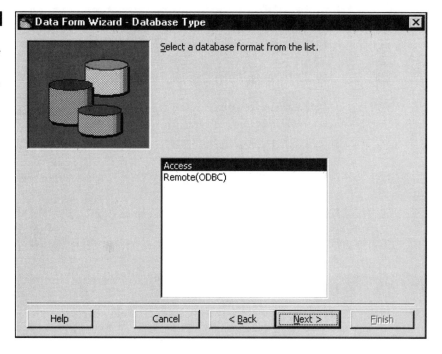

ODBC. Select the Access database type and click the Next button to go to the Database step, shown in Figure 10-23.

Enter the name of the database into the Database Name text box. If it is a file-based database, such as Access or dBase, you must enter both the path and filename. For this example, use the Northwind database. Click the Next button to continue on to the Form step of the Data Form Wizard, shown in Figure 10-24.

Click the Browse button to use an Open dialog box to locate a database file.

SELECTING A FORM LAYOUT AND BINDING TYPE

This is the most powerful step of the Data Form Wizard. From here, you can determine how data is displayed and what method is used to

FIGURE 10-23

The Data Form Wizard must know exactly which database the form uses

▼

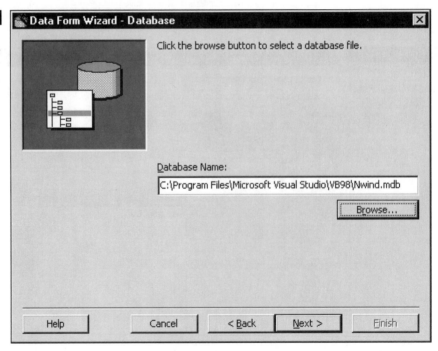

FIGURE 10-24

The Data Form Wizard presents several possible layouts for the form

▼

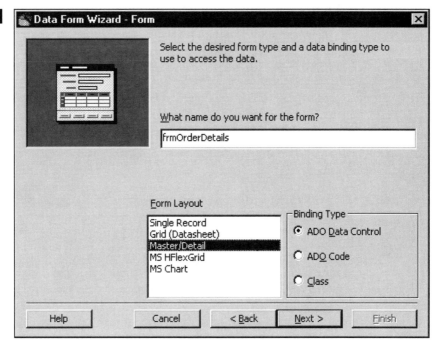

access the data. You also name the form in this step. The Binding Type option buttons refer to the way that data is drawn from a database, or the way that controls are bound to data. Controls can be bound using any of the following:

▼ ADO Data Control

▼ ADO Code

▼ Class

The ADO Data Control option uses the same ADO Data Control that you have already worked with in this chapter. ADO Code and Class both use code to access data instead of a control that is placed on the form. For now, use the ADO Data Control because you are already familiar with it.

Several options are available for the layout of the form, which determines how the data is displayed. The following sections describe each of these options.

Creating Single Table Forms

Four layouts are available for forms that display the data contained in a single table. The following are those layouts:

- ▼ Single Record
- ▼ Grid (Datasheet)
- ▼ MS HFlexGrid
- ▼ MS Chart

Note

The MS Chart layout only works with the ADO Code binding type.

Choosing the Single Record layout produces a form that displays one record at a time. Any of the other three choices displays multiple records simultaneously. After selecting a single table layout and clicking the Next button, you are prompted to identify the record source,—the table or query where the records are coming from. Figure 10-25 shows the Record Source step for a single table layout. The following section discusses the use of this part of the Wizard.

Creating a Master/Detail Form

A master/detail layout displays a single record from one record source and all of the records related to it from another record source. Select the Master/Detail layout and click the Next button. Figure 10-26 shows the Master Record Source step.

Select the Orders table from the Record Source dropdown list box. This causes the Available Fields list box to fill with the fields from the Orders table. The arrow buttons work as in all other Windows applications: a single arrow adds or removes the selected item, and a double arrow adds or removes all items. Add the CustomerID, OrderID, and ShipRegion fields to the Selected Fields list box. Now you can use the up or down arrow button to change the order in which these fields will appear. You can also use the Column to Sort By dropdown list box to force the records to appear in an order based upon a particular column. Click the Next button when finished making your selections.

FIGURE 10-25

A single table form has only one record source

▼

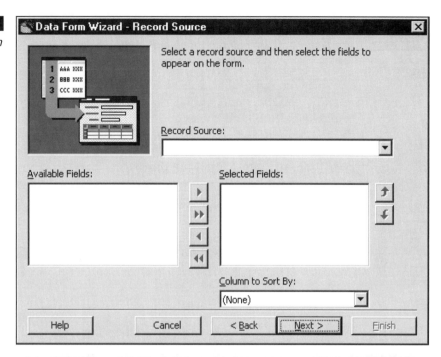

FIGURE 10-26

The Master Record Source step is nearly identical to the Record Source step

▼

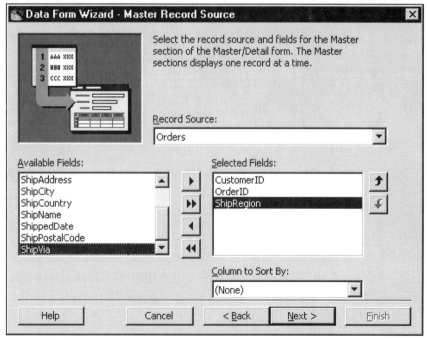

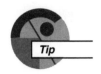

You can sort by a column that is not in the Selected Fields list box.

Now you must add a detail record source. Select the Order Details table and all of its fields, as shown in Figure 10-27. Click the Next button to continue.

In order to display the correct detail records for a master record, you must identify which field relates the detail record source to the master data source. In this case, the OrderID field relates detail records to master records; all records in Order Details with an OrderID of 1 are related to the record in Orders with an OrderID of 1. Select the OrderID field in the Master and Detail list boxes, as shown in Figure 10-28, and click the Next button.

FIGURE 10-27

The detail data source lists all of the records related to the master data source
▼

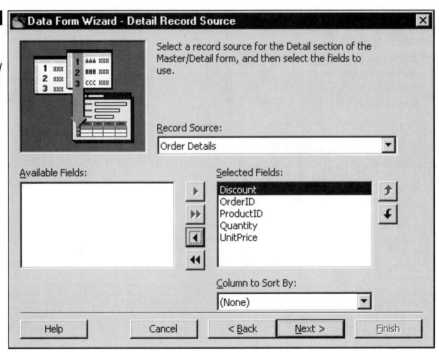

FIGURE 10-28

The Record Source Relation step defines the master/detail relationship

▼

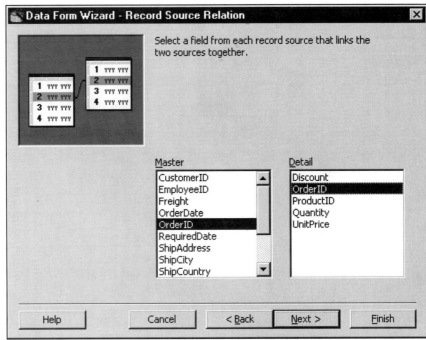

COMPLETING THE FORM

The Control Selection step asks you to identify which controls should appear on the form. Figure 10-29 shows the possible controls. Leave all of the controls selected and click the Next button.

Show Data Control is automatically selected in the Control Selection step when you choose the ADO Data Control binding type.

The Finished! step lets you know that you have completed all of the steps and gives you a chance to save the settings you selected into a profile that can be used the next time you use the Wizard. Figure 10-30 shows this step.

To save settings to a profile, select an existing profile from the dropdown list box or click the ellipsis button to create a new profile. Click the Finish button when you are done. The Wizard works for

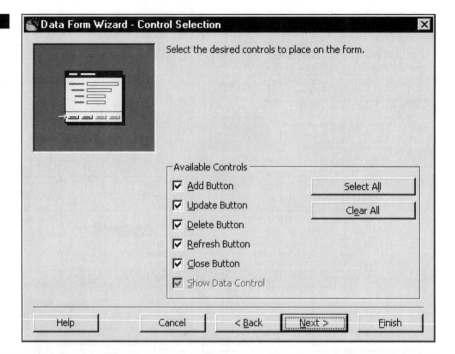

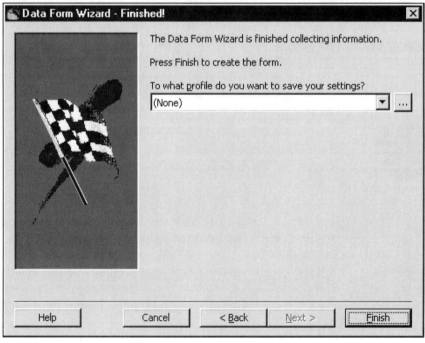

several seconds building the form and then informs you that the form has been added to the current project, as shown in Figure 10-31.

Figure 10-32 shows the newly created form. The ADO Data Control controls the display of the Order records, which controls the display of the Order Details records.

Use the code under the command buttons to learn how to use the ADO Data Control to add and delete records.

EXAMPLES

1. Figure 10-33 shows a single record form created with the Data Form Wizard.

2. Figure 10-34 shows an MS Chart form created with the Data Form Wizard.

3. Figure 10-35 shows a Grid form created with the Data Form Wizard.

FIGURE 10-31

Click the checkbox on the Data Form Completed dialog box to prevent it from displaying

▼

*Complex forms are
easily created with
the Data
Form Wizard*
▼

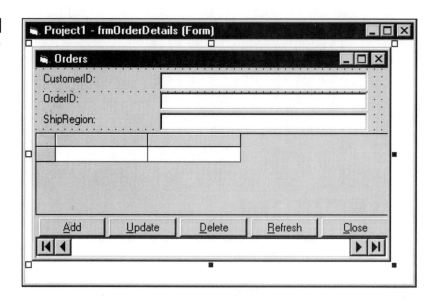

*A single record
layout form*
▼

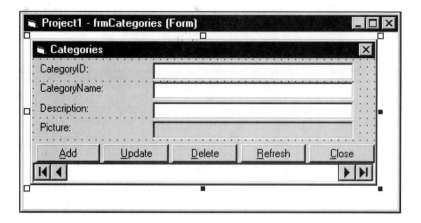

FIGURE 10-34

An MS Chart layout form
▼

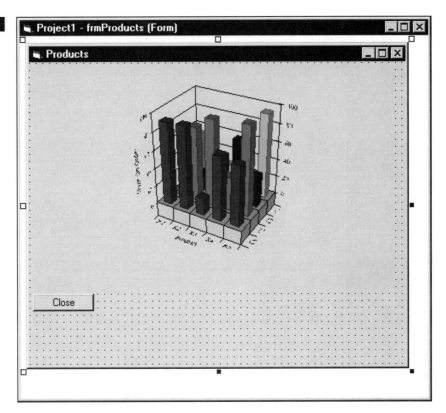

EXERCISES

1. Create a single record form with the Data Form Wizard for the Shippers table.

2. Create a master/detail form with the Data Form Wizard using the Customers table as the master and the Orders table as the detail.

FIGURE 10-35

A Grid layout form
▼

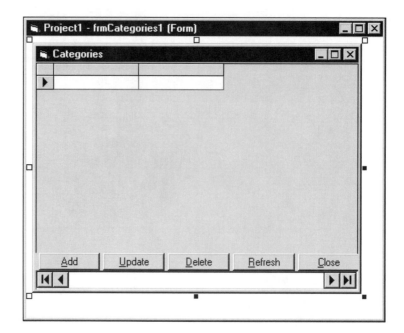

Mastery
Skills Check

1. What class does the FSO object come from?

2. What object is used to actually open a file?

3. What code must you add for the ADO Data Control to allow the user to navigate the records of a database?

4. What is the quickest way to format a DataGrid Control?

5. What are the two basic types of forms that the Data Form Wizard is capable of creating?

11

Using the Internet and an Intranet

chapter objectives

The Internet and company intranets hold large amounts of information and continue to grow every year. Many applications already exist that make it possible to access this information. It is unlikely that you will want to spend the time to write a replacement for your Web browser or your email client, but you might want to add some of their functionality to your applications.

Visual Basic provides several controls that allow information to be exchanged across the networks that make up the Internet and corporate intranets. With these controls, you can use the communication ability of a network to send and receive messages and other information between your applications. In addition, you can give your applications the ability to exchange information with other applications, such as Web servers, FTP servers, and MAPI mail systems.

Review

Skills Check

You should be able to correctly answer the following questions before beginning this chapter:

1. How do you release the resources being used by an FSO object?
2. How do you read all of the text in a file?
3. What controls can display data that is retrieved using the ADO Data Control?
4. How do you put a DataGrid control into edit mode?
5. Which type of form created by the Data Form Wizard uses more than one table or query to create a form?

11.1 *U*SING THE WINSOCK CONTROL

The Winsock control allows applications to communicate with each other on the same computer or over any type of network connection, including the Internet. It offers two methods to accomplish this communication:

▼ Transmission Control Protocol (TCP)

▼ User Datagram Protocol (UDP)

Each of these methods allows applications to send data back and forth. However, the manner in which they perform this task differs. These differences determine which method is best for an application. The following sections discuss the advantages and disadvantages of TCP and UDP.

In order to use the Winsock control, you must first add it to your project using the Components dialog box. Then, you add the control to one of the forms in your application, set its properties, and write the code that handles the communication. The following sections discuss the protocols available to use with the Winsock control.

UNDERSTANDING TCP

TCP is based upon a stable connection. One application connects to another and that connection is continually maintained in order to send data back and forth between the two applications. One of the applications acts as a server and the other as a client. To use a Winsock control for a TCP connection, its **Protocol** property must be set to 0 – sckTCPProtocol.

Note

TCP should be used when large amounts of data are to be sent and when it is important that a constant connection be maintained.

Setting up a TCP Server

A Winsock control acting as a server only requires that a single property be set. The **LocalPort** property must be set so that the control knows which port to listen for connection requests on. This property uses a **Long** data type.

When a server application is started, you must also call the **Listen** method of the control. This forces the control to listen for connection requests on the port specified in the **LocalPort** property. A connection request triggers the **ConnectionRequest** event. Calling the **Accept** method of the Winsock control in this event establishes the connection.

Setting Up a TCP Client

A Winsock control acting as a client must know the port that the server is listening on. This information is placed in the **RemotePort** property, but this is only half of the information needed to connect to the server. Remember that the server can be on any machine that the computer can reach using a network connection. So, the client must know the location of the server.

The **RemoteHost** property specifies the location of the server. This property can contain either the computer name of the server or its IP address. Both types of addresses are specified in the Network dialog box, which is opened by choosing Properties from the Network Neighborhood shortcut menu. An IP address is a numeric address that can uniquely identify a computer. Computer names are basically an alias for another type of address, such as an IP address. However, the computer name can be more descriptive and intuitive because it uses text instead of numbers. After setting these properties, call the **Connect** method to establish a connection to the server.

Sending Data Between TCP Clients and Servers

Once a connection is established, data can be sent between the two applications using the **SendData** and **GetData** method. Either the client or the server can use the **SendData** method to send data. When the data arrives at the other side, the **DataArrival** event occurs. This event should contain a call to the **GetData** method, which retrieves the data that has been sent. See the Examples section for a complete example of this process.

A TCP connection must be closed before the RemoteHost or RemotePort properties can be changed.

UNDERSTANDING UDP

UDP differs from TCP in that it doesn't require a connection to be maintained for communication to occur. It is called a connectionless protocol. Both applications can act as client and server in UDP, and they are commonly called peers instead of client and server. However, each peer must be able to perform the action of both a client and a server. To use a Winsock control for a UDP connection, its **Protocol** property must be set to 1 – sckUDPProtocol.

Each computer must set its **LocalPort** property to a port that it will listen on. This is accomplished by binding the control to a local port, using the **Bind** method. The **Bind** method also reserves a port so that no other application can use it. Then, the other computer must have its **RemotePort** property set to that same port and its **RemoteHost** property set to the other computer. Now, either computer can send data to the other using the **SendData** method, which causes the **DataArrival** event to occur in the other computer. At this point, the **GetData** method is used to retrieve the data.

Note — *UDP should be used when small amounts of data are to be sent and when a process will send or receive data at unpredictable times.*

EXAMPLES

1. Complete the following steps to create a chat program that uses the Winsock control with the TCP protocol:

   A. Create a Standard EXE and add the controls shown in Table 11-1 with the properties listed.

Object	Property	Value
Form	Name	FrmClient
	Caption	Client
Command Button	Name	CmdConnect
	Caption	Connect
Text Box	Name	TxtSendData
Text Box	Name	TxtGetData
Winsock Control	Name	TcpClient
	Protocol	0 – sckTCPProtocol

TABLE 11-1 *Controls and Properties for tcpClient* ▼

B. Add the following code to the Client form, replacing the RemoteHost property with your computer's name:

```
Private Sub Form_Load()

tcpClient.RemoteHost = "ctx"
tcpClient.RemotePort = 1001

End Sub

Private Sub cmdConnect_Click()

tcpClient.Connect

End Sub

Private Sub txtSendData_Change()

tcpClient.SendData txtSendData.Text

End Sub

Private Sub tcpClient_DataArrival(ByVal bytesTotal As Long)
Dim strData As String

tcpClient.GetData strData
txtGetData.Text = strData

End Sub
```

C. Create another Standard EXE and add the controls shown in Table 11-2 with the properties listed.

Object	Property	Value
Form	Name	FrmServer
	Caption	Server
Text Box	Name	TxtSendData
Text Box	Name	TxtGetData
Winsock Control	Name	TcpServer
	Protocol	0 – sckTCPProtocol

TABLE 11-2 *Controls and Properties for tcpServer* ▼

D. Add the following code to the Server form:

```
Private Sub Form_Load()

tcpServer.LocalPort = 1001
tcpServer.Listen

End Sub

Private Sub tcpServer_ConnectionRequest(ByVal
requestID As Long)

If tcpServer.State <> sckClosed Then
    tcpServer.Close
End If

tcpServer.Accept requestID

End Sub

Private Sub txtSendData_Change()

tcpServer.SendData txtSendData.Text

End Sub

Private Sub tcpServer_DataArrival(ByVal bytesTotal As
Long)
Dim strData As String

tcpServer.GetData strData
txtGetData.Text = strData

End Sub
```

E. Create an executable for both forms and run them. Click the Connect button to connect the Client to the Server, and then you should be able to chat back and forth between the two forms.

2. Complete the following steps to create a chat program that uses the Winsock control with the UDP protocol:

A. Create a Standard EXE and add the controls shown in Table 11-3 with the properties listed.

Object	Property	Value
Form	Name	frmPeer1
	Caption	Peer 1
Text Box	Name	TxtSendData
Text Box	Name	TxtGetData
Winsock Control	Name	udpPeer1
	Protocol	1 – sckUDPProtocol

TABLE 11-3 *Controls and Properties for udpPeer1* ▼

B. Add the following code to the Peer1 form, replacing the RemoteHost property with your computer's name:

```
Private Sub Form_Load()

udpPeer1.RemoteHost = "ctx"
udpPeer1.RemotePort = 1001
udpPeer1.Bind 1002

End Sub

Private Sub txtSendData_Change()

udpPeer1.SendData txtSendData.Text

End Sub

Private Sub udpPeer1_DataArrival(ByVal bytesTotal As
Long)
Dim strData As String

udpPeer1.GetData strData
txtGetData.Text = strData

End Sub
```

C. Create a Standard EXE and add the controls shown in Table 11-4 with the properties listed.

Object	Property	Value
Form	Name	frmPeer2
	Caption	Peer 2
Text Box	Name	TxtSendData
Text Box	Name	TxtGetData
Winsock Control	Name	udpPeer2
	Protocol	1 – sckUDPProtocol

TABLE 11-4 *Controls and Properties for udpPeer2* ▼

D. Add the following code to the Peer2 form, replacing the RemoteHost property with your computer's name:

```
Private Sub Form_Load()

udpPeer2.RemoteHost = "ctx"
udpPeer2.RemotePort = 1002
udpPeer2.Bind 1001

End Sub

Private Sub txtSendData_Change()

udpPeer2.SendData txtSendData.Text

End Sub

Private Sub udpPeer2_DataArrival(ByVal bytesTotal As
Long)
Dim strData As String

udpPeer2.GetData strData
txtGetData.Text = strData

End Sub
```

E. Create an executable for both forms and run them. You should be able to chat back and forth between the two forms.

1. Change the application in the first example so that it allows the client to specify the computer that it will connect to.

2. Change the application in the second example so that it allows either peer to specify the computer that it will connect to.

11.2 ▪ *USING THE INTERNET TRANSFER CONTROL*

The Internet Transfer control makes it possible to take advantage of two of the most popular features of the Internet: HyperText Transfer Protocol (HTTP) and File Transfer Protocol (FTP). HTTP makes it possible to view and navigate Web pages, and FTP makes it possible to transfer files between computers.

With the amount of online data available today, these two protocols can make a great addition to a program. HTTP can retrieve graphics and text from a Web site, and FTP can download files for use in an application. These and many other uses can add to an application's capabilities with the addition of the Internet Transfer control.

TRANSFERRING DATA

Transferring data with the Internet Transfer control is actually quite simple. After adding the control to a project using the Components dialog box, you must ensure that you have access to the server you are trying to get data from and call the **OpenURL** method. That's it. The data is on its way. The following is the syntax for this method:

```
Inet.OpenURL(URL)
```

URL stands for Universal Resource Locator, which can be either an FTP site or a Web server address. This is a synchronous process, meaning that no other execution occurs until all of the data arrives. The **OpenURL** methods returns the data from the site, so you should set a string variable equal to this method call to retrieve the data:

```
strData = Inet.OpenURL(URL)
```

The Internet Transfer control does not interpret data from a Web site. Web pages are returned as their HTML code, which can then be parsed to find the location of graphics and other resources or could be used to display the Web page in a Web browser.

SETTING OPTIONS

The Internet Transfer control has several options that can be used to customize the behavior of the control. However, accepting the default values for these properties normally results in the desired behavior. Two notable exceptions are the **UserName** and **Password** properties. Some servers require a user name and password before allowing access to their resources. In order to access this type of resource, you must either set the **UserName** and **Password** properties at design time or prompt the user for them and set them at run time.

Other properties, such as the **AccessType** and **Protocol**, can adjust themselves according to their environment. For example the **OpenURL** method knows which protocol is being used by the prefix on the address that it is opening—ftp for FTP and http for HTTP. Because of this, there is no need to specifically set this property unless you want to limit access to only certain types of resources.

If you are knowledgeable in using the commands of FTP and HTTP, you can use the Internet Transfer control's Execute method to execute specific commands.

EXAMPLES

1. The following code for a Click event procedure fills a text box control with the HTML code of the Microsoft home page on the Web:

```
Private Sub cmdOpenURL_Click()
txtData.Text = Inet1.OpenURL("http://www.microsoft.com")
End Sub
```

2. The following code for a **Click** event procedure fills a text box control with the contents of the root of the Microsoft FTP site listed in HTML code:

```
Private Sub cmdOpenURL_Click()
txtData.Text = Inet1.OpenURL("ftp://ftp.microsoft.com")
End Sub
```

3. The following code for a **Click** event procedure fills a text box control with the text from the file disclaimer.txt on the Microsoft FTP site:

```
Private Sub cmdOpenURL_Click()
txtData.Text =
Inet1.OpenURL("ftp://ftp.microsoft.com/disclaimer.txt")
End Sub
```

EXERCISES

1. Create a form that lets the user supply a URL to be opened and displayed in a text box.

2. Alter the form created in the first exercise so that it prompts the user for a user name and password before opening up any site.

11.3 *USING THE MAPI CONTROLS*

The Messaging Application Program Interface (MAPI) is a standard used to make it easier to write applications that take advantage of email systems. Visual Basic provides two MAPI controls that can be used together to enable applications to take advantage of MAPI-compliant email systems, such as Microsoft Exchange. These controls must be added to a project using the Components dialog box.

A computer must be on a network that has a MAPI-compliant email system, such as Exchange, and have a MAPI-compliant email client installed for the Visual Basic MAPI controls to work properly.

USING THE MAPISESSION CONTROL

The MAPISession control is used to establish a connection to a MAPI mail system. This control logs an application on to the mail system. It uses the **UserName** and **Password** properties to provide access to a mail server. Alternatively, you can specify a **True** value for the **LogonUI** property, and the installed MAPI mail system prompts the user for a valid user name and password using its own dialog box.

If the underlying mail system does not have a logon dialog box, the LogonUI property is ignored.

The MAPISession control has several other properties that determine its behavior while logging on to the mail system. For example, a **True** value for the **NewSession** property causes the control to always start a new session with the mail server. Otherwise, the control would use an existing connection if one is available. Also, a **True** value for the **DownloadMail** property causes the control to automatically download all of a user's mail when a session is started.

The **SignOn** and **SignOff** methods start and end sessions when using the MAPISession control. When the **SignOn** method completes successfully, it returns a value to the **SessionID** property, which uniquely identifies that particular session. This property is set to 0 when there is no current connection. Use the **SignOff** method to end a session and disconnect from the mail server.

USING THE MAPIMESSAGES CONTROL

After connecting to a mail system with the MAPISession control, use the MAPIMessages control to send, receive, and read messages. Set the MAPIMessages control's **SessionID** equal to the MAPISession control's **SessionID** to send and receive messages using the connection established with the MAPISession control. Table 11-5 summarizes the methods of the MAPIMessages control that are used to manage messages.

Supply a True argument to the Send method to open the message in the MAPI client application before it is sent. This allows the user to review the message and then choose to send, save, or delete it.

Method	Description
Compose	Creates a new message
Copy	Copies the current message into a new message
Delete	Deletes the current message (mapMessageDelete), recipient (mapRecipientDelete), or attachment (mapAttachmentDelete) according to the argument supplied.
Fetch	Creates a message from selected messages in the Inbox.
Forward	Forwards a message.
Reply	Replies to a message.
ReplyAll	Replies to all message recipients.
Save	Saves the current message.
Send	Sends a message.

TABLE 11-5   *MAPIMessages Control Methods* ▼

The MAPIMessages control also has many properties that are used to specify message text, recipients, and so on. Table 11-6 summarizes these properties. This control has other properties that are used to manage messages and work with the address book. For more information on all of the properties for the MAPIMessages control, find that topic in the online help file.

Tip

Attach a file to a message by setting the AttachmentPathName property equal to the full path name and filename of a file. The other attachment properties can be used to reference and position the attachment within the message.

EXAMPLES

1. The following code connects an application to a MAPI mail server using the default settings of the MAPI client and requests that the MAPI system prompt the user for a user name and password:

```
mpsSession.LogonUI = True
mpsSession.SignOn
```

Property	Description
RecipDisplayName	The name displayed for a recipient (this is usually an alias used to represent an email address).
RecipAddress	The recipient's email address.
MsgSubject	The subject line of the message.
MsgNoteText	The body of the message.
AttachmentCount	The total number of attachments.
AttachmentIndex	Index of the current attachment.
AttachmentName	Name of the current attachment.
AttachmentPathName	Full path of the current attachment.
AttachmentPosition	Position of the current attachment in the message.
AttachmentType	File type of the current attachment.

TABLE 11-6 *MAPIMessages Control Message and Attachment Properties* ▼

2. The following code connects an application to a MAPI mail server, using an existing connection if one exists, and downloads all messages:

```
mpsSession.UserName = "GUEST"
mpsSession.Password = "ANONYMOUS"
mpsSession.NewSession = False
mpsSession.DownloadMail = True
mpsSession.SignOn
```

3. The following code connects to a mail server and sends a message:

```
mpsSession.SignOn
mpmMessage.SessionID = mpsSession.SessionID
mpmMessage.Compose
mpmMessage.RecipDisplayName = "John"
mpmMessage.RecipAddress = "SMTP:john@doe.com"
mpmMessage.MsgSubject = "Automated Accounting Report"
mpmMessage.MsgNoteText = "The accounting spread sheet is
attached."
mpmMessage.AttachmentPathName =
"C:\FINANCIAL\ACCOUNTING.XLS"
mpmMessage.Send
```

EXERCISES

1. Create a form that connects to a MAPI mail server at startup using default settings and lets the user create and send a message.

2. Add a text box and the necessary code to the form created in the previous exercise to make it possible for the user to add an attachment.

Mastery Skills Check

1. What are the two protocols that the Winsock control uses?

2. Do you always have to specify the protocol used when retrieving data?

3. What property do the MAPISession and MAPIMessages controls have in common?

12

Debugging Visual Basic Applications

A s you begin your search for the bugs that inevitably find their way into the best-planned programs, your first thought might be, "There's no way that code was even executed." Or, you might just wonder exactly what did happen when the code executed. For example, did the loop execute four times or was the **ElseIf** code block executed? At this point, you could use the time-honored tradition of placing a **MsgBox** statement into your code to verify if and what portions of code are being executed. However, Visual Basic offers a more elegant approach to performing this task.

Visual Basic provides a suite of tools, collectively known as a debugger, to help you find and eliminate logic errors in your code. Logic errors use correct syntax, so the compiler doesn't flag them. But they do produce erroneous results in your program. This chapter uses a very simple program to demonstrate the use of Visual Basic's most useful debugging tools.

Review
Skills Check

You should be able to correctly answer the following questions before beginning this chapter:

1. Should TCP or UDP be used for sending small amounts of data?

2. What method is used to open a resource on a Web server or FTP server?

3. What must be present for the MAPI controls to work?

12.1 SETTING BREAKPOINTS

To set breakpoints, you must first have a program that contains executable code. This chapter uses a program that scrambles text to demonstrate the use of breakpoints. Create a new Standard EXE project. Add two text box controls, two label controls, and two command buttons to the form. Change the properties of the objects in this project as listed in Table 12-1. Then, arrange the controls on the form so that it looks similar to Figure 12-1, with txtUnscrambled under lblUnscrambled and txtScrambled under lblScrambled.

Object	Property	Value
Form	Name	frmScrambler
	Caption	Scrambler
Command Button	Name	cmdUnscramble
	Caption	Unscramble
Command Button	Name	cmdScramble
	Caption	Scramble
Label	Name	lblUnscrambled
	Caption	Unscrambled
Label	Name	lblScrambled
	Caption	Scrambled
Text Box	Name	txtUnscrambled
	Text	
Text Box	Name	txtScrambled
	Text	

TABLE 12-1 *Control Properties for the Scrambler Program* ▼

FIGURE 12-1

The Scrambler program is presented on a single form
▼

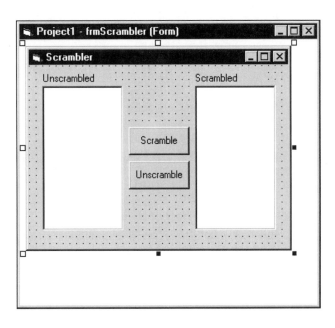

To complete the Scrambler program, add the following code to the form's code module:

```vb
Private Sub cmdScramble_Click()
Dim strTemp As String

strTemp = RearrangeText(txtUnscrambled.Text, True)
txtScrambled.Text = strTemp

End Sub


Private Sub cmdUnscramble_Click()
Dim strTemp As String

strTemp = RearrangeText(txtScrambled.Text, False)
txtUnscrambled.Text = strTemp

End Sub


Private Function RearrangeText(strText As String, blnScramble _
As Boolean) As String
Dim strChar As String
Dim strNewText As String
Dim i As Long
Dim intStringLength As Integer

intStringLength = Len(strText)

For i = 1 To intStringLength

    strChar = GetChar(strText, i)
    intChar = Asc(strChar)

    If blnScramble Then
        intChar = intChar + 20
    ElseIf Not blnScramble Then
        intChar = intChar - 20
    End If

    strChar = Chr(intChar)
    strNewText = strNewText & strChar
```

```
Next

RearrangeText = strNewText

End Function


Private Function GetChar(strText As String, intLocation As
Long) As String

GetChar = Mid(strText, (intLocation), 1)

End Function
```

The first debugger tool that you should master is the breakpoint. A breakpoint is a line of code that should halt the execution of the code right before it is to be executed. Only one breakpoint can be set for each individual line of code, but you can set a breakpoint on as many lines of code as you wish. Because each line of code is either a breakpoint or it isn't, you toggle breakpoints on and off (all breakpoints are initially off).

Note — *Only lines that contain code can have their breakpoint toggled on. If you delete the code from a line that has a breakpoint, the breakpoint is automatically toggled off when you move from that line.*

To set a breakpoint in the Scrambler program, complete the following steps:

1. Open the Code window for frmScrambler.
2. Place the cursor in the first line of code in the **Click** event procedure of cmdScramble.
3. Choose Toggle Breakpoint from the Debug menu or press F9.

After completing these steps, the Code window should look similar to Figure 12-2. Notice that a circle appears in the margin next to the line and the line becomes highlighted. By default, the circle and the highlight are red, but you can change that in the Options dialog box.

Tip — *Click once in the margin of the Code window next to a line of code to toggle the breakpoint for that line of code.*

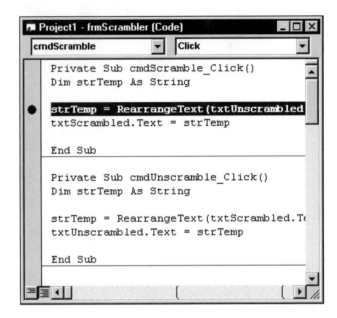

FIGURE 12-2

The margin of the Code window indicates which breakpoints have been toggled on
▼

Now, run the program and click the Scramble button. Before the line of code is executed, the execution of the program is halted and you are returned to the Visual Basic environment in debug mode. The next line to be executed is displayed in the Code window. It is highlighted with an arrow next to it in the margin, as shown in Figure 12-3.

At this point, you can click the Run button to continue the normal execution of the code or click the Stop button to close the program and return to the Visual Basic design environment. Or, as you will learn in the next section, you can step through the code, executing one line at a time. For now, click the Stop button.

Tip

To quickly toggle all breakpoints off, choose Clear All Breakpoints from the Debug menu or press CTRL-SHIFT-F9.

EXAMPLES

1. Figure 12-4 shows a code block with two breakpoints toggled on.

2. Figure 12-5 shows two separate procedures with breakpoints toggled on.

3. Figure 12-6 shows two lines of code in a row with their breakpoints toggled on.

EXERCISES

---

1. Toggle the breakpoint on for the line of code for the GetChar function of the Scrambler program.

2. Toggle the breakpoint on for the first line of code in the RearrangeText function.

3. Toggle the breakpoint on for the two statements in the If...Then statement of the RearrangeText function.

4. Toggle the breakpoint off for the first line of code in the RearrangeText function.

5. Toggle all of the breakpoints off for the Scrambler program.

FIGURE 12-3

The margin of the Code window indicates which line of code is to be executed next

▼

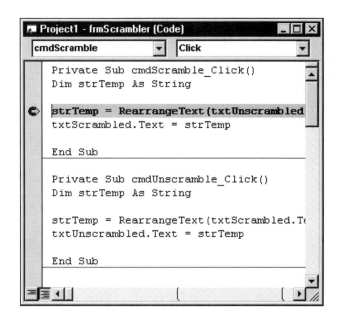

FIGURE 12-4

Multiple breakpoints can be set within a single block of code
▼

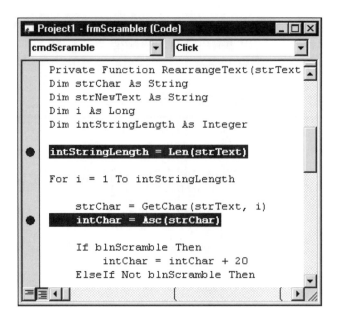

```
Private Function RearrangeText(strText
Dim strChar As String
Dim strNewText As String
Dim i As Long
Dim intStringLength As Integer

intStringLength = Len(strText)

For i = 1 To intStringLength

    strChar = GetChar(strText, i)
    intChar = Asc(strChar)

    If blnScramble Then
        intChar = intChar + 20
    ElseIf Not blnScramble Then
```

FIGURE 12-5

More than one procedure can contain a breakpoint
▼

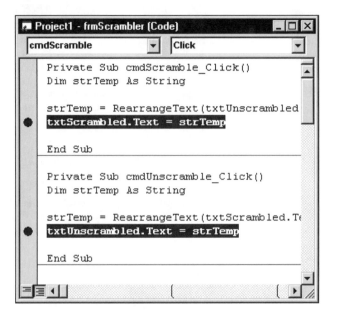

```
Private Sub cmdScramble_Click()
Dim strTemp As String

strTemp = RearrangeText(txtUnscrambled
txtScrambled.Text = strTemp

End Sub

Private Sub cmdUnscramble_Click()
Dim strTemp As String

strTemp = RearrangeText(txtScrambled.Te
txtUnscrambled.Text = strTemp

End Sub
```

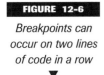

FIGURE 12-6

Breakpoints can
occur on two lines
of code in a row
▼

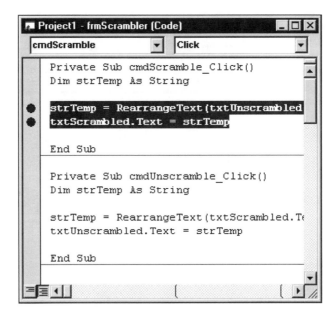

12.2 **S**_TEPPING THROUGH CODE_

Halting the execution of your code on specified lines of code can go a
long way towards finding many problems in a program. However, if
you are trying to follow the execution path that the program follows,
breakpoints become a cumbersome way of accomplishing this goal.
You would have to toggle the breakpoint on for nearly every line of
code in your program to use breakpoints to step through the execution
of each line of code in your program.

Visual Basic provides several commands for stepping through code.
These commands are available through the Debug menu and the
Debug toolbar. Choose View, Toolbars, Debug to display the Debug
toolbar, which is shown in Figure 12-7. The following sections discuss
the different ways to step through code.

STEPPING INTO CODE

Click the Step Into button to execute the current line of code. If that
line of code calls another procedure, the first line of that procedure is

FIGURE 12-7

The Debug toolbar provides access to commands from several different Visual Basic menus

▼

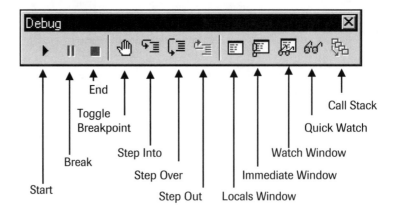

displayed. For example, toggle the breakpoint on for the following line of the RearrangeText function in the Scrambler program:

```
intStringLength = Len(strText)
```

Now, run the project. Enter some unscrambled text (for example, "Visual Basic") and click the Scramble button. Execution halts immediately before this line of code executes. Click the Step Into button until the next line of code to execute is the following, which calls the GetChar function:

```
strChar = GetChar(strText, i)
```

Press F8 to execute the Step Into command using the keyboard.

Clicking the Step Into button causes the execution of the program in the debugger to step into the execution of the GetChar function. So, that is the next piece of code executed.

The Step Into command can also be used to run a project in Visual Basic.

STEPPING OVER CODE

If you are debugging a procedure that calls many different procedures or functions—or even calls one large procedure or function—you may not want to step into a code statement. Instead, you may want to step over it. Perform the same actions as in the previous section, but click the Step Over button to execute lines of code. When you get to the line of code that calls the GetChar function, it executes without stepping into the function.

Press SHIFT-F8 to execute the Step Over command using the keyboard.

Remember that you can toggle breakpoints on in more than one procedure. So if you want to use the Step Over command to execute lines of code and you are interested in viewing the execution of a procedure that is called, you can simply toggle breakpoints on in both procedures.

STEPPING OUT OF CODE

You may find yourself stepping through a procedure that you no longer have any interest in. For example, you may have already observed what you were interested in, or you may have stepped into it by accident. If you want to resume the execution of the program, you can click the Run button. But if you just want to step out of the current procedure into the procedure that called it, click the Step Out button.

Press CTRL-SHIFT-F8 to execute the Step Out command using the keyboard.

Experiment with using the Step Out command while executing the Scrambler program. In particular, Step Out of the execution until all of the code has executed. Notice that you simply remain in the debugger. At this point you could switch to the application and continue, or you could click the Break button and then the Run button to continue using the program. If you simply switch back to the program, you are returned to the debugger the next time any code is executed.

USING OTHER OPTIONS FOR STEPPING THROUGH CODE

In addition to the most commonly used step commands, Visual Basic provides several additional ways to step through code. The following summarizes each of these methods, which are available using the Debug menu:

▼ Run To Cursor—Executes code up to the line of code that the cursor is on

▼ Set Next Statement—Moves the execution of the program to the line of code that the cursor is on

▼ Show Next Statement—Moves the debugger to the next line of code to be executed

You can also find out what code is being executed by viewing the call stack. The call stack is a list of the procedures executing. It is sorted by the order in which the procedures are called. Click the Call Stack button to view the Call Stack dialog box shown in Figure 12-8.

Select a function and click the Show button to view that function. This doesn't affect the execution point of the program. You can also

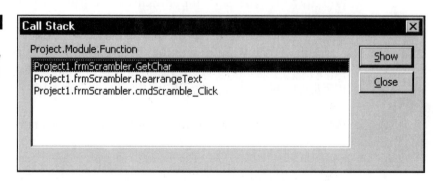

FIGURE 12-8

The Call Stack shows the order in which procedures are called

▼

double-click a function to view it. Click the Close button when you are finished viewing the procedures listed in the Call Stack dialog box.

EXAMPLES

1. Executing the Step Into command while in design mode runs the current project.

2. Executing the Run To Cursor command executes code until the execution point reaches the line of code that the cursor is currently on.

3. Executing the Step Into command always executes the next line of code.

EXERCISES

1. What happens when the Step Into command is executed if the current line of code calls another procedure?

2. What happens when the Step Over command is executed if the current line of code calls another procedure?

3. What happens when the Step Out command is executed if the current line of code calls another procedure?

12.3 *WATCHING VARIABLES*

If you have mastered the previous sections of this chapter, you now know how to halt the execution of a program on any line of code. You also know how to step through code, navigating into and out of procedures at will as you go. These techniques can tell you a lot about the execution of your code, but you need more information to be able to find errors in code that might occur in your data.

To this point, you haven't been able to view the values stored in the variables of your program. The following sections each discuss methods for viewing the values that are stored in the variables of your program and the properties of the controls that your program contains. This information, combined with the ability to halt execution and step through code, gives you the ability to locate and fix almost any bug you might encounter.

USING THE IMMEDIATE WINDOW

The Immediate window is the simplest of the three windows available for viewing the values that variables and properties contain. As with the other windows, it also lets you set these values. This window also gives you added capability of calling procedures directly from within the window.

The most basic piece of information you want to know about a variable is what value it holds. This simple fact is the key to finding almost every bug that occurs in an application.

Use the **Print** command in the Immediate window to find out what value a variable or property holds, as in the following:

```
Print varName
```

You can use a single question mark (?) instead of the Print command in the Immediate window to get the exact same results.

Print can also display the value contained in controls' properties. In Figure 12-9, the Immediate window displays the values for the strChar and intChar variables. It also shows the **Text** property of the txtUnscrambled control.

In addition to viewing the value of variables and properties, you can assign values to variables and properties. Assign values using the following syntax:

```
variable | property = newvalue
```

Figure 12-10 shows the Immediate window after it was used to change the **Caption** of Scrambler's main form to Changed. The effect of this change is immediate.

You can call other procedures or functions built into Visual Basic or your program while assigning values to variables and properties. You can even just call a procedure to see if it works properly (without assigning a value to anything).

FIGURE 12-9

The Immediate window lets you analyze variables and properties

▼

```
Immediate
Print strChar
T
?intChar
 84
|
```

USING THE WATCHES WINDOW

The Immediate window gives you access to only the most basic information about a variable or property—its value. This is all you probably need to debug simple applications, but as your applications become more complex so do your needs for information about variable and property values. The Watches window provides you with this extra information.

FIGURE 12-10

Values are assigned without delay in the Immediate window

▼

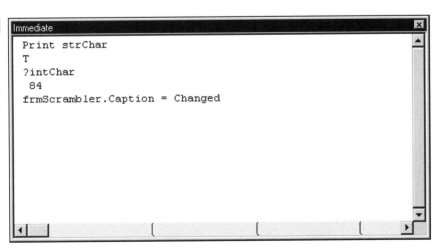

```
Immediate
 Print strChar
 T
 ?intChar
  84
 frmScrambler.Caption = Changed
```

Click the Watch Window button to open the Watches window. This window is normally docked at the bottom of the Visual Basic environment, but it can also be floating, as shown in Figure 12-11.

The Watches window displays information in a tabular format, with one row for each expression being watched. Table 12-2 summarizes the information displayed in each column of the Watches window.

You can add a watch using the Watches window. Right-click on the Watches list and choose Add Watch from the shortcut menu to open the Add Watch dialog box, which is shown in Figure 12-12.

The expression to be watched is added at the top of this dialog box. You must also specify the context in which this expression should be watched by specifying if the expression is for a single procedure or all procedures—as well as specifying a single module or all modules. Many different procedures might use the exact same variable name, and different modules can use the same name for module-level variables. So without the context information, Visual Basic can't add the watch.

The expression for a watch can be a variable or a formula that contains a variable. If the formula uses a comparison operator ($<$, $>$, $=$), the expression evaluates to a True or False value based on the results of the comparison.

The Add Watch dialog box defaults to the context and variable that the cursor is in when you open the dialog box. You can also place the cursor in a variable and click the Quick Watch button on the Debug

FIGURE 12-11
The Watches window ▼

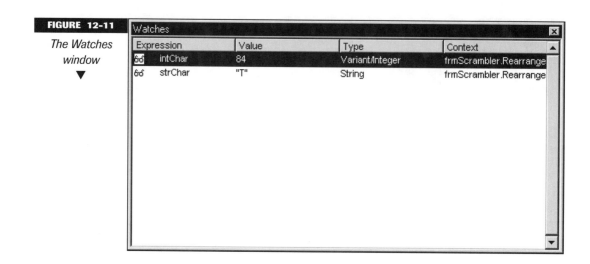

Column	Description
Expression	Displays the expression to be evaluated. This can be a variable, property, or any valid expression, such as intValue = 1, blnValue = False, or (lngValue * .75).
Value	Displays the value that the expression in the Expression column evaluates to. This is normally the value of a variable or property, but it can also indicate if an expression is True. For example, if intValue actually contained the value 1 and the expression was intValue = 1, then this column would display True.
Type	Displays the data type for the expression.
Context	Displays the context, or scope, of the expression.

TABLE 12-2   *Information Displayed by the Watches Window* ▼

toolbar to quickly view a value. Click the Add button in the Quick Watch dialog box to add the expression to the Watches window.

As shown in Figure 12-12, Visual Basic allows three types of watches to be added. The following is a brief description of each:

▼   Watch Expression—Displays the value of the expression in the Watches window

FIGURE 12-12

Specify what to watch and how to watch it in the Add Watch dialog box

▼

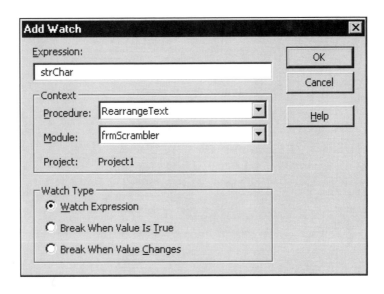

▼ Break When Value Is True—Displays the value of the expression in the Watches window and halts execution of the program when the expression evaluates to **True**

▼ Break When Value Changes—Displays the value of the expression in the Watches window and halts execution of the program when the value changes

Right-click on an expression in the Watches window and choose Edit Watch from the shortcut menu to change the watch. You can also choose Delete Watch from this shortcut menu or click the Delete button in the Edit Watch dialog box (see Figure 12-13) to remove the watch.

USING THE LOCALS WINDOW

The Locals window draws its name from the data that it displays. This window shows all of the declared variables—including properties—for the current procedure and the values of those variables. In

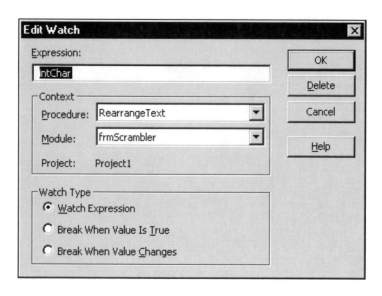

FIGURE 12-13

The Edit Watch dialog box allows watches to be changed or removed

▼

other words, it shows all of the variables that are local to the current procedure.

Click the Locals Window button on the Debug toolbar to open the Locals window. In design mode, this window is empty. At run time, this window displays all of the variables local to the current procedure, their values, and their types, as shown in Figure 12-14. The text box at the top of the Locals window shows the current procedure. As you step through code, the variables listed and their values change according to the processing of the program.

Tip

Click the button to the right of the text box displaying the current procedure to view the Call Stack window. Then, you can choose a different procedure and view that procedure's variables in the Locals window.

The Locals window lists all variables that have subvariables with a plus sign next to them. Click the plus sign to expand the tree and view the subvariables. You can change the value of a variable by clicking on the expression and then clicking on the value. Once the value is in edit mode, enter a new value and press the ENTER key or move to a different expression to change the value.

FIGURE 12-14

The Locals window automatically shows information that you must add manually to the Watches window

▼

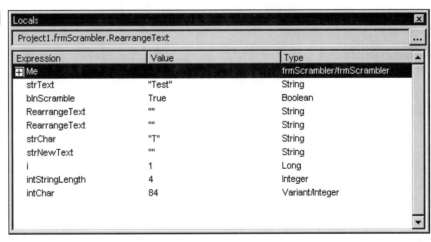

Expression	Value	Type
⊞ Me		frmScrambler/frmScrambler
strText	"Test"	String
blnScramble	True	Boolean
RearrangeText	""	String
RearrangeText	""	String
strChar	"T"	String
strNewText	""	String
i	1	Long
intStringLength	4	Integer
intChar	84	Variant/Integer

Locals

Project1.frmScrambler.RearrangeText

EXAMPLES

1. To show the value of the variable intNumber in the Immediate window, enter either of the following commands into the Immediate window:

```
Print intNumber
?intNumber
```

2. To add a watch for a global variable name gintNumber, use the settings for the Add Watch dialog box shown in Figure 12-15.

3. Figure 12-16 displays a Locals window for the Scrambler program. The expression Me refers to frmScrambler. To view the types of controls on this form, expand the Me expression and then expand the Controls expression. The controls are listed as Item 1, Item 2, and so on. The Type column indicates what type of control each item is, as shown in Figure 12-16.

EXERCISES

1. Run the GetChar function from the Immediate window.

2. Add a watch to a variable using the Quick Watch button.

3. Change the value for a variable using the Locals window.

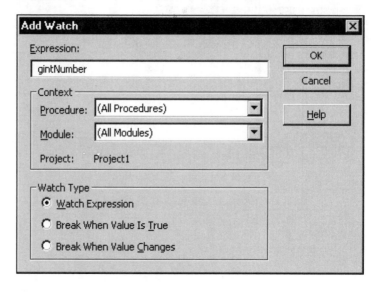

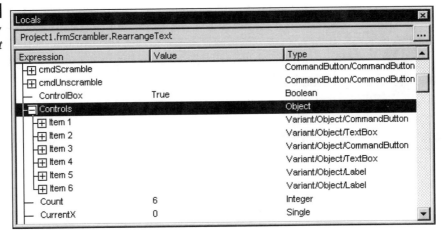

Locals		
Project1.frmScrambler.RearrangeText		...
Expression	Value	Type
⊞ cmdScramble		CommandButton/CommandButton
⊞ cmdUnscramble		CommandButton/CommandButton
— ControlBox	True	Boolean
⊟ Controls		Object
⊞ Item 1		Variant/Object/CommandButton
⊞ Item 2		Variant/Object/TextBox
⊞ Item 3		Variant/Object/CommandButton
⊞ Item 4		Variant/Object/TextBox
⊞ Item 5		Variant/Object/Label
⊞ Item 6		Variant/Object/Label
— Count	6	Integer
— CurrentX	0	Single

12.4 USING THE DEBUG OBJECT

Visual Basic provides the **Debug** object to perform basic debug actions.
It can send output to the Immediate window, and it can halt the
execution of a program. The following sections describe the methods of
the **Debug** object used to perform these tasks.

USING THE PRINT METHOD

As discussed in the previous section, you can use the **Print** command
in the Immediate window to view the values stored in variables and
properties. The **Debug** object also allows you to print these values to
the Immediate window, but it doesn't require you to halt the execution
of the program to do so.

The **Print** method of the **Debug** object prints data directly to the
Immediate window. You place a call to the **Print** method using the
following syntax directly in your procedure:

```
Debug.Print output
```

When this line executes, output is printed in the Immediate window.
Output can be a variable, property, or Visual Basic expression. If the
output contains more than one expression, either spaces or semicolons

separate them. Any data that requires formatting (such as numbers and dates) is automatically formatted using the settings for the computer.

Boolean variables print as True or False, and errors print the error code preceded by the word Error.

USING THE ASSERT METHOD

The **Debug** object has a second method that allows you to conditionally halt the execution of a program. When using the **Assert** method, you supply a **Boolean** expression as the only argument. If the expression evaluates to **False**, the execution of the program halts on the line that called the **Assert** method. Otherwise, processing continues as normal. The following is the syntax for the **Assert** method:

```
Debug.Assert booleanexpression
```

The **Boolean** expression can contain several parts, but they must all evaluate to **True** or **False**. Use the **And** and **Or** keywords to join the different **Boolean** expressions into a single expression that evaluates to **True** or **False**.

Debug.Assert method calls only work in the design environment. Visual Basic does not include these in any executables that are created.

EXAMPLES

1. The following code shows how you could print the uncoded characters in the RearrangeText function and then print the coded character, including a space in between each pair:

```
Private Function RearrangeText(strText As String,
blnScramble As Boolean) As String
Dim strChar As String
Dim strNewText As String
Dim i As Long
Dim intStringLength As Integer

intStringLength = Len(strText)
```

```
For i = 1 To intStringLength

    strChar = GetChar(strText, i)
    intChar = Asc(strChar)

    If blnScramble Then
        intChar = intChar + 20
    ElseIf Not blnScramble Then
        intChar = intChar - 20
    End If

    Debug.Print "Uncoded: "; strChar

    strChar = Chr(intChar)
    strNewText = strNewText & strChar

    Debug.Print "Coded: "; strChar
    Debug.Print

Next

RearrangeText = strNewText

End Function
```

2. The following code shows how you could add **Debug.Assert** method calls to the RearrangeText function to check for certain situations:

```
Private Function RearrangeText(strText As String,
blnScramble As Boolean) As String
Dim strChar As String
Dim strNewText As String
Dim i As Long
Dim intStringLength As Integer

intStringLength = Len(strText)

For i = 1 To intStringLength

    strChar = GetChar(strText, i)
    intChar = Asc(strChar)

    Debug.Assert strChar <> "A"

    If blnScramble Then
```

```
        intChar = intChar + 20
    ElseIf Not blnScramble Then
        intChar = intChar - 20
    End If

    Debug.Assert intChar < 95

    strChar = Chr(intChar)
    strNewText = strNewText & strChar

  Next

  RearrangeText = strNewText

End Function
```

EXERCISES

1. Add code to the GetChar function that prints the text that the character is being drawn from, the position it should be drawn from, and the character that is going to be returned.

2. Add code to the RearrangeText function that stops execution if a space character is encountered.

Mastery
Skills Check

1. What is the quickest way to toggle off all of the breakpoints in a module?

2. If you are stepping through the code of procedure B that was called by procedure A, how do you execute the line of code in procedure A after the line that called the procedure B?

3. Can you change the values of variables and properties in the Immediate window?

4. What effect do calls to **Debug.Assert** have on executable files that are distributed to users?

13

Handling Errors

chapter objectives

13.1 Dealing with Errors

13.2 Using the Resume Statement

13.3 Using the Err Object

A fter reading and hopefully using this entire book, you should now be able to develop at least simple Visual Basic applications. As you develop more applications, your skills will increase and so will the complexity of your programs. These more complex programs normally provide more functionality to their users, but they also introduce more opportunities for errors to occur. The last chapter showed you how to find errors in the design environment; this chapter shows you how to plan for them and handle them in the run-time environment.

Things that tell you a program is having a problem are very confusing to the average user of computer programs. They don't know how to—and probably don't want to—read a cryptic error message. For this reason, well-planned Visual Basic applications that place a premium on operating in a continuous manner, without displaying unpredictable behavior to users, employ some type of error handling.

The following sections describe the Visual Basic code required to trap and handle run-time errors. This code is very similar from one procedure to another and should become second nature to you after you get into the habit of adding it to all of your procedures. After reading this chapter, you should incorporate error handling into all of your applications to prevent them from shutting down abruptly or providing users with confusing messages.

Review

Skills Check

You should be able to correctly answer the following questions before beginning this chapter:

1. On which line of code does a breakpoint cause the execution of code to be halted?

2. How would you cause a line of code to be executed without stepping into any procedures called from that line of code?

3. Does the Locals window only display the values for variables in the currently executing procedure?

4. What are the two methods of the **Debug** object, and what do they do?

13.1 ▰ **D**EALING WITH ERRORS

Visual Basic provides many tools for handling run-time errors. You must add code to the procedures of your application to take advantage of these tools. This added code detects when errors occur and handles them in a fashion that you determine to be best for the users of your application. You might anticipate some of these errors, but the true power of handling run-time errors comes from its ability to handle unanticipated errors without losing data or confusing the user. After dealing with the error, error handling code helps the program continue its normal operation.

This sounds like a repetitive task that you might want to create a single procedure to handle. Unfortunately, all Visual Basic errors are handled locally. In other words, each procedure must have its own error handling code. You can, however, create a generic error handling routine that the error handling code of each procedure could call. Regardless of how you decide to handle it, each of your procedures should contain code that does the following tasks:

1. Trap errors

2. Handle errors

3. Continue program execution

Caution

If an error occurs in a procedure with no error handling that was called by another procedure, the error is passed to the calling procedure. To avoid confusion as to exactly where an error is occurring, all procedures should contain error handling code.

TRAPPING ERRORS

Visual Basic executables immediately alert users when an error occurs. As discussed previously, the default error messages provided are usually not very intuitive for the average user. Also, the user is normally forced to stop execution of the program because of the error.

Trapping errors is the process of detecting and intercepting errors before the user is alerted to them. A single line of code is all that is required to trap an error, although more lines are required to actually handle the error. The **On Error** statement traps errors and uses the following syntax:

```
On Error Goto line
```

This statement causes execution of the program to move to the point in the procedure where the line parameter is. The line parameter can specify either a line label or line number. See the following section for an example of a line label.

A simpler variation of the **On Error** statement causes the next line after the line that caused the error to execute following the error. This is useful when trapped errors require no special handling and the flow of the program's execution isn't affected. The following is the syntax for using the **On Error** statement in this manner:

```
On Error Resume Next
```

Use the On Error Statement with the following syntax to disable error handling in a procedure: On Error GoTo 0

HANDLING ERRORS

The **On Error** statement redirects execution of your program into a procedure's error handler when an error occurs. It is within the error handler that processing occurs to actually handle and deal with the error. The first example in the Examples section shows a basic framework for a procedure with an error handler.

An error handler can call other procedures. So, you could write generic error handlers for similar procedures and have all of the code in a single procedure—making it easier to maintain.

The processing occurs after the **On Error** statement to make sure that all possible errors are trapped. To prevent the error handling routine from being executed when there are no errors, an **Exit Sub** is added right before the error handler. Error handling code frequently uses information from the **Err** object, which is discussed in the "Using the Err Object" section.

In a procedure that contains an error handler, execution is redirected to the error handler any time that an error occurs. If another error occurs within the error handler, Visual Basic then behaves as it would have without the error handler—displaying the default error message.

REDIRECTING THE PROGRAM FLOW

Code that is added to handle the processing of an error should also direct the execution of the program after the error has been taken care of. The "Using the Resume Statement" section discusses the redirecting of a program's execution after handling an error.

EXAMPLES

1. The following shows a basic framework for a procedure with an error handler. This framework is incomplete, however. See the "Using the Resume Statement" section on how to complete this basic framework.

```
Private Sub ErrorExample()

On Error GoTo ErrorHandler

'Do Some Processing

Exit Sub

ErrorHandler:
    MsgBox Err.Description

End Sub
```

2. The following shows a procedure that continues execution on the line after the line of code that caused an error:

```
Private Sub ErrorExample()

On Error Resume Next

'Do Some Processing

Exit Sub
```

3. The following shows a procedure that disables error handling:

```
Private Sub ErrorExample()

On Error Resume Next

On Error GoTo 0

'Do Some Processing

Exit Sub
```

EXERCISES

1. Add an error handler to any procedure. Then, read the following section to see how to complete the error handler

2. Add an error handler to any procedure that resumes execution on the line following the line of code that caused an error.

13.2 **U**SING THE RESUME STATEMENT

After an error has been handled, the execution of the program needs to continue in an orderly fashion. That was the whole reason for handling the error yourself instead of accepting the default Visual Basic behavior. In addition, Visual Basic is left in a sort of error limbo unless a **Resume** statement is used to specifically restart the normal flow of execution in a program.

The End Sub statement at the end of a procedure would terminate the procedure after an error handler had completed its task, but the Err object and the Visual Basic environment would not be reset. If this happens, the system begins to behave unpredictably.

The **Resume** statement is used to reset the Visual Basic program's environment and can also redirect programming to perform specific tasks. The following sections discuss the variations of the **Resume** statement.

USING RESUME LABEL

Just as the **On Error** statement sends the flow of execution into an error handler using a label, the error handler can send the flow of execution back into a procedure using a label. The syntax for this use of the **Resume** statement is as follows:

```
Resume label
```

The label must appear in the same procedure; the **Resume** statement can't send execution into a different procedure. A procedure could have several labels used for continuing processing after an error, but that can indicate that the procedure needs to be split into multiple smaller and more focused procedures.

The code that execution is redirected to by the error handler might simply stop the execution of the procedure. In some situations, the statements following the redirection label may do more than simply end the procedure. For example, the code might set variables, close database connections or files, and so on.

USING RESUME NEXT

Some procedures may have errors that need to be handled but don't necessarily affect the processing being done in the procedure. In this case, the procedure would normally need to continue execution starting at the line immediately after the line that caused the error. The following statement in the error handler causes that to happen:

```
Resume Next
```

If any processing occurs in the procedure that is adversely affected by any errors that occur, the error handler should take care of the situation before using the **Resume Next** statement. Otherwise, the error will still cause unpredictable behavior in the application.

USING RESUME

Certain procedures might require that they complete their execution regardless of the occurrence of any errors. For example, financial or medical applications might contain procedures that deal with very important information and require errors to be handled and execution of the entire procedure to run to completion. For these situations, the **Resume** statement is used without any other keywords:

```
Resume
```

This causes the execution of the program to continue starting with the line that caused the error. Assuming that the error handler corrected the circumstances that caused the error, the procedure should then be able to run to completion.

Caution

The Resume statement by itself redirects program flow to the line that caused the error. If the error handler hasn't resolved the problem, the error will occur again, causing an endless loop.

EXAMPLES

1. The following procedure contains an error handler that redirects execution using a label:

```
Private Sub ErrorExample()

On Error GoTo ErrorHandler

'Do Some Processing

ExitProcedure:
Exit Sub

ErrorHandler:
    MsgBox Err.Description
    Resume ExitProcedure

End Sub
```

2. The following procedure redirects program flow to the next line after the line that caused an error after the error handler runs. So if an error occurs while executing intSum = 1 + 1, the execution resumes at intSum = 2 + 2 after the error handler runs.

```
Private Sub ErrorExample()
Dim intSum As Integer

On Error GoTo ErrorHandler

intSum = 1 + 1
intSum = 2 + 2
intSum = 3 + 3

ExitProcedure:
Exit Sub

ErrorHandler:
    MsgBox Err.Description
    Resume Next

End Sub
```

3. The following procedure redirects program flow to the line that
   caused an error after the error handler runs. So if an error occurs
   while executing intSum = 1 + 1, the execution resumes at
   intSum = 1 + 1 after the error handler runs.

```
Private Sub ErrorExample()
Dim intSum As Integer

On Error GoTo ErrorHandler

intSum = 1 + 1
intSum = 2 + 2
intSum = 3 + 3

ExitProcedure:
Exit Sub

ErrorHandler:
    MsgBox Err.Description
    Resume

End Sub
```

EXERCISES

1. Write a procedure that increments a counter to 100. Include an error handler that halts execution of the program if the counter is greater than 50 when the error occurs and continues execution if the counter is 50 or less when the error occurs.

2. Alter the procedure from the previous example so that it continues execution on the line after the line that caused an error.

13.3   USING THE ERR OBJECT

Any time that an error occurs in Visual Basic code, the **Err** object is immediately activated. The **Err** object is a special object designed specifically for dealing with errors. It has properties and methods that help make error handling easier. This information also makes it easier to identify the source of an error.

The Err object is created by Visual Basic and has a global scope. You don't have to write any code that creates an Err object or worry about it not being available to any procedures.

USING ERR OBJECT PROPERTIES

The **Err** object has several properties that are populated when an error occurs. These properties can be used to determine the best way to handle a situation. For example, you could use these properties to handle different errors in distinct ways. The following sections discuss the most commonly used properties of the **Err** object.

Err.Description

The **Description** property of the **Err** object contains a brief description of the error that has occurred. Many times, this is not the message that you want to show to users of your application. However, it can be used for errors that you couldn't anticipate or don't want to specifically handle.

Err.Number

The **Number** property of the **Err** object contains the number for a specific error. Several errors might be similar enough to have the same description, but each would have its own number. For example, a procedure might have three errors that you plan for and specifically want to handle. To do this, you would check for the three error numbers and process them accordingly. Then, you could also add some other code to handle any other situation that falls outside of the three specifically handled errors.

The Number property of the Err object can be used to determine exactly what happened in an application and display a very specific message to the user, instead of using the default description provided by Visual Basic.

Err.Source

Visual Basic has the ability to use the resources of other applications in its procedures. This is a very powerful tool, but it can cause some difficulty when handling errors. Other programs have their own set of error codes that most likely don't match up with Visual Basic's own error numbers. To be able to handle error codes coming from different applications, the **Err** object has a **Source** property.

The **Source** property contains the source of an error. For example, if you take advantage of Microsoft Word's resources in your code and an error is generated by an action performed in a Word application, the **Err** object is activated and the **Source** property is set to Word.Application.

Errors that occur in a standard module have a source equal to the project name; errors that occur in a class module have a source equal to the project name and class name (project.class).

USING ERR OBJECT METHODS

Situations may arise where you need to generate an error of your own. If so, you need to use the **Raise** method of the **Err** object. Calling this method generates a run-time error in a procedure. The following sections contain more information on the **Raise** method and the **Clear** method of the **Err** object.

Err.Raise

The **Err** object provides the **Raise** method to allow programmers to generate their own run-time errors. Many things could cause this to be necessary, such as a missing file, lost network connection, or bad data. Table 13-1 describes the arguments of the **Raise** method. The **Raise** method has the following syntax:

```
Err.Raise number, source, description, helpfile, helpcontext
```

When defining the error number for a class module, it should always be added to the constant vbObjectError, such as vbObjectError + 513.

If you use the **Raise** method and do not specify any of the optional properties, those properties will retain any previous settings they contained. This normally won't be a problem, but if you ever find that you need to reset the properties of the **Err** object, you can use the **Clear** method, which the following section discusses.

Argument	Description
Number	This is the only argument required; all others are optional. It is a Long data type that identifies the error. Visual Basic uses numbers 0 through 512, but all others up to 65,535 are available as user-defined errors.
Source	Specifies the object that generated the error. Should follow the project.class source naming convention. Programmatic ID is used if no source is provided.
Description	Describes the error that has occurred. If no description is given, the method attempts to map the error number to a defined Visual Basic error and use that description. Otherwise, the method places "Application-defined or object-defined error" in this property.
Helpfile	Path to a helpfile.
Helpcontext	Context ID identifying a specific topic in the help file specified in the helpfile property.

TABLE 13-1 *Arguments for the Raise Method of Err Object* ▼

Err.Clear

To clear all of the properties of the **Err** object, use the **Clear** method. This method is normally called automatically. For example, the **Clear** method is automatically called in any of the following situations:

▼ Any **Resume** statement

▼ Any time the procedure that generated the error is exited

▼ Any **On Error** statement

The **Clear** method of the **Err** object has the following syntax:

```
Err.Clear
```

EXAMPLES

1. The following procedure shows how to provide the user with a message that combines the error number and error description provided by the **Err** object:

```
Private Sub ErrorExample()

On Error GoTo ErrorHandler

'Do Some Processing

ExitProcedure:
'Perform Cleanup
Exit Sub

ErrorHandler:
    MsgBox Err.Number & " " & Err.Description
    Resume ExitProcedure

End Sub
```

2. The following procedure shows how to handle different types of errors by using the **Number** property of the **Err** object. These error numbers can be found in the Visual Basic help file by searching for the topic "Trappable Errors."

```
Private Sub ErrorExample()

On Error GoTo ErrorHandler

'Do Some Processing
```

```
ExitProcedure:
'Perform Cleanup
Exit Sub

ErrorHandler:
     Select Case Err.Number
          Case 7 'Out Of Memory
               'Process Error
          Case 11 'Division By Zero
               'Process Error
          Case 53 'File Not Found
               'Process Error
          Case Else 'Unanticipated Error
               MsgBox Err.Number _
                  & " Generated by " _
                  & Err.Source _
                  & ": " & Err.Description
               Resume ExitProcedure
          End Select
End Sub
```

3. The following statement raises an error in an application:

```
Err.Raise 513, "MyProject.MyClass", "This is my error."
```

4. The following statement raises the "Out Of Memory" error:

```
Err.Raise 7
```

EXERCISES

1. Write a function called ErrorMessage that concatenates the error number, description, and source into a string and then returns the string.

2. Write a statement that raises an error for a class called Free that is in a project called Error.

3. Write a statement that raises a "File Not Found" error.

Mastery
Skills Check

1. What statement is used to trap errors?

2. What statement is used to redirect the flow of execution after an error is handled?

3. What is the syntax for creating an **Err** object?

A

Answers

CHAPTER 1

1.1 EXERCISES

1. Run Visual Basic from the Start menu and double-click the ActiveX Control in the New tab of the New Project dialog box.

2. Choose Options from the Tools menu. Click the Environment tab of the Options dialog box and select Create default project option button. Finally, click the OK button to put the change into effect.

3. Click the Close button in the Visual Basic title bar. If asked if you would like to save your changes, click the No button.

1.2 EXERCISES

1. Click the Close button on the Project Explorer's title bar.

2. Press CTRL + R.

3. Right-click on the Project Explorer and choose Dockable from the shortcut menu, so that the Dockable option is unchecked.

4. Make the Project Explorer undockable and click its Maximize button.

5. Click the Project Explorer's Restore button.

6. Right-click on the Project Explorer and choose Dockable from the shortcut menu, so that the Dockable option is checked. Then, double-click the Project Explorer's title bar.

1.3 EXERCISES

1. Click on the sizing handle in the lower-right corner of a form in the Object window and drag it until the Object size box reads 5760 x 2880.

2. Double-click the title bar of a form in the Object window.

3. Click on a form in the Form Layout window and drag it down and to the left until the Object coordinates box reads 1000, 1000.

4. Right-click on a form in the Form Layout window and choose Center Screen from the Startup Position submenu of the shortcut menu.

5. Click the Close button on the title bar of the Form Layout window and then choose Form Layout Window from the View menu.

1.4 *EXERCISES*

1. Open a form in the Object window. Then, select the Caption property, type My Form, and press the ENTER key.

2. Select 2-Center Screen for the StartUpPosition property of a form.

3. Open the property page for the Font property by selecting the property and clicking the ellipsis button on the far right side of the property. Then, select size 10, bold, Courier, and click the OK button.

4. Select the BackColor property and click the down arrow to open the dropdown list box. Click the System tab and choose Active Title Bar.

5. Select the BackColor property and click the down arrow to open the dropdown list box. Click the Palette tab and choose White, which is the box at the top left.

6. Right-click on the Properties window and choose Description from the shortcut menu to either make the Description Pane appear or disappear.

7. Click the Close button on the title bar of the Properties window and press F4.

1.5 *EXERCISES*

1. Click on the TextBox control in the Toolbox. Then, click on a form and drag the shape that you want the control to be.

2. Click on the TextBox control in the Toolbox. Then, click on a form and drag the shape that you want the control to be.

3. Press CTRL+T. Click the Microsoft Common Dialog Control 5.0 checkbox in the list on the Controls tab of the Components dialog box and click the OK button.
4. Right-click on the Toolbox and choose Add Tab from the shortcut menu. Type Internet in the New Tab Name dialog box and click the OK button.
5. Select the Internet tab. Press CTRL+T. Click the Microsoft Internet Controls checkbox in the list on the Controls tab of the Components dialog box and click the OK button.
6. Right-click on the Internet tab and choose Delete Tab from the shortcut menu.

1.6 EXERCISES

1. Start Visual Basic or choose New Project from the File menu. Double-click the Standard EXE icon in the New Project dialog box. Choose Save Project from the File menu. Select or create a project folder and enter FirstProject for the filename. Then, click the OK button.
2. Open FirstProject and choose Add Form from the Project menu. Double-click the Form icon in the Add Form dialog box.
3. Open FirstProject and choose Add User Control from the Project menu. Double-click the User Control icon in the Add User Control dialog box.
4. Choose Add Project from the File menu. Double-click the Standard EXE icon in the New Project dialog box. Select the new project in the Project Explorer and press CTRL+S. Create or select a project folder and enter SecondProject for the filename.
5. Right-click on the User Control and choose Remove UserControl1 from the shortcut menu.

1.7 EXERCISES

1. Select a form. Choose Print from the File menu. Click the Current Module option button and click the Form Image

checkbox. The Code and Form As Text checkboxes should not be checked. Click the OK button.

2. Choose Print from the File menu. Click the Current Project option button. Click the OK button.

3. Select a form. Choose Print from the File menu. Click the Current Module option button and click the Form Image checkbox. The Form As Text checkbox should not be checked. Click the OK button.

4. Choose Print Setup from the File menu or click the Setup button on the Print dialog box.

1.8 **E*XERCISES***

1. Choose Make Project1.exe from the File menu. Click the Options button on the Make Project dialog box. Click the Compile tab of the Project Properties dialog box and click the Compile to Native Code option button. Click the OK button and select your hard drive in the Save in dropdown list box of the Make Project dialog box. Type Native in the File name text box and click the OK button.

2. Choose Make Project1.exe from the File menu. Click the Options button on the Make Project dialog box. Click the Compile tab of the Project Properties dialog box and click the Compile to P-Code option button. Click the OK button and select your hard drive in the Save in dropdown list box of the Make Project dialog box. Type Pseudo in the File name text box and click the OK button.

3. Press F5.

4. Press CTRL + F5.

***M*ASTERY SKILLS CHECK**

1. The Recent tab gives you the quickest access to the last project that you worked on.

2. To view the code for a form, select the form and click the View Code button.

3. Use the Resolution Guides in the Form Layout window.

4. The following are the properties that control the appearance of a form:

   ▼ Appearance

   ▼ BackColor

   ▼ BorderStyle

   ▼ Caption

   ▼ FillColor

   ▼ FillStyle

   ▼ FontTransparent

   ▼ ForeColor

   ▼ Palette

   ▼ Picture

5. The Toolbox has 20 tools by default, but this number can vary if you add more controls.

6. Yes, you can create a new project while you have a project open.

7. Choose Print from the File menu. Click the Current Project option button and click the Form Image checkbox. The Code and Form As Text checkboxes should not be checked. Click the OK button.

8. Press Ctrl + F5.

CHAPTER 2

REVIEW SKILLS CHECK

1. The three ways to start Visual Basic are the following:

   ▼ Using the Start menu

   ▼ Using a program shortcut

   ▼ Opening a file with a registered file type

2. To view a form in the Object window, select the form and click the View Object button.

3. Yes, you can specify the position at which a form appears.

4. Property pages are used to set complex properties.

5. There are two ways to add a control to a form:

▼ Select a control and then draw it on a form

▼ Double-click a control to add it to the center of a form

6. No, project files do not contain code.

7. Visual Basic can only print one project at a time.

8. No, projects are compiled according to the options that are chosen in the Make and Compile tabs of the Project Properties dialog box.

2.1 ▮ *EXERCISES*

1. Open the Editor tab Options dialog box and enter 2 in the Tab Width text box.

2. Open the Editor tab Options dialog box and click the Drag-and-Drop Text Editing checkbox, so that it is unchecked.

3. Click the Procedure View button to view one procedure at a time and click the Full Module View button to view the entire module.

4. Open the Editor Format tab of the Options dialog box. Select Syntax Error Text in the Text List and choose 12 from the Size dropdown list box.

2.2 ▮ *EXERCISES*

1. Naming conventions create a standard way of naming objects and variables. This makes it easy to create meaningful names. It also makes code more readable and easier to work with.

2. The commonly used prefix for the name of a form is frm.

3. The commonly used prefix for the name of a Label control is lbl.

4. The prefix for a variable that holds a currency value is cur.

5. The prefix for a variable that holds a user-defined string value is ustr.

███ 2.3 ███ **E**XERCISES

1. The maximum value of an Integer data type is 32,767.

2. The variable name 55intSpeedLimit is not valid because it begins with a number.

3. The following is a variable declaration for a variable that holds a two-digit number:

```
Dim bytTwoDigitNumber As Byte
```

4. The following declares two variables; one that holds the name of a city and one that holds a two-letter abbreviation for a state:

```
Dim strCityName As String
Dim strState As String * 2
```

5. The function CDate converts variables to a Date data type.

6. The value FRI is retrieved from the array by using strDaysOfWeek(5).

███ 2.4 ███ **E**XERCISES

1. The following is a declaration for a public procedure named MyFirstProcedure:

```
Public Sub MyFirstProcedure()

End Sub
```

2. The following is a declaration for a private function named MyFirstFunction that returns a Variant data type:

```
Private Function MyFirstFunction() As Variant

End Function
```

3. The following is a declaration for a module-level variable named dblCalculatedValue:

```
Dim mdblCalculatedValue As Double
```

4. The following is a declaration for a global variable that stores the results of a question during a lie-detector test:

```
Dim gblnLieDetectorResult As Boolean
```

This variable could be named nearly anything, but it should definitely be a Boolean variable, and it is always good to use descriptive names.

2.5 *E*XERCISES

1. Subroutines do not return a value.

2. To return a value from a function, set the function name equal to the value that should be returned.

3. The following is an example of a function call to a function named GetAccountBalance that accepts an integer account number and places the return value in a Currency variable:

```
curCurrentBalance = GetAccountBalance(intAccountNumber)
```

4. Yes, an event can cause code to be executed, but no, it doesn't do it on its own. An event procedure must be declared and code added to it for an event to actually cause code to be executed.

*M*ASTERY SKILLS CHECK

1. The Code window is used to view and edit Visual Basic code.

2. The use of naming conventions makes it easy to identify the data type of any variable without seeing its declaration.

3. All variables have to be declared in a module if the Option Explicit statement appears in the declarations section.

4. Global variables declared in one module and module-level variables declared as public can be used anywhere in an application.

5. Either directly or indirectly, Windows users cause events to happen in Visual Basic applications.

◼◼◼ *C*HAPTER 3

◼◼◼ *R*EVIEW SKILLS CHECK

1. All variables in a module must be explicitly declared if the Option Explicit statement appears at the top of the module. This statement can be typed in manually or added by clicking the Require Variable Declaration checkbox on the Editor tab of the Options dialog box.

2. Naming conventions are used for both objects and variables.

3. The data type that a variable is declared with determines what kind of data it can hold.

4. Scope determines where a variable can be used.

5. Subroutines do not always correspond to certain events, although some are triggered by the occurrence of an event.

◼ 3.1 ◼ *E*XERCISES

1. To make a Label control automatically adjust its size to display all of its text, set the AutoSize property to True.

2. If you double-click a Label control, the Code window opens to the control's Click event procedure. The Click event procedure is automatically declared if it doesn't exist.

3. To place the value contained in a text box into a variable, assign the Text property of the TextBox control to the variable.

4. If you double-click a TextBox control, the Code window opens to the control's Change event procedure. The Change event procedure is automatically declared if it doesn't exist.

3.2 **E**XERCISES
_____

1. If the Cancel property for a command button is set to True, that button's Click event can be triggered by pressing the ESC key.

2. Yes, the Default and Cancel properties can both be set to True for a command button.

3. The Click event procedure of a button named cmdClickMe would look like the following:

```
Private Sub cmdClickMe_Click()

End Sub
```

4. After adding a call to the procedure DoSomething to the Click event of cmdClickMe, the procedure would be as follows:

```
Private Sub cmdClickMe_Click()
    DoSomething
End Sub
```

3.3 **E**XERCISES
_____

1. A form with four option buttons would look like the following:

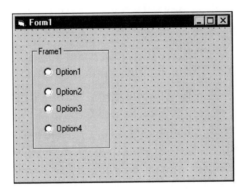

Option buttons don't have to be placed within frames, but it is good practice to do so because it is less confusing to the user.

2. Yes, option buttons have a double-click event.

3. No, checkboxes don't have a double-click event.

4. To reference the value of an option button or checkbox, use dot notation. The following are examples:

```
blnOptionButtonValue = optOptionButton.Value
intCheckboxValue = chkCheckBox.Value
```

3.4 EXERCISES

1. The AddItem method accepts two parameters: item and index. Item specifies the actual item being added and is required. Index specifies the location where the item should be added. The index parameter is optional and shouldn't normally be used.

2. Use the RemoveItem method to remove an item from a list box.

3. The contents of a list box or combo box are held in the List property. This property behaves like an array variable.

4. The ItemData property holds values that correspond to the contents of a list box or combo box, but are not displayed.

5. You know that a user entered a value into a list box or combo box if the ListIndex property is equal to -1.

3.5 EXERCISES

1. The Drive property of a drive list box is a run time-only property. It cannot be set while designing a form.

2. The Path property of the directory list box controls which directory is displayed.

3. The Change event procedure is triggered when the current directory is changed in the directory list box.

4. To display only files with a TXT extension in a file list box, set the Pattern property to *.txt.

5. The Path property of the directory list box and the file list box is only available at run time.

EXERCISES

1. Place several controls on a form and use the Align submenu of the Format menu to align the controls in different ways.

2. Place several controls on a form and use the Make Same Size submenu of the Format menu to make the controls the same size. The last form that you select determines the length or width that is used.

3. Place several controls on a form. Then, select all of the controls and choose Horizontally from the Center in Form menu.

4. Choose Lock Controls from the Format menu.

EXERCISES

1. A control array can only contain one type of control.

2. If a control is part of a control array, it has a value in its Index property and there are other controls that are the same type and have the same name.

3. The index of the control that caused an event is passed to the event procedure for the control.

4. To change the width and height of a command button when it is clicked if it's part of a control array, use the following code:

```
Private Sub cmdCommandButton_Click(Index As Integer)
    cmdCommandButton(Index).Width = intNewValue
    cmdCommandButton(Index).Height = intNewValue
End Sub
```

EXERCISES

1. The TabIndex property determines where a control is in the tab order.

2. The Menu, Timer, Data, Image, Line, and Shape controls are not included in the tab order.

3. Invisible controls remain in the tab order, but they are skipped when it is their turn to receive focus.

4. An ampersand before a letter in the caption makes that letter the access key for the control.

5. To display an ampersand in a label, set the UseMnemonic property to False or place two ampersands in a row.

*M*ASTERY SKILLS CHECK

1. Users can enter data on a form using the TextBox control.

2. The Click event is most commonly used for command buttons.

3. Option buttons are mutually exclusive, and checkboxes are not.

4. Combo boxes use a dropdown list box, which takes up less space than a normal list box.

5. The directory list box displays the directory structure of a disk drive.

6. Use the Make Same Size submenu of the Format menu to quickly make a group of controls the same size.

7. More than one control can have the same name if the controls are the same type. This creates a control array.

8. The TabIndex property determines which control gets the focus when the TAB key is pressed.

*C*HAPTER 4

*R*EVIEW SKILLS CHECK

1. The Text property of text boxes is a String data type.

2. Yes, command buttons can have access keys.

3. Option buttons are mutually exclusive, and checkboxes are not.

4. The values contained in list boxes and combo boxes are stored in the List property, which is treated like an array variable.

5. Directory list boxes display a folder hierarchy that represents a directory structure.

6. The quickest way to make a group of controls the same size is to use the Make Same Size submenu of the Format menu.

7. Controls in a control array must be of the same type.

8. When the tab order for a control is changed, the tab order for other controls is updated automatically by Visual Basic.

4.1 *EXERCISES*

1. String variables are not all the exact same type. There are variable-length and fixed-length strings.

2. Different types of strings hold different amounts of data. Variable-length strings can hold around two billion characters, and fixed-length strings hold about sixty-four thousand characters.

3. To declare a local string variable that holds the value of a license number, you could use the following declaration (any variable name works, but it should be descriptive):

```
Dim strLicenseNumber As String
```

4. To assign a license number of MPR274 to the variable declared in the previous exercise, use the following line of code:

```
strLicenseNumber = "MPR274"
```

5. To assign the license number from a text box named txtLicenseNumber, use the following code:

```
strLicenseNumber = txtLicenseNumber.Text
```

4.2 *EXERCISES*

1. The character code for uppercase P is 80, and the character code for lowercase P is 112.

2. When a positive number is converted to a string using the Str function, an extra space is added to the beginning of the string. No space is added when the CStr function is used.

3. What CStr is supplied a Boolean argument, it returns a string containing the value "True" or "False".

4. Use the Asc function to find out the character code for the first letter in a string variable.

EXERCISES

1. The & operator should be used when concatenating strings.

2. To join string values stored in variables strValue1 and strValue2 into a single string stored in the variable strNewValue, use the following line of code:

```
strNewValue = strValue1 & strValue2
```

3. The result of the following is "What does this do?"

```
"What does " & "this do?"
```

4. The result of the following is 20.

```
"10" + 10
```

5. The result of the following is "10.10".

```
"10" + ".10"
```

EXERCISES

1. The UCase, StrConv, and Format functions can be used to convert a string to all uppercase letters.

2. The LCase, StrConv, and Format functions can be used to convert a string to all lowercase letters.

3. The StrConv function can be used to convert a string to initial capital letters.

4. The Format function can be used to format dates and times.

5. The following function converts a string argument to uppercase, proper case, and lowercase. Then, it concatenates the three different cases of the string together, separated by commas, and returns that value.

```
Private Function Converter(MyString As String)
    Dim strTemp As String
    strTemp = UCase(MyString) & ","
    strTemp = strTemp & StrConv(MyString, vbProperCase) &
","
```

```
        strTemp = strTemp & LCase(MyString)
        Converter = strTemp
   End Function
```

4.5 EXERCISES

1. Use the Len function to find the length of a string.

2. Use the following to build the string "XXXOOOXXX" using the String function:

   ```
   String(3, "X") & String(3, "O") & String(3, "X")
   ```

3. The RTrim function removes trailing spaces.

4. No, you cannot remove the spaces from the middle of a string using the Trim function.

5. To obtain the text from a string variable removing the first two characters and the last two characters, use the following:

   ```
   Mid(strExample, 3, Len(strExample) - 4)
   ```

4.6 EXERCISES

1. To find the second occurrence of a string within a string, use the InStr function and specify a starting point after the first occurrence of the string.

2. The StrComp function compares two strings.

3. Use the Option Compare Text statement to make comparisons default to a text comparison.

4. To find out if a string contains the letters A, F, or G, use the following statement:

   ```
   strExample Like "*[a,f,g]*"
   ```

MASTERY SKILLS CHECK

1. The following is a declaration for a fixed-length string with a size of 5 characters:

   ```
   Dim strFiveLong As String * 5
   ```

2. Use the Asc function to find the character code for the letter Q, which is 81.

3. The & concatenation operator should be used when working with strings.

4. Use the StrConv function to make the first letter of each word in a string capitalized. The following syntax would be used:

```
strExample = StrConv(strExample, vbProperCase)
```

5. The Trim function removes the leading and trailing spaces from a string. LTrim removes leading spaces and RTrim removes trailing spaces.

6. The Option Compare statement affects the default comparison method for a module.

CHAPTER 5

REVIEW SKILLS CHECK

1. Strings can be declared to hold a specific number of characters by declaring a fixed-length string.

2. ASCII is a subset of the ANSI character set.

3. The & operator should always be used when concatenating strings.

4. The StrConv function can be used to capitalize the first letter of each word in a string.

5. The Left, Mid, and Right functions allow you to isolate and use only a portion of a string.

6. Binary is the default compare method, which can be changed using the Option Compare statement.

5.1 EXERCISES

1. The Integer data type should be used to store numbers less than 100 that have no fractions.

2. The Currency data type should be used if there can be no rounding errors.

3. Numeric variables can be set equal to a string if the string contains a numeric value.

4. The IsNumeric function determines if a string holds a numeric value.

5. The characters &H must precede a hexadecimal number.

5.2 EXERCISES

1. The following statement adds two negative numbers together:

```
intResult = -1 + -2
```

2. The following statement multiplies two numbers together:

```
intResult = 5 * 5
```

3. The following statement determines the remainder of dividing one number by another:

```
intRemainder = 12 MOD 5
```

4. Within an expression, the arithmetic operators are evaluated in the following order:

^ Operator

- Operator (indicating negative value)

* and / Operator

\ Operator

MOD Operator

+ and - Operator

5. Parentheses can be used to override operator precedence.

5.3 **E** XERCISES

1. The Sgn function determines the sign of a number.

2. The Abs function determines the value of a number regardless of the sign.

3. The following statement sets dblLogValue equal to the log of 2.7:

```
dblLogValue = Log(2.7)
```

4. The following statement sets dblSquareRoot equal to the square root of the value contained in the variable dblMyValue:

```
dblSquareRoot = Sqr(dblMyValue)
```

5. The trigonometric functions are the following:

Atn

Cos

Sin

Tan

5.4 **E** XERCISES

1. Pass a negative number as the seed value to generate the same random number every time you call the Rnd function.

2. The Rnd function uses the last number generated as the seed value after the first time that it is called.

3. If no seed value is specified, the Randomize statement obtains the seed value from the system timer.

4. The following code generates a completely random number each time it is called:

```
Randomize
dblRandomNumber = Rnd
```

MASTERY SKILLS CHECK

1. The Single, Double, and Currency data types can handle numeric values that have fractions.

2. Parentheses can dictate the order in which numeric operators should be used.

3. The Exp function is sometimes called the antilogarithm.

4. Pass the same negative seed value to the Rnd function to generate the same random number each time you call the Rnd function.

CHAPTER 6

REVIEW SKILLS CHECK

1. If it contains a valid numeric value, a string variable can be used to assign a value to a numeric variable.

2. When using numeric operators, operator precedence determines which operations are performed first. For example, all multiplication is performed before any addition.

3. The Abs function returns the absolute value of a number.

4. The Randomize statement executed without any parameters before the Rnd function ensures that a truly random number is generated.

6.1 **E**XERCISES

1. The following statement sets y equal to 2 if x equals 1:

```
If x = 1 Then y = 2
```

2. The following statement sets y equal to 2 if x equals 1, and if x isn't equal to 1, it sets z equal to 3 if y equals 2:

```
If x = 1 Then
    y = 2
ElseIf y = 2 Then
    z = 3
End If
```

3. The following is the code for this exercise:

```
If txtFirstNumber + txtSecondNumber = txtSum Then
    lblResult.Caption = "Correct"
Else
    lblResult.Caption = "Incorrect"
End If
```

6.2 EXERCISES

1. There is no Select Case ElseIf statement.

2. The following is a Select Case statement that checks the variable intSomeNumber for each of the following values: 1, 2, 3, 4, 5.

```
Select Case intSomeNumer
    Case 1

    Case 2

    Case 3

    Case 4

    Case 5

End Select
```

3. The following is the code for this exercise:

```
Select Case strSomeLetter
    Case a To m
        lblCharacterType.Caption = "first half of
alphabet"
    Case n To z
```

```
        lblCharacterType.Caption = "second half of
alphabet"
    Case Else
        lblCharacterType.Caption = "not part of alphabet"
End Select
```

6.3 **EXERCISES**

1. The Do statement is more flexible than the While statement because it has several different possibilities for its syntax.

2. The following Do statement adds the text "I will learn Visual Basic" to the string variable strText until the string is greater than 255 characters long:

```
Do Until Len(strText) > 255
    strText = strText & "I will learn Visual Basic"
Loop
```

3. The following Do statement only executes if the integer variable intNumber is greater than 10:

```
Do While intNumber > 10

Loop
```

4. The following Do statement executes at least once, but then only executes if the integer variable intNumber is greater than 10:

```
Do

Loop While intNumber > 10
```

6.4 **EXERCISES**

1. The following is the code for this exercise:

```
Private Function MyFiller(strChar As String * 1, intNum
As Integer) As String
Dim intCounter As Integer
```

```
For intCounter = 1 To intNum
    MyFiller = MyFiller & strChar
Next intCounter

End Function
```

2. The following is a For statement nested within another For statement:

```
Dim intOuterLoop As Integer
Dim intInnerLoop As Integer

For intOuterLoop = 1 To 5
    For intInnerLoop = 1 To 5

    Next intInnerLoop
Next intOuterLoop
```

3. The following is the code for this exercise:

```
Dim vntControl As Variant
Dim intCounter As Integer

For Each vntControl In frmMain.Controls
    If TypeName(vntControl) = "TextBox" Then
        intCounter = intCounter + 1
        vntControl.Text = "This is text box #" &
Str(intCounter)
    End If
Next vntControl
```

6.5	***E*XERCISES**

1. The Exit For statement immediately halts the execution of a For loop. Afterward, the line of code immediately following the Next clause is the next line of code executed.

2. The Exit Do statement immediately halts the execution of a Do loop. Afterward, the line of code after the Loop clause is the next line of code executed.

3. The following is the code for this exercise:

```
Dim intCounter As Integer
Dim intGolfer As Integer
```

```
Dim strTemp As String
Dim strScore As String
Dim strGolfer(1 To 10) As String
Dim intScore(1 To 10, 1 To 18) As Integer

Do
    strTemp = InputBox( _
      "Enter golfer name.", _
      "Golf Score Calculator")
    If strTemp = "" Then
        Exit Do
    Else
        intGolfer = intGolfer + 1
        strGolfer(intGolfer) = strTemp
    End If
    For intCounter = 1 To 18
        strScore = InputBox( _
            "Enter hole #" & Str(intCounter) & _
            " score for " & strGolfer(intGolfer) & ".", _
            "Golf Score Calculator")
        If strScore <> "" Then
            intScore(intGolfer, intCounter) = _
                intScore(intGolfer, intCounter) +
Int(strScore)
        Else
            Exit For
        End If
    Next intCounter
Loop While intGolfer <= 10
```

MASTERY SKILLS CHECK

1. Code blocks for an If statement do not require code. In fact, the absence of code can sometimes make the objective of the code more clear.

2. In a Select statement, the expression that is being compared to the different cases is evaluated one time.

3. The following syntax of the Do statement executes the code block for the statement at least once:

```
Do
    [code block]
Loop While|Until condition
```

4. A start and end value does not always have to be provided to the For statement. The For Each statement draws its start and end value from the lower and upper bound of the array that is being used.

5. The line of code immediately after the Loop clause is executed after an Exit Do statement.

CHAPTER 7

REVIEW SKILLS CHECK

1. Use the ElseIf clause to test for more than one condition when using the If statement.

2. The expression in the Select statement is evaluated only once, regardless of how many comparisons are made in the statement.

3. Place the While/Until clause at the end of a Do statement, to ensure that the code block is executed at least once.

4. The default step value of the For statement is 1.

5. The first line of code following the loop containing an Exit statement is executed after the Exit statement.

7.1 EXERCISES

1. The following statement uses the MsgBox function to inform a user that their hard drive is nearly full:

```
MsgBox ("Your hard drive is almost full.")
```

2. The following statement adds the critical icon to the dialog box displayed in the previous exercise:

```
Result = MsgBox ("Your hard drive is almost full.",
vbOKOnly + vbCritical)
```

3. The following code block creates a dialog box:

```
Dim strMessage, strTitle As String
Dim Result As VbMsgBoxResult
Dim Style As VbMsgBoxStyle

strMessage = "Do you want to save " _
   & "the changes you made to Document1?"
strTitle = "Microsoft Word"
Style = vbYesNoCancel + vbExclamation
Result = MsgBox(strMessage, Style, strTitle)
```

4. The following code recreates the results of the fourth example in this section, using a Select statement instead of an If statement:

```
Dim strMessage, strTitle As String
Dim Style As VbMsgBoxStyle
Dim Result As VbMsgBoxResult

strMessage = "Click a button to see a confirmation."
strTitle = "Dialog Box Demonstration"
Style = vbYesNoCancel + vbInformation + vbDefaultButton3

Select Case MsgBox(strMessage, Style, strTitle)
Case vbYes
    MsgBox ("You clicked the Yes button.")
Case vbNo
    MsgBox ("You clicked the No button.")
Case vbCancel
    MsgBox ("You clicked the Cancel button.")
End Select
```

7.2 EXERCISES

1. The following code block creates a dialog box using the InputBox function until the user enters the text "stop":

```
Dim strMessage, strTitle, strResponse As String

strMessage = "Enter the magic word."
strTitle = "Stop Me"
```

```
Do
    strResponse = InputBox(strMessage, strTitle)
Loop Until strResponse = "stop"
```

2. The following code block uses the InputBox function to ask for two numbers to add together and then displays the results in a dialog box:

```
Dim strMessage, strTitle, strResponse As String
Dim lngNumber1, lngNumber2, lngSum As Long
Dim Result As VbMsgBoxResult
Dim Style As VbMsgBoxStyle

strTitle = "Find the Sum"

strMessage = "Enter first number (must be valid number)."
Do
    strResponse = InputBox(strMessage, strTitle)
Loop Until IsNumeric(strResponse)
lngNumber1 = CLng(strResponse)

strMessage = "Enter second number. (must be valid
number)"
Do
    strResponse = InputBox(strMessage, strTitle)
Loop Until IsNumeric(strResponse)
lngNumber2 = CLng(strResponse)

lngSum = lngNumber1 + lngNumber2
strMessage = "The product of the two numbers is " &
lngSum
Style = vbOKOnly + vbInformation
Result = MsgBox(strMessage, Style, strTitle)
```

7.3 **E***XERCISES*

1. Any project can use the CommonDialog control if it is contained in that project's Toolbox.

2. CommonDialog controls have no optimum size—they are not visible to users.

E*XERCISES*

1. The following is the code for this exercise:

```
dlgFileOpen.Filter = "Word documents (*.doc)|*.doc|" _
    & "Excel workbooks (*.xls;*.xlb)|*.xls;*.xlb|" _
    & "Access databases (*.mdb)|*.mdb|" _
    & "Any files (*.*)|*.*"
dlgFileOpen.FilterIndex = 1
dlgFileOpen.ShowOpen
```

2. The following is the code for this exercise:

```
dlgFileSave.Filter = "Word documents (*.doc)|*.doc|" _
    & "Excel workbooks (*.xls;*.xlb)|*.xls;*.xlb|" _
    & "Access databases (*.mdb)|*.mdb|" _
    & "Any files (*.*)|*.*"
dlgFileSave.FilterIndex = 1
dlgFileSave.DefaultExt = "doc"
dlgFileSave.ShowSave
```

E*XERCISES*

1. The following code block prompts the user for a color and then changes the BackColor property of a list box to that color:

```
dlgColor.ShowColor
lstBox.BackColor = dlgColor.Color
```

2. The following is the code for this exercise:

```
dlgColor.DialogTitle = "Select a Color"
dlgColor.ShowColor
lstBox.BackColor = dlgColor.Color
```

E*XERCISES*

1. The following code block shows a Font dialog box without the underline, strikethrough, and color options. Then, it shows the Font dialog box with them:

```
dlgFont.Flags = cdlCFBoth
dlgFont.ShowFont

dlgFont.Flags = cdlCFBoth + cdlCFEffects
dlgFont.ShowFont
```

2. The following code block prompts the user for font properties and then uses those properties to create a new font object and set its properties:

```
Dim f As New StdFont

dlgFont.ShowFont
f.Name = dlgFont.FontName
f.Size = dlgFont.FontSize
f.Bold = dlgFont.FontBold
f.Italic = dlgFont.FontItalic
f.Underline = dlgFont.FontUnderline
f.Strikethrough = dlgFont.FontStrikethru
```

7.7 EXERCISES

1. The following code block opens a Print dialog box that defaults to printing 3 copies:

```
dlgPrint.Copies = 3
dlgPrint.ShowPrint
```

2. The following code block opens a Print dialog box that defaults to printing 1 copy, has a possible print range of 5 to 25, and does not affect the default printer:

```
dlgPrint.Copies = 1
dlgPrint.PrinterDefault = False
dlgPrint.Min = 5
dlgPrint.Max = 25
dlgPrint.FromPage = 5
dlgPrint.ToPage = 25
dlgPrint.ShowPrint
```

7.8 **E**XERCISES

1. The following code block displays the contents of the Windows help file that goes directly to all of the information that has to do with starting something:

```
dlgHelp.HelpFile = "C:\WINDOWS\HELP\WINDOWS.HLP"
dlgHelp.HelpKey = "starting,"
dlgHelp.HelpCommand = cdlHelpPartialKey
dlgHelp.ShowHelp
```

2. The following code block displays the Windows help file:

```
dlgHelp.HelpFile = "C:\WINDOWS\HELP\WINDOWS.HLP"
dlgHelp.HelpCommand = &HB
dlgHelp.ShowHelp
```

MASTERY SKILLS CHECK

1. The vbMsgBoxResult data type stores the results of the MsgBox function.

2. The InputBox function returns a String data type.

3. To add a CommonDialog control to a form, you must first add the control to the project using the Components dialog box. Then, add the control to a form by double-clicking on it in the Toolbox.

4. Use the DefaultExt property to specify a default extension for filenames obtained using the CommonDialog control's Save As dialog box.

5. Colors are specified in Visual Basic using RGB colors.

6. The Flags property of the CommonDialog control must be set to cdlCFScreenFonts, cdlCFPrinterFonts, or cdlCFBoth to open a Font dialog box.

7. If the PrintDefault property is set to True when opening a Print dialog box, any changes made in the dialog box immediately affect the default printer.

8. To show help on how to use a help file, set the Flags property to cdlHelpHelpOnHelp.

CHAPTER 8

REVIEW SKILLS CHECK

1. The MsgBox function is able to display seven different buttons:

   ▼ OK

   ▼ Cancel

   ▼ Abort

   ▼ Retry

   ▼ Ignore

   ▼ Yes

   ▼ No

2. The InputBox function returns an empty string ("") if the user clicks the Cancel button or presses the Esc key.

3. The CommonDialog control cannot be resized.

4. The index of the first filter defined for the CommonDialog control's Save As dialog box is 1.

5. The letters in RGB stand for Red, Green, and Blue.

6. The CommonDialog control supports screen fonts and printer fonts.

7. To force changes made in the Print dialog box of the CommonDialog control to immediately affect the default printer, set the PrintDefault property to True.

8. The HelpCommand property of the CommonDialog control determines the behavior of the ShowHelp method.

8.1   EXERCISES

1. The following image shows a menu structure that resembles Visual Basic's Run menu:

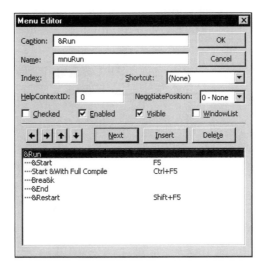

2. The following image shows a menu structure that resembles
   Visual Basic's Add-Ins menu:

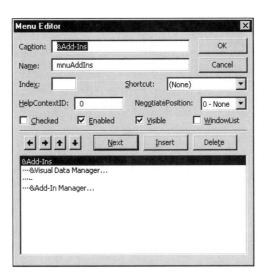

3. The following image shows a series of submenus, naming them according to the level of submenu that they are:

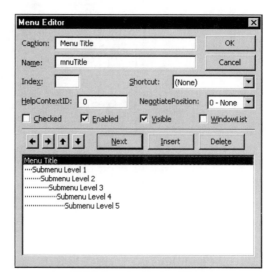

EXERCISES

1. The quickest way to create a Click event procedure for a menu command is to select the command in the Form window.

2. To have mnuEdit's Click event make the Text Color submenu invisible if the ForeColor of the text box is not black or red, add the following code:

```
If txtText.ForeColor <> RGB(0, 0, 0) And _
    txtText.ForeColor <> RGB(255, 0, 0) Then
    mnuEditTextColor.Visible = False
Else
    mnuEditTextColor.Visible = True
End If
```

| 8.3 | **E**XERCISES |

1. The following is the code for this exercise:

```
Private Sub Form_MouseDown(Button As Integer, _
Shift As Integer, X As Single, Y As Single)

If Button = vbMiddleButton Then
    PopupMenu mnuFileNewForm
End If

End Sub
```

2. The following is the code for this exercise:

```
Private Sub Form_MouseDown(Button As Integer, _
Shift As Integer, X As Single, Y As Single)

If Button = vbLeftButton Then
    PopupMenu mnuFileNewForm, , , , mnuFileNewFormText
End If

End Sub
```

MASTERY SKILLS CHECK

1. Move menu items around within the Menu Editor by using the arrow button in the left-middle portion of the dialog box.

2. Create Click event procedures for menu titles and submenu titles by writing their declaration and the code for them in the Code Editor.

3. By default, popup menus appear left-aligned at the x and y coordinates of the mouse pointer and respond only to selections made with the left mouse button.

CHAPTER 9

REVIEW SKILLS CHECK

1. Use a hyphen (-) to add a separator bar to a menu.

2. The fastest way to add code to a menu item is to select the menu item in the Form window.

3. Use the button argument passed to the MouseDown event to determine which mouse button caused the event.

9.1   EXERCISES

1. The following is the code for the Click event procedure:

```
Private Sub cmdPrint_Click()
PrintForm
End Sub
```

2. The following is the code for the Click event procedure:

```
Private Sub cmdPrint_Click()
Dim F As Form

frmOne.Load
frmTwo.Load
frmThree.Load
frmFour.Load
frmFive.Load

For Each F In Forms
```

```
        If Instr(F.Caption, "4") <> 0 Then
            F.PrintForm
        End If
    Next
    End Sub
```

9.2 ◾ **E**XERCISES

1. The second printer in the Printers collection is addressed in the following manner:

   ```
   Printers(1)
   ```

2. The following For statement steps through each of the printers in the Printers collection:

   ```
   Dim P As Printer

   For Each P In Printers
       'Do something with P
   Next
   ```

3. The next-to-last printer in the Printers collection is addressed in the following manner:

   ```
   Printers(Printers.Count - 2)
   ```

9.3 ◾ **E**XERCISES

1. Use the following statement to set the default printer to the last printer in the Printers collection:

   ```
   Set Printer = Printers(Printers.Count - 1)
   ```

2. Use the following statement to change the properties of the Printer object so that its default printer always matches the Windows default printer:

   ```
   Printer.TrackDefault = True
   ```

3. Use the following statement to set the properties of the Printer object so that it will print 3 copies of everything:

```
Printer.Copies = 3
```

4. Use the following statements to set the Font property of the Printer object to 8 point bold Courier:

```
Printer.Font.Name = "Courier"
Printer.Font.Bold = True
Printer.Font.Size = 8
```

9.4 EXERCISES

1. The following code uses the Circle method to draw several ellipses and circles so that they have the appearance of a pair of eyes:

```
Printer.Circle (1000, 1000), 1000, , , , 0.6
Printer.Circle (1000, 1000), 500
Printer.Circle (1000, 1000), 200
Printer.Circle (3500, 1000), 1000, , , , 0.6
Printer.Circle (3500, 1000), 500
Printer.Circle (3500, 1000), 200
Printer.EndDoc
```

2. The following code uses the Line method to draw a triangle:

```
Printer.Line (0, 500)-(500, 0)
Printer.Line (500, 0)-(1000, 500)
Printer.Line (1000, 500)-(0, 500)
Printer.EndDoc
```

3. The following code uses the Print method to print a numbered list of the names of all the controls on a form:

```
Dim intCounter As Integer

For intCounter = 0 To Controls.Count - 1
    Printer.Print intCounter + 1; _
      Controls(intCounter).Name
Next
Printer.EndDoc
```

4. The following code prints a separate page for each control on a form that lists the type of control and the control's name

```
Dim i, intIndexMax As Integer

intIndexMax = Controls.Count - 1
For i = 0 To intIndexMax
    Printer.Print TypeName(Controls(i))
    Printer.Print Controls(i).Name
    If i < intIndexMax Then
        Printer.NewPage
    End If
Next

Printer.EndDoc
```

*M*ASTERY SKILLS CHECK

1. When you call the PrintForm method, the image of the current form is printed.
2. The index of the first printer in the Printers collection is 0.
3. The Set statement is used to set the default printer.
4. The KillDoc method terminates a print job.

*C*HAPTER 10

*R*EVIEW SKILLS CHECK

1. Zero is the index of the first printer in the Printers collection.
2. The Set statement is used to change the default printer.
3. The EndDoc method sends the contents of the Printer object to the current printer device.

EXERCISES

1. The following code creates a TextStream object:

```
Dim fso As Object
Dim ts As Object

Set fso = CreateObject("Scripting.FileSystemObject")
Set ts = fso.OpenTextFile("C:\FILE.TXT")
ts.Close
Set fso = Nothing
```

2. The following code creates a text file named EXERCISE.TXT on the root of the C: drive:

```
Dim fso As Object
Dim ts As Object

Set fso = CreateObject("Scripting.FileSystemObject")
Set ts = fso.OpenTextFile("C:\EXERCISE.TXT", 8, True, -2)
ts.Close
Set fso = Nothing
```

3. The following code opens the text file named EXERCISE.TXT on the root of the C: drive:

```
Dim fso As Object
Dim ts As Object

Set fso = CreateObject("Scripting.FileSystemObject")
Set ts = fso.OpenTextFile("C:\EXERCISE.TXT")
ts.Close
Set fso = Nothing
```

4. The following code deletes the text file named EXERCISE.TXT on the root of the C: drive:

```
Dim fso As Object

Set fso = CreateObject("Scripting.FileSystemObject")
fso.DeleteFile "C:\EXERCISE.TXT", True
Set fso = Nothing
```

E*XERCISES*

1. The following code creates a new text file named NEW.TXT on the root of the C: drive:

```
Dim fso As Object
Dim ts As Object

Set fso = CreateObject("Scripting.FileSystemObject")
Set ts = fso.OpenTextFile("C:\NEW.TXT", 8, True, -2)
ts.Close
Set fso = Nothing
```

2. The following code opens the text file created in the previous example and adds several lines of text to it:

```
Dim fso As Object
Dim ts As Object

Set fso = CreateObject("Scripting.FileSystemObject")
Set ts = fso.OpenTextFile("C:\NEW.TXT", 8)
ts.WriteLine("This is the first line of text.")
ts.WriteLine("This is the second line of text.")
ts.WriteLine("This is the third line of text.")
ts.Close
Set fso = Nothing
```

3. The following code opens NEW.TXT and reads every other line of text starting with the first one:

```
Dim fso As Object
Dim ts As Object

Set fso = CreateObject("Scripting.FileSystemObject")
Set ts = fso.OpenTextFile("C:\NEW.TXT")

Do While Not ts.AtEndOfLine
    ts.ReadLine
    ts.SkipLine
Loop

ts.Close
Set fso = Nothing
```

4. The following code opens NEW.TXT and reads the entire file one character at a time:

```
Dim fso As Object
Dim ts As Object

Set fso = CreateObject("Scripting.FileSystemObject")
Set ts = fso.OpenTextFile("C:\NEW.TXT")

Do While Not ts.AtEndOfLine
    ts.Read(1)
Loop

ts.Close
Set fso = Nothing
```

10.3 ***E*XERCISES**

1. To add to the form built in this section that lists the fields from the Categories table by adding an Image control to display the picture for a category, place an Image control on the form. Then, set the DataSource property to the ADO DataControl and set the DataField property to Picture.

2. To create a form that displays the data from the Shippers table of the Northwind sample database, add an ADO DataControl to a form that points to the Shippers table. Then, add a text box control for each field in the Shippers table. Finally, set the DataSource property for each text box to the ADO DataControl and set the DataField property of each text box to one of the fields.

3. To create a form that displays the ProductID, ProductName, and Discontinued fields from the Products table of the Northwind sample database, add an ADO DataControl to a form that points to the Products table. Then, add three text box controls to the form. Finally, set the DataSource property for each text box to the ADO DataControl and set the DataField property of each text box to one of the fields being displayed.

10.4 **E**XERCISES

1. To create a form that allows the user to view the records of the Northwind sample database Customers table, add an ADO DataControl to a form that points to the Customers table. Then, add a DataGrid to the form. Set the DataSource property for the DataGrid to the ADO DataControl. Finally, right-click on the DataGrid and choose Retrieve Fields from the shortcut menu.

2. To make it possible to add and delete records in a DataGrid, open the property pages and select the AllowAddNew and AllowDelete checkboxes.

10.5 **E**XERCISES

1. To create a single record form with the Data Form Wizard for the Shippers table, select Single Record in the Form step of the Wizard and select the Shippers table in the Record Source step. Then, finish answering the Wizard's questions.

2. To create a master/detail form with the Data Form Wizard using the Customers table as the master and the Orders table as the detail, select Master/Detail in the Form step of the Wizard. Select the Customers table in the Master Record Source step and the Orders table in the Detail Record Source step. Then, select the CustomerID field in the Master and Detail list boxes of the Record Source Relation step. After that, finish answering the rest of the Wizard's questions.

10.6 **M**ASTERY SKILLS CHECK

1. The FSO object is in the Scripting class.

2. The FSO object is used to actually open a file; the TextStream object is used to read and write to a file.

3. You don't have to add any code to the ADO Data Control to allow the user to navigate the records of a database.

4. The quickest way to format a DataGrid control is to right-click on it and choose Retrieve Fields from the shortcut menu.

5. The two basic types of forms that the Data Form Wizard is capable of creating are single table forms and master/detail forms.

▆▆▆▆ *C*HAPTER 11

▆▆▆▆ *R*EVIEW SKILLS CHECK

1. To release the resources being used by an FSO object, set the FSO object equal to Nothing.

2. Use the ReadAll method of the TextStream object to read all of the text in a file.

3. Any control that can be bound to a data source can display data that is retrieved using the ADO Data Control.

4. To put a DataGrid control into edit mode, right-click on it and choose Edit from the shortcut menu.

5. A master/detail form created by the Data Form Wizard uses more than one table or query.

▆▆ 11.1 ▆▆ *E*XERCISES

1. To change the application in the first example so that it allows the client to specify the computer that it will connect to, remove the form's Load event procedure, add a text box to the form named txtRemoteHost, and change the Click event procedure of cmdConnect to the following:

```
Private Sub cmdConnect_Click()
```

```
tcpClient.RemoteHost = txtRemoteHost.Text
tcpClient.RemotePort = 1001
tcpClient.Connect
```

```
End Sub
```

2. To change the application in the second example so that it allows either peer to specify the computer that it will connect to, add a text box named txtRemoteHost and a button named cmdConnect to each form. Then, change the form's Load event procedure to be the Click event procedure for the button and set the RemoteHost property equal to txtRemoteHost.Text instead of a hard-coded string.

11.2 *EXERCISES*

1. To create a form that lets the user supply a URL to be opened and displayed in a text box, add an Internet Transfer control, two text boxes (txtURL and txtDisplay), and a button (cmdOpenURL) to a form. Then, add the following procedure to the form:

```
Private Sub cmdOpenURL_Click()

txtDisplay.Text = Inet1.OpenURL(txtURL.Text)

End Sub
```

2. To alter the form created in the first exercise so that it prompts the user for a user name and password before opening up any site, change the Click event procedure to the following:

```
Private Sub cmdOpenURL_Click()

Inet1.UserName = InputBox("Enter User Name")
Inet1.Password = InputBox("Enter Password")
txtDisplay.Text = Inet1.OpenURL(txtURL.Text)

End Sub
```

EXERCISES

1. To create a form that connects to a MAPI mail server at startup using default settings and lets the user create and send a message, add the following code to a form like the one shown below (each control displays its Name, except for the MAPISession (mpsSession) and MAPIMessages (mpmMessage) controls):

```
Private Sub cmdSend_Click()
mpmMessage.Compose
mpmMessage.RecipAddress = txtRecipAddress.Text
mpmMessage.ResolveName
mpmMessage.MsgSubject = txtMsgSubject.Text
mpmMessage.MsgNoteText = txtMsgNoteText.Text
mpmMessage.Send

End Sub

Private Sub Form_Load()

mpsSession.SignOn
mpmMessage.SessionID = mpsSession.SessionID

End Sub
```

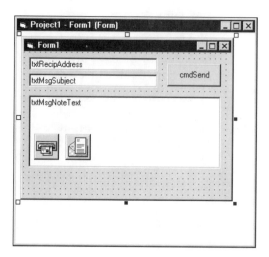

2. Add a text box (txtAttachment) and the following line of code before the message is sent to the form created in the previous exercise to make it possible for the user to add an attachment:

```
mpmMessage.AttachmentPathName = txtAttachment.Text
```

MASTERY SKILLS CHECK

1. TCP and UDP are the two protocols that the Winsock control uses.

2. You do not always have to specify the protocol being used when retrieving data using the Internet Transfer control.

3. The MAPISession and MAPIMessages controls have the SessionID property in common.

CHAPTER 12

REVIEW SKILLS CHECK

1. UDP should be used for sending small amounts of data.

2. The OpenURL method of the Internet Transfer control is used to open a resource on a Web server or FTP server.

3. A MAPI-compliant mail system must be in use for the MAPI controls to work properly.

12.1 EXERCISES

1. To toggle the breakpoint on for the line of code for the GetChar function of the Scrambler program, click in the margin to the left of the line of code.

2. To toggle the breakpoint on for the first line of code in the RearrangeText function, click in the margin to the left of that line of code.

3. To toggle the breakpoint on for the two statements in the If...Then statement of the RearrangeText function, click in the margin next to those lines of code.

4. To toggle the breakpoint off for the first line of code in the RearrangeText function, click in the margin next to that line of code.

5. Choose Clear All Breakpoints from the Debug menu to toggle all of the breakpoints off for the Scrambler program.

▐ 12.2 ▐ **EXERCISES**

1. If the Step Into command is executed and the current line of code calls another procedure, execution moves into that procedure.

2. If the Step Over command is executed and the current line of code calls another procedure, that procedure is called and execution moves to the next line of code.

3. If the Step Out command is executed and the current line of code calls another procedure, the rest of the current procedure is executed and execution moves back to the procedure that originally called the current procedure.

▐ 12.3 ▐ **EXERCISES**

1. To run the GetChar function from the Immediate window, enter a command similar to the following in that window:

```
GetChar("STRING", 3)
```

2. To add a watch to a variable using the Quick Watch button, place the cursor within that variable in the Code window and click the Quick Watch button on the Debug toolbar. Then, click the Add button on the Quick Watch dialog box.

3. To change the value for a variable using the Locals window, select the variable in the Locals window and change its Value column.

12.4	**E**XERCISES

1. Add the following code to the GetChar function after the existing line of code to print the text that the character is being drawn from, the position it should be drawn from, and the character that is going to be returned:

```
Debug.Print strChar
Debug.Print intLocation
Debug.Print GetChar
```

2. Add the following code to the RearrangeText function to stop execution if a space character is encountered:

```
Debug.Assert strChar <> " "
```

MASTERY SKILLS CHECK

1. The quickest way to toggle off all of the breakpoints in a module is to choose Clear All Breakpoints from the Debug menu.

2. If you are stepping through the code of procedure B that was called by procedure A, you click the Step Out button to execute the line of code in procedure A after the line that called procedure B.

3. You can change the values of variables and properties in the Immediate window.

4. Calls to Debug.Assert have no effect on executable files that are distributed to users.

CHAPTER 13

REVIEW SKILLS CHECK

1. A breakpoint causes the execution of code to be halted on the line that the breakpoint is set on—before that line is executed.

2. To cause a line of code to be executed without stepping into any procedures called from that line of code, use the Step Over command from the Debug menu or the Debug toolbar.

3. The Locals window displays the values for variables in the currently executing procedure and the current form.

4. The Debug object has two methods: Print and Assert. Print places values in the Immediate window and Assert halts the execution of the program depending upon conditions specified when the Assert method is called.

13.1 EXERCISES

1. To add an error handler to any procedure, use the On Error statement.

2. To add an error handler to any procedure that resumes execution on the line following the line of code that caused an error, place the following at the beginning of the procedure:

```
On Error Resume Next
```

13.2 EXERCISES

1. The following is the code for this exercise:

```
Private Sub ErrorExample()
Dim intSum As Integer

On Error GoTo ErrorHandler

Do
    intSum = intSum + 1
Loop Until intSum = 100

ExitProcedure:
Exit Sub

ErrorHandler:
    MsgBox Err.Description
    If intSum < 50 Then
        Resume
    Else
```

```
        Exit Sub
    End If

End Sub
```

2. The following continues execution on the line after the line that caused an error:

```
Private Sub ErrorExample()
Dim intSum As Integer

On Error GoTo ErrorHandler

Do
    intSum = intSum + 1
Loop Until intSum = 100

ExitProcedure:
Exit Sub

ErrorHandler:
    MsgBox Err.Description
    If intSum < 50 Then
        Resume Next
    Else
        Exit Sub
    End If

End Sub
```

13.3 $\blacksquare$**XERCISES**

1. The following is the code for this exercise:

```
Private Function ErrorMessage() As String
Dim strTemp As String

strTemp = "Error Number: "
strTemp = strTemp & Err.Number
strTemp = strTemp & Chr(10)
strTemp = strTemp & "Source: "
strTemp = strTemp & Err.Source
strTemp = strTemp & Chr(10)
strTemp = strTemp & "Error Description: "
strTemp = strTemp & Err.Description
```

```
ErrorMessage = strTemp

End Function
```

2. The following statement raises an error for a class called Free that is in a project called Error:

```
Err.Raise 513, "Error.Free", "This is my error."
```

3. The following statement raises a "File not found" error:

```
Err.Raise 53
```

*M*ASTERY SKILLS CHECK

1. The On Error statement traps errors.

2. The Resume statement redirects the flow of execution after an error is handled.

3. An Err object does not have to be created; Visual Basic automatically creates this object and makes it available to all parts of an application.

Glossary

A

ACCELERATOR KEY

An accelerator key, or shortcut key, is a combination of keystrokes that activates a control or performs a command. For example, ALT-F4 causes Windows applications to exit, and ALT-W activates the Windows menu in most Windows applications. Accelerator keys allow the user to use the keyboard to perform actions normally completed using the mouse.

ACTIVEX

A programming standard established so that components and controls developed in different languages—or the same language—for Windows applications could communicate with each other.

ACTIVEX DATA OBJECTS (ADO)

ADO is an object hierarchy designed to make it easy to access databases from many different languages. This technology is similar to Data Access Objects (DAO) and Open Database Connectivity (ODBC), which Microsoft previously encouraged developers to use. Microsoft now asks that developers use ADO in all of their data access applications.

ANSI

The American National Standards Institute (ANSI) is an organization that defines specifications for communications and encoding, including programming languages and computer systems.

API

An Application Programming Interface (API) is a set of methods defined so that developers can take advantage of particular resources while creating applications. For example, the Windows API allows developers to take advantage of Windows resources. In most cases, Visual Basic makes the method call to the Windows API for you when you execute commands in your Visual Basic procedures and functions.

ARGUMENT

A value passed to a procedure or function. This value can be any of the Visual Basic data types. Arguments are also referred to as parameters.

ARRAY

A collection of data stored in a single variable. Each value in the array is referenced using an index or subscript, with each value having a unique index number to identify it. Data stored in an array can be any of the Visual Basic data types.

ASCII

The American Standard Code for Information Interchange (ASCII) is a code that assigns characters to the numbers 0 to 255. The American National Standards Institute defined ASCII to make it possible for computers and computer peripheral devices to transmit text between each other.

ASYNCHRONOUS

Asynchronous tasks continue without waiting for any other task to complete. For example, if an asynchronous process called a procedure, the process would continue without waiting for that procedure to run to completion.

 B

BASIC

Beginner's All Purpose Symbolic Instruction Code (BASIC) is a programming language originally developed to teach computer science students programming skills. It became very popular and has been used in many programming environments since its introduction.

BITMAP

A bitmap file contains all of the information necessary to display an image on a Windows computer.

BLOB

Binary Large Object (BLOB) is a type of database field that is used to store large files that contain large amounts of binary data. Video files or even computer applications are commonly stored in this type of database field.

BOOLEAN

The Boolean data type has a value or either True or False. Visual Basic equates a True Boolean value to –1 and a False Boolean value to 0.

BREAKPOINT

A breakpoint is a designated line of code in a program. Execution of the program should be halted before that line is executed. This provides developers a chance to examine program variables and to step through code in order to identify problems with code and fix them.

BUFFER

A buffer is a designated memory space that is used for a single purpose. That purpose could be to store the value of a variable or to temporarily store data being communicated to or from an application.

 C

CASE SENSITIVE

Case sensitivity defines whether a query or comparison takes the case of letters into consideration. If a query or comparison is case sensitive, all letters must match exactly (including upper or lower case) in order for a value to be returned in a query or a True value returned by a comparison. Otherwise, the case does not have an effect, which makes it case insensitive.

CHECKBOX

Checkbox controls display a value of True or False. When an X appears in a checkbox, it is considered checked, which indicates a True value.

If an X doesn't appear in a checkbox, it is considered unchecked, which indicates a False value. Clicking a checkbox control toggles it between being checked and unchecked.

CHILD

The term child refers either to a window that is the child of an MDI parent window or to an object that is the child of a parent object.

CLASS

A class is the definition from which objects are created. The definition includes information such as properties, methods, and events. The properties of objects created from a single class are what make each object unique.

CLASS MODULE

Class modules are the Visual Basic files that contain class definitions. Each class must be stored in its own class module.

CLIENT

Client is a generic term that refers to any component or application that uses the service of another component or application. An application that accesses data through a database server is a client of the database server because it uses the services of the database server. In the same way, a component on a form that uses the services of another component on the same form is also a client. It is a client of the component whose services it is using, even though they are both on the same form in the same application.

CLIENT/SERVER

Client/Server refers to an architecture that defines the ability of components and applications to make services available to other components and applications. Components and applications that make their services available to others are called servers, while components and applications that use services are called clients. A component or application can be both a client and a server.

CLIPBOARD

The Windows clipboard is a resource that allows data to be temporarily stored in memory. The clipboard, and the data it contains, is available to all Windows applications. Applications can place data on the clipboard and copy data from the clipboard. However, the clipboard can only contain one set of data at any one time. So, any time new data is placed on the clipboard, the data it previously contained is lost.

CODE

See source code.

CODE EDITOR

Visual Basic's Code Editor is the window where all Visual Basic code is added and modified.

COMBO BOX

The Combo Box control is a text box control combined with a dropdown list box control. This combination gives a user the ability to either enter text or select text from the dropdown list box.

COMMAND BUTTON

Command button controls are placed on forms to give users the ability to control the flow of an application. Clicking the mouse over a command button triggers the Click event of the command button, which causes the code associated with the event to be executed. The most common uses of command buttons are the OK and Cancel buttons, which almost every Windows dialog box contains.

COMMENT

Comments are used to document applications' procedures. They are text that appears within code for descriptive purposes only and do not affect execution. To create a comment in Visual Basic, place a single quote (') in front of the comment text.

COMMON DIALOG CONTROL
The Common Dialog control is included with Visual Basic to provide access to the most commonly used dialog boxes in Windows, such as file, color, font, and so on.

COMPILE
Code is compiled when it is converted to an executable file.

COMPONENT
A component is an object or unit of code that provides service(s) through a clearly defined interface.

COMPONENT OBJECT MODEL (COM)
The Component Object Model (COM) defines a standard set of interfaces that allows components to be created that can communicate and interoperate with each other, regardless of the language they were created with.

CONSTANT
A constant is a reference to a value that never changes. Constants are usually defined to make code more clear. For example, True is a constant for the value –1.

CONTROL
Controls are objects that perform a single task for an application. They are normally graphical, such as the command button and text box controls, but can be also be non-graphical like the Common Dialog control.

 D

DATA ACCESS OBJECTS (DAO)
Data Access Objects is an object hierarchy defined to allow database access. Starting with Visual Basic 6, ADO should be used instead of DAO.

DATABASE
A database contains information that is organized into tables.

DATABASE TABLE
Database tables store information categorized into columns, which are also called fields. A single row of data columns is called a record.

DATA TYPE
Data Type refers to the types of values that can be stored or used for a particular variable or procedure call.

DEBUG
Debugging an application is the process of finding and eliminating errors that occur in the code.

DESIGN TIME
Applications are created and modified during design time, which refers to any time that the application is not running.

DROPDOWN LIST BOX
A dropdown list box contains a list of values that can be selected. The selected value cannot be edited.

DYNAMIC LINK LIBRARY (DLL)
A dynamic link library (DLL) is a group of executable procedures that are placed in a single file, which has the DLL extension.

 E

EMPTY
Variant variables that have not been assigned a value contain an Empty value. Variants that refer to an object can be set to the Empty value to free the resources that the object is using.

ENUMERATED DATA

Enumerated data has a distinct number of possible values that are usually associated with constant values. For example, True and False could be thought of as the enumerated data for a property that accepts only those two values.

ERROR TRAPPING

Error trapping is the process of catching errors in an application and handling them instead of letting Windows handle the error message. This makes it possible for applications to continue execution even if an error occurs.

EVENT

An event is any occurrence that the Windows operating system receives a message for. For example, the mouse moving across the screen triggers a series of mouse move events. When creating Visual Basic applications, the Click event becomes very useful for allowing the user to control the flow of the application.

EVENT PROCEDURE

Event procedures are blocks of code that automatically execute any time a particular event is triggered.

EXECUTABLE

Executables are the files used to run applications.

EXPRESSION

This is any combination of Visual Basic variables, delimiters, and operators that results in a single value.

 F

FOCUS

The control or window that is currently selected on the screen has the focus. Only one control can have the focus at any one time.

FILE TRANSFER PROTOCOL (FTP)

The File Transfer Protocol (FTP) allows users to transfer files between computers.

FUNCTION

A function is a procedure that returns a value.

 ## G

GIF

CompuServe developed the Graphics Interchange Format (GIF) to display images.

 ## H

HTML

The Hypertext Markup Language (HTML) is used to create documents that are viewed using Web browsers, which interpret the HTML in order to display a formatted page of graphics and text. HTML pages can also contain links to other HTML pages or any other type of file.

 ## I

IDE

IDE is an acronym for Integrated Development Environment. An IDE is a programming environment that combines several different programming tools into a single, integrated piece of software.

INDEX

An index is a number that uniquely identifies a value that is stored in an array variable.

INHERITANCE
Inheritance describes the ability of objects to inherit properties and methods from their parent objects.

INSTANCE
An instance is the actual object created from a class module.

INSTANTIATE
An object is instantiated when a new instance is created from a class module.

INTERNET
A large group of networks that are all interconnected. The Internet has many access points, which makes it widely available.

INTRANET
An intranet is a private network that is not widely available to users. Intranets are usually only available to the workers within the organization that controls the intranet.

J

JET
Jet is Microsoft's desktop database engine, which is built into Visual Basic and many other Microsoft applications.

JPEG
The Joint Photographic Experts Group (JPEG or JPG) is a compressed file format for graphics files that allows detailed graphics to be stored in small files.

K

KEYWORD

Words that have a special meaning in Visual Basic. They are part of Visual Basic and cannot be separated from their defined meaning. For example, you can't use keywords as variable names.

 L

LOGIC ERROR

An error that causes an application to produce erroneous data, but does not create a syntax error in the code.

 M

MENU

Menus allow commands to be grouped together and presented in a graphical hierarchy.

METHOD

Methods are the actions that an object can perform. A method call is the action of forcing the object to perform one of these actions.

MODAL

A modal form is one that must be closed before any other windows in an application can be accessed.

MODELESS

Any other form can be accessed at the same time that a modeless form is open.

MODULE

Visual Basic code is stored in files called modules.

MULTIPLE DOCUMENT INTERFACE (MDI)

The term MDI is used to describe applications made up of a parent window that contains a number of child windows.

 N

NULL

A variable contains a Null value if it contains no value or its value is not known.

 O

OBJECT

An object is any entity within Visual Basic that has its own set of properties and/or methods. Variables can also be thought of as objects. Examples of objects include forms, command buttons, and text boxes.

OBJECT LINKING AND EMBEDDING (OLE)

Object Linking and Embedding (OLE) is an older programming standard that is similar to ActiveX. For the most part, ActiveX has replaced OLE in Windows applications.

OCX CONTROLS

An OCX control is a synonym for an ActiveX control.

OPEN DATABASE CONNECTIVITY (ODBC)

Open Database Connectivity (ODBC) is an API that can be used to write applications that can access data from a variety of database systems.

OPERATOR

An operator is a symbol or keyword that performs an operation on one or more values, such as addition or multiplication.

OPTION BUTTON

Option button controls allow users to select a mutually exclusive value. When more than one option button is contained on a form, only one can be selected at any one time.

 P

PARENT

A window that is in control of one or more child windows or an object that other objects are descended from.

PARAMETER

See argument.

PROJECT

Visual Basic projects are a group of files that form an application, control, or any combination of the two.

PROPERTY

Properties are values that describe an object and control its behavior. Some properties are only available at run time, some properties are read-only, and some properties are both. A read-only property cannot be changed.

PROPERTY PAGE

A property page is dialog box that can be provided with ActiveX controls to allow users to set custom properties of the control.

 Q

QUERY

A query is a question that is posed to a database. The database returns any data that matches the criteria provided in the query. Queries are written using SQL.

R

RAPID APPLICATION DEVELOPMENT (RAD)

Rapid Application Development is a method of quickly developing computer programs. Visual Basic supports RAD through its visual development environment.

READ-ONLY

Any property or other attribute that is read-only cannot be deleted or modified.

RECORD

A record is a single row from a database table.

RECORDSET

A recordset is a group of records that are being referred to as a single unit. Recordsets are made up of one or more records.

REGISTRY

The registry is a Windows database that contains detailed information about the software and hardware being used on a particular machine.

RUN TIME

Run time refers to any time a Visual Basic application is running. The application could have been started from within Visual Basic or using an executable file. Some properties are only available at run time.

 S

SCOPE

Scope refers to the time in which a variable or procedure is available to your application. Attempting to access values that are not in the scope of the current procedure can cause errors or unpredictable behavior.

SERVER

A server is an application or component that provides services to other applications and components. Server can also refer to a computer that provides services to other computers.

SHORTCUT MENU

A shortcut menu or context-sensitive menu is a menu that appears when the user right-clicks on an object. The menu shows actions that can be performed on the object that was clicked.

SOFTWARE DEVELOPMENT KIT (SDK)

An SDK contains detailed information about a piece of software. It may also contain tools specifically designed to work with that software. Developers use SDKs to write applications to work specifically with the software that the SDK is for.

SOURCE CODE

Source code refers to the text and characters that make up an application. The code controls the behavior of the application.

SQL

SQL stands for Structured Query Language. It is the language developers use to program and work with databases.

STATEMENT

A statement is a group of Visual Basic keywords and variables that work together to perform some action.

SUBROUTINE

Subroutines are sets of code that perform specific tasks.

SYNCHRONOUS

Synchronous tasks are unable to continue their execution until, after calling another procedure, that procedure responds back that it is completed.

SYNTAX

Syntax refers to the rules that must be followed when writing Visual Basic code. These rules define how keywords, variables, and operators can be used.

SYNTAX ERROR

A syntax error occurs when a keyword or variable is used improperly or misspelled. Visual Basic cannot compile an application with a syntax error; it must be fixed before the program can be compiled into an executable file.

 T

TAB ORDER

A form's tab order is the order in which controls receive focus when the user presses the TAB key.

TCP/IP

Transmission Control Protocol/Internet Protocol (TCP/IP) is the standard used to facilitate communication between computers. Many networks, including the Internet, use TCP/IP as their main form of communicating.

TEXT BOX

A text box control displays text or accepts textual input provided by the user.

TITLE BAR

The title bar is the area at the top of a form that contains a descriptive title, as well as the minimize, maximize, and close buttons.

TOOLBAR

A toolbar is a graphical representation of menu commands. Each command is represented by an icon, which indicates what the toolbar button does.

TOOLBOX

Visual Basic's toolbox provides a way to add controls to forms. All controls and components available to a project are displayed in the toolbox. The controls are dragged from the toolbox and dropped onto forms.

TWIP

Visual Basic uses twips as a unit of measurement. A twip is 1/1440 of an inch.

 U

UNICODE

Unicode defines a character set, similar to ASCII. However, Unicode has the ability to define over 65,000 characters, which makes it very useful when dealing with languages that have thousands of characters.

 V

VARIABLE

A variable refers to a named reference that is used to store values in an application.

VARIANT

The variant data type can be used with any data type, but it does not take on any of the features or limitations of the data type that the data would normally be assigned to. It is best used when the data type will be unknown.

W

WIZARD

Wizards interview a user and use the answers to complete the task that the Wizard is specific to.

Z

Z-ORDER

The z-order is the order in which controls are placed on a form. It controls which controls are displayed as being on top of other controls.

Index